ADVERTISING RESOURCE HANDBOOK

Keith Adler, Ph.D.

A Sourcebook for People Who Advertise

ADVERTISING RESOURCES, INC.
P.O. BOX 6136, EAST LANSING,
MICHIGAN 48826

Library of Congress Cataloging in Publication Data

Adler, Keith.
    Advertising resource handbook.

    Bibliography: p.
    Includes index.
    1. Advertising--Handbooks, manuals, etc.
I.Title.
HF5823.A165   1989   659.1   88-8004
ISBN 0-923044-01-9

TRADEMARKS

Adobe, Adobe Illustrator and PostScript are registered trademarks of Adobe Systems, Incorporated. Adworks is a trademark of Concept Publishing Systems. Aldus PageMaker is a registered trademark, and Aldus FreeHand is a trademark of Aldus Corporation. Apple is a registered trademark, and Macintosh is a trademark of Apple Computer, Inc.. Cendata is a trademark of the U.S. Bureau of the Census. CompuServe is a trademark, and Comp-u-store and Electronic Mall are trademarks of CompuServe Information Services, Inc. Cricket Presents in a trademark of Cricket Software, Inc. Deneba Software and Canvas are trademarks of Deneba Systems, Inc. Dialog is a registered trademark, and DialogLink is a trademark of Dialog Information Services. Disclosure is a registered trademark of Disclosure Information Group. DisplayAdBuilder is a trademark of Digital Technology, Inc. Expert Choice is a trademark of Decision Support Software. FlowMaster is a trademark of Select Microsystems, Inc. GeoQuery is a trademark of Odesta Corporation. IBM is a trademark of International Business Machines Corporation. Letraset is a registered trademark, and ImageStudio is a trademark of Esselte Pendaflex Corporation in the United States, of Letraset Canada Limited in Canada, and of Esselte Letraset Limited elsewhere. LightYear is a trademark of Thoughtware, Inc. Lotus 1-2-3 is a trademark of Lotus Development Corporation. MacPaint is a trademark of Claris Corporation. Microsoft is a registered trademark, and Microsoft Excel and PowerPoint are trademarks of Microsoft Corporation. Moody's is a registered trademark of Moody's Investor Services, Inc. More is a trademark of Living Videotext, Inc. Prism is a trademark of Tempus Development Corporation. QuarkXpress is a trademark of Quark, Inc. Digital Darkroom and AutoTrace are trademarks of Silicon Beach Software, Inc. ThunderScan is a registered trademark of Thunderware, Inc. VALS is a trademark of SRI International. WetPaint is a trademark of Dubl-Click Software, Inc. What's Best! is a trademark of General Optimization, Inc.

Without Carol and Susan, I could never have finished this book. It's dedicated to victims of abuse, and people who have the patience to help them.

Contents

Illustrations

Preface

This is a book about advertising. It's not a textbook; it's a sourcebook. It was written to provide descriptions of the vocabulary used by advertising professionals, and more. With the vocabulary is the reasoning behind advertising and marketing strategy. This reasoning is essential to understanding the process of advertising.

In this book you'll find a wide breadth of topics covered from the social impact of advertising to the nitty gritty of advertising research. Concise analysis was the goal for many of the discussions presented here. As a book, the *Advertising Resource Handbook* offers both the old and new. A list of copywriting books begins with 1940 editions that are priceless; the idea of *structured strategies* for advertising and marketing appears here first.

Advertising is pluralistic. There are many different ways to do advertising effectively. There are just as many ways to do it ineffectively. Different strategies may be equally effective; but all strategies have to be accountable. When strategies are built on explicit reasoning, their effectiveness can be challenged and monitored. They can also be improved, and honed to precision.

Advertising isn't hocus pocus. It's not some mystical force that only weird, crazy people understand. Advertising can be both creative and effective. It can also be both uncreative and ineffective. People who do advertising well understand people, and why they behave the way they do. Sometimes cravings for glitz, glitter and glamour confuse people who advertise. Advertising is a very simple process.

You have to communicate the best information about your product or company to people who are ready to hear it. If the message is clear, more people will understand it. If the message is exciting and interesting, more people will remember it. If people remember your message, there's a better chance they'll use the information to buy your products. Regardless of what you say about your product, some people will reject it.

Competition is what's tough in advertising. Consumers are bombarded with messages from you and your competitors. Unless your message stands out, it can get lost in the clutter. As soon as you get a good idea, someone else will copy it. It doesn't matter. As long as you can think of a better idea, you can stay ahead of the competition.

This book is about the raw materials and tools of competition in advertising. These tools aren't substitutes for a sharp mind, a sensitive perception of consumer wants and needs, or the stamina to work long hours through the night. The tools presented here offer another perspective into the advertising process.

For those unfamiliar with the advertising industry, Part One offers a quick review of the relationships between the major players in the industry. It reviews some of the oldest arguments against advertising, and some continuing complaints. Part Two reviews the interrelationship between marketing and advertising because many managers try to solve unrelated marketing problems by advertising more often. Others develop advertising programs which have no connection to their overall marketing strategy. When marketing and advertising strategy are interlocked, both can have greater impact. Part Three examines the advertising campaign process sequentially, and offers *structured strategies* and a way to develop highly integrated campaigns for marketing, sales promotion, advertising and public relations. Several new applications for computers are highlighted; none are overrated. Part Four discusses four types of advertising briefly, because each area could be the focus for an entire analysis: business advertising, retail advertising, public relations advertising and inter-national advertising. Finally, another view of advertising presentations is offered because nothing is more fundamental in the life of an advertising professional.

Like all books about advertising, separating issues and techniques into chapters and sections disguises the dynamic and unpredictable nature of advertising processes. Some people thrive on the unpredictability; others don't. Techniques, tools and constant adjustment offer the best chances for making advertising more predictable.

Some of the discussions presented here aren't popular. Hopefully, a number of the discussions will be stimulating, challenging and useful. Without apology, this book was written from an educator's viewpoint. After teaching advertising to more than 20,000 students it would be impossible to do otherwise. Comments and suggestions should be sent to: Keith Adler, Department of Advertising, Michigan State University, East Lansing, Michigan 48824.

A special thanks should be given to Doyle Fellers and Dave Hunt for having the guts to hire me as a copywriter for $100 a week, many years ago. The money wasn't great and the hours were crazy; but it was fun.

Three super friends, and great proofreaders helped eliminate many glitches and mistakes: Regan LaMothe, Sandy Ducoffe and Regan Kania. The mistakes that remain were my responsibility.

1
Advertising Contrasts and Collisions

Critics of advertising often blame many of society's ills on the evils of advertising, yet these same individuals are the first to think advertising can help them promote themselves, religion, or a myriad of other social causes. We have to examine the attacks on advertising in order to understand why people criticize it. As you'll see, some attacks are justified; some aren't.

Three Types of Advertising Criticism

Three types of criticism can be made about advertising; 1) a **product criticism** criticizes advertising because a specific ad is linked to a product of questionable taste; 2) a **process criticism** is connected to the way advertising is done, such as the use of **deception** in advertising messages or the use of too many advertisements by a medium, called **clutter**; 3) a **content criticism** is made when the words or pictures in an advertisement or commercial are found objectionable by an audience. These three types of criticism lie at the heart of whether advertising is considered "good" or "bad" by a specific audience.

Since product and content criticisms are related to a viewer's attitude toward a product, illustration, or statement, they are typically made by consumers. Deception, a process criticism, may result in consumer dis-satisfaction with a product; but it has also become an important topic with government legislators. Legislators feel deception results in unfair market advantage for the deceptive company, and may be especially harmful to less educated audiences, such as the young children targeted by **children's advertising**. Clutter is a criticism important to the businessperson because it means the effectiveness of an advertisement may be diminished. For marketers and advertisers "good" and "bad" advertising refers to the effectiveness of an advertisement, rather than its social, moral or political implications.

While studies by **Steven Greyser** found the consumer less interested in advertising than other day to day concerns, there are significant social criticisms about the **negative stereotypes of women and minorities** which may be portrayed in or perpetuated by advertising.

Four Characteristics of Advertising Definitions

In order to study advertising more effectively, it must be separated from other communication and marketing concepts. Books about advertising attempt to make this separation by offering strong **definitions of advertising**. The definitions are used to distinguish advertising from **communication, propaganda, publicity, sales promotion** and **marketing**.

All definitions of advertising use **four criteria** to separate advertising from the concepts above. Advertising is defined as **controlled information**. In other words, within the bounds of legality the advertiser determines what is said, and pays to have his or her message put on the air or in a print ad. This separates advertising from publicity, where the advertiser does not pay to have the message published. Nor does he or she have control over how the message appears in print. <u>Definitions require an</u> **<u>identified source</u>** for the advertising message to separate advertising from propaganda, where the source is unidentified. **Persuasive communication** isolates advertising from everyday communication where persuasion is not necessarily the goal. Sales promotion uses direct incentives to get a response from consumers, rather than the persuasive information in advertising. By restricting advertising to a **mass media channel**, definitions of advertising distinguish between the personal selling situations for most marketing interactions, and the media influence of advertising.

Even though most books use these four criteria, almost all fail to incorporate the dynamic nature of the **process of advertising** into the definition. Advertising starts with the initial decision to advertise and continues until final evaluation occurs. Many managers consider advertising an investment because there is a cumulative effect of advertising over time. But for the purpose of study, advertising is considered to begin with the first advertising planning and to end after the evaluation of an advertising campaign.

Systems Approach Explains How Advertising Relates

One useful way for social scientists to look at advertising would be through an approach called the **systems perspective**. This approach allows the researcher to set boundaries for the system to be studied. Within the system, individual processes can be studied. In advertising, the individual processes of planning, creating, or evaluating advertising could be studied. More importantly, the systems perspective would be a useful perspective to explain the interrelationship of advertising as a system, with other systems, like the social system, the economic system, the political system, a marketing system, or the environment.

Study Questions

❏ What characteristics of an audience would determine whether they thought an advertisement was "good" or "bad"? How is this different from what an advertiser might think?

❏ What type of criticism would be made by a consumer who objected to a photograph of a "nude" model in an advertisement? What type of criticism would be made when a consumer criticized deceptive photographic lighting which made an older person look young in order to sell a beauty product?

❏ What advantage does a process definition of advertising have over a non-process definition of advertising?

❏ With what systems in society does advertising conflict?

❏ Where does the responsibility for bad advertising lie when the criticism of an ad is based upon content criticisms? Process criticisms? Product criticisms?

❏ How does a definition of advertising differentiate it from marketing, publicity, propaganda, interpersonal communication, sales promotion, and marketing?

Perspectives on Advertising You Shouldn't Miss!

Stephen Fox (1984), *The Mirror Makers: A History of Twentieth Century American Advertising,* (New York: Random House). An outstanding history of American advertising, written superbly from a historian's perspective.

Claude C. Hopkins (1966), *My Life in Advertising / Scientific Advertising,* (Chicago: National Textbook). An inside perspective of advertising and promotion which shows the conflict, the genius, and egos that produce advertising's most important commodity...ideas.

David Ogilvy (1986), *The Unpublished David Ogilvy,* (New York: Crown Publishers). Another sketch of an advertising legend.

An interesting debate about the cultural and social effects of advertising can be seen by reading the following article and responses. Richard W. Pollay (1986), "The distorted mirror: reflections on the unintended consequences of advertising," *Journal of Marketing,* 50 (April), 18-36. Morris B. Holbrook (1987), "Mirror, mirror on the wall, what's unfair in the reflections on advertising?" *Journal of Marketing,* 51 (July), 95-103. Richard W. Pollay (1987), "On the value of reflections on the values in 'the distorted mirror,'" *Journal of Marketing,* 51 (July), 104-110.

2
Advertising and Its Environment

When advertising is viewed as one element of society, we can easily see how different social forces have had an impact on the advertising industry. Some forces can be reacted to or controlled by advertisers. Others cannot. Factors which cannot be controlled or influenced by advertisers make up the **environment** in which advertising operates. Factors which can be controlled or influenced are part of the marketing **system,** or some other social system. This distinction between systems and environments permits more careful analysis of the interaction between outside forces and the advertising process.

Advertising in the Communication Environment

Advertising messages are just one type of message received by consumers every day. The total messages taken in by consumers make up the **communication environment**. Through **interpersonal communication** with friends, associates and workers, consumers form opinions, likes, and dislikes about products and services. One essential difference between the messages of interpersonal communication and advertising messages is that **all advertising messages have persuasion as their goal**. By definition, an advertiser is trying to change opinions, buying preferences, or attitudes in the consumer every time advertising space or time is purchased. Not all interpersonal communication is designed to persuade. In fact, there are situations in close interpersonal relationships where partners are offended by persuasion because it indicates self-interest, rather than a concern for one's partner.

Many debates about the role of information and persuasion in advertising have occurred. Some researchers have tried to separate informative elements from persuasive elements in advertising. Government regulators would rather see more information than persuasion in advertising. Yet as long as the advertiser determines which information is selected for an advertising message, it will be favorable to his or her product. Advertisers argue that persuasion does not guarantee deception in an advertising message.

The communication environment becomes more confusing when one considers the effect of news messages on the consumer. Journalists teach and believe in objective reporting. But countless distortions of news events and issues occur because of a reporter's slant or attitudes toward an issue. Magazines, newspapers, and television networks have attempted to attract larger audiences by adopting a specific approach to the news. These news messages, whether informative or persuasive, also become part of the consumer's attitudes toward products and companies.

Like persuasion in interpersonal communication or journalism, the key to deception lies in the **motives of the source** of the message. An unethical partner, an unethical journalist, or an unethical advertiser will use persuasion in a deceptive manner. Determining the ethics of any message source is not an easy task.

Conflicting messages in the communication environment can pose special problems for the advertiser. Conflicting messages can come from different media channels, such as discrepancies between interpersonal and news sources. Or conflicting messages can be sent by a single advertiser. This often occurs in retail advertising when a store's advertising claims friendly service and store salespersons are not nearly as friendly as the advertising suggests.

Advertising as a Process in the Marketing System

The **four P's**, a view of the marketing system developed by McCarthy[1], divides the processes of marketing into four categories. **Product** refers to factors associated with product development. **Price** includes those factors related to product or service pricing. **Place** refers to factors associated with how and where the product is distributed. **Promotion** encompasses all those factors and processes which relate to promoting and selling the product or service. Together the four P's are called the **marketing mix**. The marketer manipulates the marketing mix to achieve maximum profitability.

Advertising is only one element of the promotion category, or **promotion mix.** **Personal selling**, **sales promotion**, **advertising**, and **public relations** are the other tools in the promotion mix which are used to sell the product. It's easy to underestimate the importance of personal selling when we focus on advertising; but personal selling receives the heaviest emphasis in the promotion mix for many products. Wherever there is an extended chain of distribution through wholesalers and jobbers or a limited number of buyers, personal selling remains the dominant element in the promotion mix. Advertising plays a major role in the promotion mix when a company wants to establish a brand preference for a nationally distributed product. This is why a marketer's decision to establish a national brand is so important. Selecting an effective **brand name** and providing enough national advertising to establish preference, or a "**brand franchise**," is critical to a product's success.

---

[1]E. Jerome McCarthy and William D. Perreault (1987), *Basic Marketing* 9th Edition, (Homewood, Illinois: Irwin), 37-40.

When Advertising Conflicts with Other Systems

There are four possible ways an advertiser, or the advertising industry can respond to pressure from an outside system. The response used is determined by the amount of force exerted by the outside system.

An outside system can directly control advertising. When broadcast cigarette advertising was criticized for its role in promoting a dangerous product, the political system responded with a ban on cigarette commercials in the broadcast media. Print advertisements were required to have highly visible product warnings. This was an instance where control was exerted over an entire industry. Many individual advertisers have been directly controlled through the pressure of the legal system and litigation by the government and consumers.

Pressure can be exerted on the industry or a single advertiser to change unfair practices. When an advertiser violates a norm in the social system by putting negative images in advertisements, consumers often protest. If the protest is large enough, or noticed by lawmakers, an advertiser will often change his or her advertising practice because of the pressure. The "Frito Bandito" was removed as a trade character when less than five percent of the Latin American population objected to it as a negative stereotype.

Self-regulatory standards can be adopted by advertisers to prevent outside control. This is the basis for the entire advertising self-regulatory system. By policing itself the advertising industry accomplishes two goals. It reduces the influence of outside systems on the industry, and attempts to maintain standards which establish credibility as a professional industry.

Advertising can ignore the influence of other systems. This response would be expected when an outside system has little power or influence. It's a dangerous response for advertisers, because small groups of dissatisfied consumers can use the mass media to gain more power, visibility and influence.

Advertising and Environmental Change

The "computer revolution" and "information age" are phrases which have become buzzwords in this decade. How might these changes in the communication environment affect advertising?

Most futurists predict that information will become more accessible to consumers. More information will be available about products. Longer commercials, called **infomercials** have already appeared on cable television channels. More detailed information about consumers will be available to marketers and advertisers. Accuracy of predicting consumer purchase patterns will be improved because of scanner data at the supermarket. Product purchasing patterns will change because more goods will be purchased through alternative mail-order sources. Instant information will lead to lower inventories. Information itself will become an important product. Competitive sources of information will reduce the cost of information to the consumer and the advertiser.

Advertisers will respond with new ways to distribute product information. Computer databases with catalog shopping have already appeared. Alternative sources of information will be used when the audiences are large enough for major advertisers. This trend can be seen in the growth of cable television advertising. Growth of advertising in any new advertising medium parallels audience size and quality.

Study Questions

❑ How does the promotion mix differ from the marketing mix? How does the promotion mix differ for different types of products?

❑ How are advertising messages different from other types of communication messages?

❑ How can conflicting messages in the communication environment create problems for an advertiser?

❑ What are some likely consequences of the "information age" on the way advertising is done?

❑ In what ways can an advertiser, or the advertising industry, respond to pressure from outside systems?

New Technology: Innovation and Aftermath

"Technology Creates New Press Release Channels," *O'Dwyer's PR Services Report,* March, 1988 v. 2 no. 3 p. 1,18. Public relations departments begin distributing corporate news via satellite, computers, regional and national newswire, facsimile machines, and electronic mail.

"New billboard-painting process employs computerized 'artist',"*Marketing News,* February 15, 1988 v. 22 no. 4 p. 1,2. Computer generation of billboard artwork revolutionizes the printing industry.

"VCR tapes offer new era for ads,"*USA Today,* April 24, 1988 v. 6 no. 156 p. 1A. In attempts to monitor all TV audiences, ScanAmerica develops a system to monitor viewing of videotapes.

"CBS may tie rates to buying patterns," *Advertising Age,* March 21, 1988 v. 59 no. 12 p. 10. Because of reductions in audience reported by People-Meter meaurements, CBS attempts to develop a return on investment (ROI) model of television rates.

Advertising and
the Economic System

Advertising scholars and economists have debated the importance of advertising and its effect on consumers since advertising started. The issues and debates are important because economists have a powerful influence upon the economic system, and the resulting regulations governing advertising. For all of the arguments made against advertising, advertising experts cite counterarguments which support their side of the issue. Fundamental differences between the two groups can be partially explained by the assumptions they each make about how consumers behave. Still other differences can be seen in their opposing views of the free market system.

Two Models of Consumer Behavior

Economists assume consumers act rationally. In searching for products, they reason out decisions based upon information from many sources. Decision-making behavior is deliberate. If the consumer makes a mistake, it's the result of imperfect information upon which a decision has been made. Information is used and integrated into behavior without evaluation of the source of the message. **An economic consumer searches for products using utility as the criterion for choice among competing products.**

From the economists' perspective of a consumer, it's easy to see why persuasion and deception in advertising are important issues. Faulty information from advertising can lead to the purchase of products which aren't needed by the consumer. This wastefulness exhausts important financial resources needed for other goods and services. **Puffery, or** exaggerated claims in advertising, can persuade a consumer to pay more for a product than what it is worth. **Price** is an important attribute to communicate about products for the economist, because price helps a consumer evaluate the differences between products. Consumer choice, the economist believes, should be determined by product value not distorted product information.

Advertisers contend consumers are able to evaluate messages effectively. Through experience consumers become wary and careful about product decisions. He or she can evaluate the source of messages effectively and determine the validity of claims made in advertising. If the consumer buys something he or she doesn't need, the responsibility lies with the consumer not the advertiser. The advertiser would also suggest consumers have a right to act impulsively, without reason, if they choose.

These are obvious oversimplifications of the economic and advertising models of consumer behavior; but they highlight important differences. Actually consumers can act according to both models of behavior, or neither. Consumer behavior in the marketplace is more flexible than either academic model allows. Each model of consumer behavior has been developed on the basis of philosophical assumptions about human behavior which are consistent with the theories of each discipline. The assumptions made are simplifying assumptions which allow economists and advertisers to make predictions about behavior.

From research about consumer behavior, we know consumers tend to act more like the economic model when purchases are extremely important to them. This situation is called **high involvement** with the product. When involvement with the product is low, other decision criteria may provide more accurate predictions of how consumers will behave.

Advertising in the Free Market

Economists argue that **advertisers should be constrained** in the free market system for several reasons. They believe the free market system doesn't always punish deceptive advertisers, and deception may lead to unequal power for firms in the marketplace. With large advertising budgets an advertiser can create myths about a product which lead to unfair compe-tition. Myth creating power was evident in the popular belief that Listerine mouthwash was an effective sore throat remedy. Despite $11 million worth of corrective advertising, the myth persisted.

Advertisers suggest that **a businessperson acts out of self-interest**, and in order to please consumers and maintain a profitable stance, he or she must act in a responsible manner. Economists disagree and say self-interest is not a powerful enough driving force for the market system.

The **Robinson-Patman Act** (1936) was one form of constraint designed to improve competition between firms. It outlawed trade deals from manu-facturers which sold products of comparable quality to different buyers at different prices. In recent years, manufacturers have been accused of violating the Robinson-Patman Act through the use of **cooperative advertising** allowances. With cooperative advertising, the manufacturer usually pays part of the advertising cost to support product distribution. But huge advertising allowances effectively result in a reduced per unit cost of a product for the purchaser.

Based upon their beliefs about utility, economists favor **technological innovation** for product improvement rather than **market differen-tiation**. Technological innovation adds characteristics to the product which make it a better value. Market differentiation simply adds characteristics which distinguish the product from competitors, without necessarily adding value. The phrase "**added value**" has been used by economists to describe the increased price of branded merchandise when compared to unbranded merchandise of equal quality. They suggest the difference in price delivers no significant improvement in product value. One court case, the **Borden Case**, held that different prices for branded versus unbranded products were acceptable because the brand had been used to build more consumer confidence in the product. Some advertisers also believe consumers have a right to purchase a product for its psychological benefits rather than utilitarian attributes. So if a consumer wants to pay more for a well known brand, that's his or her decision.

Economists argue that **advertising raises the price of goods**. Advertisers counter this argument by showing that increased demand for the product will ultimately lead to lower costs. Early **toy advertising** in the U.S., France, and Great Britain has been used to support the advertisers case. In the U.S. "fair trade" laws were abolished and advertising permitted. Demand for toys increased and prices declined. In Great Britain, "fair trade" laws were maintained, advertising was allowed. There was no increase in demand or lower prices. In France where no advertising was allowed, there was no increase in demand or lowering of prices. Similar reductions in the price of optical services have been shown when price advertising was permitted. The emphasis on price advertising has been a sensitive issue for persons using **professional advertising**.

Medical and legal experts contend professional advertising causes several problems. It moves consumers, or service users, to other providers; it doesn't increase demand for services. Therefore it may actually increase the price of professional services to the consumer. Also, the quality of care for consumers may diminish because of increased demand at one or a few providers. Price advertising tends to establish "price" as the most important attribute for a medical or legal service, and price may not be the best criterion for a medical or legal decision.

Several other arguments have been made by economists about the negative effect of advertising in the marketplace. Examples that support both sides of the arguments can be found. Economists argue that large advertising budgets lead to **industrial concentration** where one or a few large firms control the market structure and product offerings to consumers. They also argue that large expenditures on advertising create **barriers to entry** for small fledgling firms.

Information Issues in Advertising

Information is an important concept to both advertisers and economists. Economists favor price information. Governmental regulatory agencies would like to see more information in advertisements. The **Federal Trade Commission** (FTC) favors **comparative advertising** where two products are directly compared because of the increased information in the ads. Most advertising researchers have found ads with product comparisons use more information cues than non-comparison ads. But remember, advertisers who prepare comparative advertising copy will not put unfavorable information cues in an ad for their product. In terms of advertising effectiveness there are more important issues related to comparative advertising. For example, research shows that putting a competitor's name in your ad may significantly boost your competitor's sales.

If we examine fashion advertising in national magazines, not much information about product construction, quality, or materials will be found in the advertisements. We might ask what benefits the consumer is using to make a decision about the product. Clearly, the look or the style may be subjective **psychological attributes** of the product. But these psychological attributes can be very important to the product purchaser. As long as the consumer has discretionary income to spend, utility may not be the criterion for product choice. For some products where consumer involvement is low, purchasers may not want more information about the product. Direct incentives from sales promotions may be a more effective promotional strategy.

Study Questions

❏ What are the major arguments advertisers have made against advertising?

❏ How does deception in advertising relate to economic arguments about market power and free competition?

❏ What are the characteristics of an economic model of human behavior? What about an advertising model of behavior?

❏ How can cooperative advertising be used to create unfair advantages in the marketplace?

❏ What do economists feel about product development and improvement?

Projected Expenditures on Advertising by Media

"Commerce Dept predicts hot year: Ad spending should climb by 10%," *Advertising Age*, January 11, v. 59 no. 2, 1988.

Advertising Age reported Commerce Department, advertising expenditure estimates for 1988. The Commerce Department projected a 10% growth to $120 billion. Growth is expected to continue at about 9% through 1992. Expenditures for all media are projected as follows: television, $26.6 billion; radio, $8.4 billion; newspaper, $31.7 billion; direct mail, $20.1 billion; magazine, $9 billion; outdoor, $1.1 billion.

Advertising Creates
Social Conflicts

The norms of society pose a special problem for advertisers. To sell products effectively the advertiser has to show that he or she understands the problems and interests of the consumer. By understanding the problems, interests and motives, the advertiser can design messages which tell how his or her product can provide solutions for the consumer's problems. If the advertiser violates **social norms** consumers will be angered and fail to buy company products.

Sometimes an advertiser may target consumers who have different normative beliefs than the general public. This has been the case with Calvin Klein underwear advertising. Calvin Klein print advertisements have been criticized by women's groups and consumers, but the ads continue to be used because the purchasing audience is not offended by the ads. The advertisements target and attract an audience through their use of nudity and sex appeals.

The **strategic dilemma** for an advertiser is to decide whether portrayals of people in advertisements will picture life as it is, as it should be, and as it is fantasized. If we picture people like they are, we are perpetuating the normative view of society with its present stereotypes. If we show life as it should be, we are making judgments about how others should live. When we show fantasies in advertising we are gambling that a large segment of our audience has similar fantasies. This strategic dilemma is at the heart of most social criticisms of advertising, including protests about nudity, the use of sexual appeals , and negative racial and role stereotyping.

Advertising Violates Social Norms

There are many criticisms of advertising which are based on the violation of social norms by advertisers. Some have claimed advertising is immoral because of these criticisms. Others find it a question of taste in the presentation of production information.

Advertising creates materialism is the strong claim made by many supporters of regulation for children's advertising. A softer version of the claim would be advertising supports materialism, rather than creating it. This criticism is related to an economic criticism of advertising which says advertising makes us buy things we don't need or want. The materialistic

argument claims advertising makes the consumer want more and more
products to satisfy a growing list of wants.

Product advertising appears everywhere. Tracing the influence of
product advertising to specific consumer behavior has been extremely difficult. Social scientists have focused on the interaction between reference
group influence and media influence. An early model of communication was
based on the **two-step flow hypothesis**. Opinion or infuence leaders
received information about products from the media and influenced people
who trusted them. The hypothesis has only received marginal support. It
has been modified several times to include more steps in the influence
process. Researchers now suggest a multi-step flow of influence from the
mass media to individual behavior, but the relationship has not been
precisely defined.

Advertising exhibits poor taste in its presentation of some sales
messages. Complaints about personal hygiene products, laxatives, and
medicinal remedies top this list of criticisms. Some critics dislike the
content of the ads; others complain about the timing of advertising messages. Seeing ads for hemorrhoidal preparations during the dinner hour
and objections to condom advertising are two examples of these criticisms.

Advertising exploits nudity and sexual appeals to get attention.
Examples of advertisements that exploit sex or nudity can be found in many
different media. There are a few important issues. Advertisers suggest
nudity may be **relevant** or **irrelevant** to the product being advertised.
Partial nudity in an advertisement for bath soap which is filmed in a
shower may be acceptable because the nudity is relevant to the product. A
nude model draped over an automobile hood selling paste wax for cars is
neither relevant nor acceptable.

Sexual appeals also have a degree of relevancy or irrelevancy based on
characteristics of the product being sold. If a product is likely to be purchased to make oneself more attractive to the opposite sex, sexual appeals
may be more relevant to that product. Many critics believe that advertising with sexual appeals has been used by advertisers to create new sexual
symbols from everyday products, like automobiles.

These critics believe advertising has created false needs in consumers, a
view held by many economists. The critics would ask why we as consumers
have developed a need for mouthwash, cosmetics, and many other personal
hygiene products. Sexual appeals they claim, have contributed to the
growth of these products.

Cross-cultural differences in the norms for nudity can be seen clearly by
comparing European advertising with advertising from the U.S. European
commercials have much more nudity and tend to shock American audiences. Consumers notice, or attend to, messages which violate existing
social norms. Norms against nudity in advertising are strong, but they're
often violated.

Advertising lies to sell products. Most advertisers would say lying
can only sell a bad product once. Because of governmental regulation of
national advertising, it's rare to see a blatant lie in national advertising

copy. William Weilbacher[2] created several categories of truth in advertising. He said advertising copy could contain claims which ranged from **blatantly false** statements to **whole truth**, where undersirable effects were included in the ad copy. Between the extremes can be found **true but deceptive** claims, and claims which contain **puffery** or exaggeration. While deception in advertising cannot be accepted or justified, puffery has been supported because of its relationship to interpersonal communication. In normal communication, we exaggerate daily. The person who ran a 12 second dash in high school reports faster times as he or she gets older. Advertisers believe consumers can decipher these exaggerations.

Responsible advertisers know the value of repeat sales in customers so they are careful to preserve consumer trust. Deceptive ads are most prevalent today in media where little screening of ads is done by media management, and with local advertisers where regulations are difficult to enforce.

Advertising deceives children. Because of a child's susceptibility to persuasion and inexperience with products, children's advertising has been monitored most by consumer action groups and government regulators. Much research has been done about the damaging effects of advertising on young people. Research has found that children do not develop defenses against persuasive claims until they are about eight years old. Therefore, much of the regulation has been designed to protect children from persuasive advertising during children's programming time periods. Definite breaks for commercials must be inserted in programs. Trade characters cannot be used in a commercial if the same character appears in the program. Parental action groups are still concerned about programming which contains commercial trade characters because the program may create a feeling for the trade character which can be later associated with a product. Like adults, programming influence seems to be more important to a child's behavior than advertising influence.

Advertising creates and perpetuates negative stereotypes. Two areas have been particularly troublesome. Research has shown that **sex-role stereotyping** has occurred in advertising. Women's role portrayals have not been as diverse as men's role portrayals. More limits have been placed on the roles portrayed by women in ads. Negative stereotypes of women as sex objects continue to appear in advertisements. These criticisms will be examined in the next chapter.

Racial stereotyping has also occurred. Minority groups have been negatively portrayed. Early characterizations of blacks in advertisements were atrocious; portrayals today have resulted in criticisms. Hispanic Americans have been dissatisfied with their portrayals in advertising, and with the lack of ethnic sensitivity shown by large advertisers. Under-representation of minorities continues to be a problem in advertising campaigns.

---

[2]William Weilbacher (1984), *Advertising* 2nd. Edition, (New York: Macmillan), 506-509.

Changes in the portrayal of women and minorities have occurred at a pace approximately parallel to activism and protest in society. When protesting voices were loud and frequent, changes occurred rapidly. During quieter times there has been less tendency to change. In fairness to advertisers, many saw the changing norms of society and incorporated changes into their advertising programs. Not all have changed; some never will.

Advertising creates insecurities in people. Advertisers promise to make you thin, physically and sexually attractive, and rich. Here the role of the advertiser is probably overshadowed by the same person's role as a product manufacturer. Products are developed to meet the needs or wants of a consuming public. Product purchases are votes of approval from a consuming public to the manufacturer. The advertising may enhance or accelerate the desire for those products. But continued growth depends upon consumer interest and sales.

How Conflicts are Resolved

Violation of social norms by advertisers is probably most noticed by religious groups, political conservatives, and special interest groups. One historic battle placed Jerry Falwell against the major television networks in his "Clean Up TV" campaign. In print advertisements, he attempted to get consumers to boycott advertisers who supported questionable television programming. Several manufacturers were sensitive to the criticism, but consumers didn't present a uniform stand against the advertisers.

Advertisers often overreact to criticism because they have a vested interest in an audience. An audience represents a potential group of product purchasers. Profitability is determined by the ability of the advertiser to demonstrate responsibility and concern for his or her consuming public.

An advertiser cannot help but respond to criticism when an audience can show its strength and power. For example, until recently advertisers were not organized to meet the needs of Hispanic consumers in this country. But changes in the demographic composition of society has stimulated a change in industry attitudes. Advertising agencies specializing in Hispanic markets have emerged, and national advertising campaigns have been tailored to Hispanic audiences.

Study Questions

❏ What is the strategic dilemma for advertisers when determining how to portray life in a commercial or advertisement?

❏ What is the relationship of social norms to judgments of poor taste and nudity in advertising?

❏ How are different groups of consumers affected by deception in advertising?

❏ What justification can be made for puffery in advertising?

❏ How can an advertiser determine the relevancy or irrelevancy of nudity or sexual appeals to his or her advertising campaign?

❏ What is stereotyping? How have stereotypes in advertising reflected social norms? How have they lead to criticism of advertising, and change in advertising content?

Classic Readings in Sex-role Stereotyping

Alice Embree (1970), "Media images 1: Madison Avenue brainwashing - the facts," in Robin Morgan (Ed.), *Sisterhood is Powerful*, (New York: Vintage Books), 194-212.

Lucy Komisar (1971), "The image of woman in advertising," in Vivian Gornick and Barbara K. Moran (Eds.), *Woman in Sexist Society*, (New York: Basic Books), 207-217.

Alice E. Courtney and Sarah Wernick Lockeretz (1971), "A woman's place: An analysis of the roles portrayed by women in magazine advertisements," *Journal of Marketing Research*, 8 (February), 92-95. Louis C. Wagner and Janis B. Banos (1973), "A woman's place: A follow-up analysis of the roles portrayed by women in magazine advertisements," *Journal of Marketing Research*, 10 (May), 213-214. Ahmed Belkaoui and Janice M. Belkaoui (1976), "A comparative analysis of the roles portrayed by women in print advertisements: 1958, 1970, 1972," *Journal of Marketing Research*, 13 (May), 168-172.

Alice E. Courtney and Thomas W. Whipple (1974), "Women in TV Commercials," *Journal of Communication*, 24 (Spring), 110-118.

Major Steadman (1969), "How sexy illustrations affect brand recall," *Journal of Advertising Research*, 9 (March), 15-19.

5
Advertising and the Portrayal of Women

Much has been written about how advertisers have misused women in advertisements and commercials. Many of the criticisms are related to **negative stereotyping**, as indicated earlier. But some of the criticisms are more stinging and universal. The criticisms about women and advertising could have been analyzed in the previous chapter; but there are important reasons to examine them separately.

The problem acquires more importance when you consider that negative portrayals of women in advertising have existed as long as advertising itself. If the cumulative effects are considered, there has probably never been an advertising problem that has influenced more people. Despite research which shows diminished effectiveness of advertising with the use of negative portrayals, the negative images persist.

Advertising images have been examined, analyzed, and exposed from several different perspectives. **Erving Goffman** studied advertising images as reflections of rituals and norms of society in *Gender Advertisements*. In *The Hidden Persuaders*, **Vance Packard** argued that many national advertisers were using sophisticated motivational research to manipulate helpless consumers. The end result of some research was the use of sexy female models to sell cars, and a host of other products.

Adopting only one approach to the study of women's role portrayals and stereotyping can cause generalization errors about advertiser motives which may be inaccurate. For example, if you view all advertising images as reflections of societal norms, then you could easily argue that the norms are inappropriate. This position could justify the behavior of an unethical advertiser who was perpetuating negative stereotypes of women through his or her illustrations in advertisements. If you believe every image in advertising is a subversive attempt to manipulate, then no image can be accepted as a normative reflection of human behavior. From this position, all advertiser motives are unethical and unacceptable. For this reason, before we examine what researchers have found about role portrayals and negative stereotyping, the concept of "meaning" should be discussed.

What does an ad mean?

This short discussion of meaning is not meant to be an exhaustive discussion of the philosophy of meaning. What we need is a practical discussion which will help us understand how advertising illustrations and copy communicate or influence an audience.

Donald P. Cushman, a respected communication theorist, developed a typology of meaning based on increasing levels of standardization in language. He said there were four levels of meaning, **intrapersonal**, **interpersonal**, **organizational**, and **societal**. Intrapersonal meaning is the very personal feeling or emotion you get when you see a picture or hear words that touch you. For example, if you've had a bad experience with a dog, possibly bitten badly, the word dog, or a picture of a dog can have a dramatic effect upon you. You can't describe the feeling very well to others because it's just how you feel. Unless they've had a similar experience, they can't fully understand your feelings.

After you develop a close interpersonal relationship with another person, you talk and develop meanings which are special to the two of you. One of the best examples of this interpersonal meaning can be seen in the line, "...they're playing *our* song." Couples in this situation have experienced a feeling together during the playing of a specific song. Again, it's not necessarily how everyone feels about the song. With both intrapersonal and interpersonal meaning, standardization doesn't go beyond you and another person. It doesn't have to because the meanings you have developed permit you to communicate effectively with the other person. It's only when you need to coordinate your behavior with many other people that standardized meanings get more important.

When we go on the job and assemble the *Busy Buddy Jig-Saw Machine* with 90 other people, we have to have organizational levels of meaning. Remember, meaning is connected to terminology and names in the following way. The "left cantilevered saw release" has to mean the same thing to everyone on the job, or else we can't produce the saw. When we have to coordinate a job like the saw, one piece of machine, the **object**, can only have one **name** and one **meaning**. Philosophers call the name a symbol, because it stands for the physical object in our conversations. The meaning is called a **referrent** because it refers to the object or symbol.

There's one other type of meaning we should include when we're talking about doing a specific job, **episodic meaning**. When we're on the assembly line making saws, we develop names for entire sequences of events. For example, if I'm doing the *quality control check*, I may be performing 24 different operations. But, all of the operations together make up the *quality control check*. When I tell other people on the job what I do, they all know because quality control check means a specific thing to them. *Quality control check* is the name of a sequence or **episode**, the operations performed are the episodic meaning. Here again, one episode has only one episodic meaning because if we don't have **unambiguous meaning** the job won't get done. Organizational meanings are good examples of highly standardized meanings. Many meanings in society aren't quite so standardized.

Societal meaning could be defined as the agreed upon meanings we have as members of society in order to work together. Unfortunately, because our language is so complex, **one object or symbol doesn't have one referent.** Let's prove it. Take the symbol "pig." What does it refer to? A four-legged mammal that produces piglets and bacon? A dirty little kid? A brutal police officer? How do we know what it means? We depend upon the **context** to determine which referent or meaning to use. If we're talking to farmers it's probably the first meaning. If we're talking to bruised protesters, it's probably the last. For verbal language, the dictionary gives us a list of symbols or words and their possible referrents. We usually call these **denotative meanings. Connotative meanings** are the emotional feelings we connect to denotative meanings because of our experiences.

There are no dictionary definitions for nonverbal images or pictures, so determining the meaning of an advertising illustration is even more complex. Erving Goffman used advertising illustrations as evidence of rituals in society which demonstrated the subservient roles portrayed by women. The strength of his arguments depends upon the accuracy between the illustrations he selected and the viewer's ability to see evidence of the ritual without being told. As viewers, it's very easy to suggest possible meanings for an ad; but there are several possible meanings for advertising visuals, too. If we wanted to be scientific about it, we would list the meanings according to their usage, like the dictionary. The issue is complicated by the vagueness of nonverbal images. Here's what the meaning discussion says about determining what an ad means.

When a critic of advertising says an advertisement shows a negative stereotype of women, a sizeable group of viewers should be able to see the negative stereotype without being prompted. Many popular critics try to **assign meanings** to advertisements, rather than relying on this consensus of viewers. Consensus isn't meant to mean majority, just a countable number. **Wilson Bryan Key** has sold thousands of books by assigning sexual meaning to phallic-like images in advertising. Some of the same mistakes were made in *Killing Us Softly: Advertising's Image of Women,* a film created from a slide presentation by **Jean Kilbourne.** But, *Killing Us Softly* is a film that should be seen by every advertising person, even though most wouldn't agree with this statement. Here's why.

Kilbourne criticized and dramatized many of the most common arguments women have had against advertisers. She provided evidence of negative stereotyping and questionable copy appeals in print advertising. She also expressed strong disapproval of ads where women were posed in sexually-subservient positions, and where illustrations featured violence against women.

Evidence for the socialization effects of advertising were never presented, even though that was the basis for her criticism of the advertising. Her case would have been stronger had she focused on the content of advertising, rather than introduce the economic arguments about advertising making women buy things they didn't need. For emphasis, she sometimes assigned abusive meanings like "mock rape" to illustrations, even though the meanings were much more ambiguous.

Like Key, Kilbourne argued every part of an illustration had special manipulative meaning because advertisers spend so much money on advertising. *Killing Us Softly* illustrated many truths about the way women have been portrayed in advertising. It also certainly attributed more power to advertising than it probably has. Exaggeration and emotionalism were used in place of accurate intellectual statements for some of the arguments made against advertising. Despite the errors, the film makes people re-examine portrayals of women in advertising.

What Do We Know about Women in Advertising?

Several trends have been found in studies about how women are portrayed in advertising. Not surprising are the findings which say role portrayals for women have been more limited than role portrayals for men. Studies have also found irritation and conflict associated more with the context of the woman's role, rather than the role. When household products were shown in a household context, neither women's activists nor non-activists were upset with the characterizations. Brand recall was reduced when sexy models appeared in test advertisements. The models proved to be a distraction from the selling goal of the advertisements.

In addition to the complaints made by *Killing Us Softly*, many women have questioned the new portrayals of women in a variety of roles. Some women have said it's wrong to portray a woman with a briefcase, because women don't occupy those roles yet. This complaint takes us back to the strategic dilemma of whether to show roles like they are or as they should be. Fortunately, some advertisers have found a key. In studies about which ads were preferred by women, there have been common elements across the winners.

Jockey for Her, Pepsi, and Levis 501 Jeans were found to be favorite ads among women. In each of the advertisements or commercials, the ads showed women in expanded roles. But, instead of using a model to portray the role, actual women were used in the ads. In using actual case histories, the advertisers found an instance where the expanded and actual roles were identical.

Study Questions

❑ How are verbal and nonverbal meaning different or similar?

❑ Why is it difficult or impossible to assign meaning to illustrations or photographs in advertisements?

❑ How does an advertising medium affect the meaning of its advertisements? Think about the context of the message.

❑ What has advertising research found about the portrayal of women in advertising?

❑ What kind of images are disliked and preferred by women in advertising?

❑ Why are some advertisers likely to respond to criticisms by women's groups? Why are others not likely to respond?

Women in Advertising: Activist and Professional Groups

Women Against Violence Against Women, 543 N. Fairfax Ave., Los Angeles, CA 90036. An activist organization dedicated to the elimination of images in the mass media which show physical, sexual, and psychological violence toward women.

Women Against Pornography, 358 W. 47th St., New York, NY 10036. A feminist organization whose goal is to change public opinion about pornography and its negative influence on popular culture. Bestows advertising awards.

Women in Advertising and Marketing, 4200 Wisconsin Ave., N.W., Suite 106-238, Washington, DC 20016. A professional organization of women in advertising and marketing. Promotes professional contact among members.

Women in Communications, Inc., P.O. Box 9561, Austin, TX 78766. Professional society for journalism and communications. Sponsors awards, and career activities. Many college chapters.

Women in Production, 211 E. 43rd St., New York, NY 10017 4. Professional organization of women working in the publishing industries, including: magazine publishing, print vending and buying, advertising production, and book publishing.

Advertising Women of New York, 153 E. 57th St., New York, NY 10022. Women who hold executive or administrative capacities in adver-tising, public relations, marketing, research, or promotion.

Advertising Regulation
and Industry Responses

Whenever public protests over the ethics and standards of advertising have achieved critical mass, two responses have occurred. The government has passed legislation to regulate advertising activities, and the advertising industry has attempted to soften the effects through self-regulatory action. This is not meant to imply there is two-way negotiation between government regulators and advertising industry spokespersons. Government regulators clearly have the power to enact laws which constrain the advertising industry; but political considerations sometimes temper the regulators. In general, the regulatory environment for advertising tends to reflect the regulatory philosophy of the presidential administration at the time.

Many governmental agencies have minor responsibilities for regulating advertising practices. Here, we'll discuss the more general Federal acts and issues which control the advertising process. Several court decisions involving advertisers and the FTC have assigned responsibility and penalties for deceptive practices. In this way the laws regulating advertising have been clarified. A few other cases have attempted to establish the First Amendment rights of advertisers.

Even though self-regulation has often been a measure to avert pending regulation, this doesn't mean it's impotent as a regulatory force. In some cases like children's advertising, self-regulatory pressure has been more efficient than governmental regulation. Arguments for and against self-regulation are important because they are the basis for support or opposition to the actions of self-regulatory agencies.

Constrasting governmental regulation with industry self-regulation can be deceiving. It might appear that there is little interdependency between the two systems. It would be easy to conclude that advertising has little power against governmental bodies and legislation. But the recent history of the **Florida Advertising Tax**, as it has been known, suggests otherwise. The effects of the Florida tax on services demonstrate important interdependencies between advertising and the economic system which are critical considerations for representatives of government and industry.

The Acts of Governmental Regulation

After years of freewheeling advertising claims, the early 1900's brought a period of exposes and reform movements. The claims made in patent medicine advertising were so outrageous, newspapers and magazines began reviewing and refusing advertising. The forerunner of the American Advertising Federation, the Associated Advertising Clubs of America, called for "Truth in Advertising," and developed an early code of practices. *Printer's Ink* magazine published the **Printer's Ink Model Statute**, which became the model for many state laws regulating advertising.

In 1914, the **Federal Trade Commission Act** established the **Federal Trade Commission** to regulate "...unfair methods of competition." A few years later in the **Sears Roebuck v. FTC** case, a court decision supported the extension of this regulation to advertising, since it was believed deceptive advertising could lead to unfair competition. Sears claimed they could provide lower sugar and tea prices because they were a large company. The claim was found to be false, and the action upheld because smaller competitive firms could be harmed by the deception. Also in 1914, the **Clayton Act** was passed to prohibit price discrimination by manufacturers. It's revision, the Robinson-Patman Act, later proved to be important for advertisers.

In 1931, a dramatic change in regulatory practices was caused by the **FTC v. Raladam** case. The Supreme Court said the FTC could not stop false advertising, unless it could show damage to competitors. Notice how this action limited the FTC's power to regulate deceptive advertising to competition between firms. It didn't protect consumers from deceptive practices.

The **Robinson-Patman Act** in 1936, outlawed price discrimination which interferred with competition. Companies could not charge different prices for products of the same quality, unless the different prices were established to meet competitive pressure. One test of the Robinson-Patman Act occurred with the **Borden case**. The FTC claimed Borden's higher prices for branded milk resulted in price discrimination because there was no difference in quality between branded and unbranded milk. Borden claimed the branded milk was more accepted by the consumer because of a reputation established through national advertising. Borden insisted the enhanced reputation was a difference in quality. A circuit court agreed. The Supreme Court deferred to the circuit court decision.

In 1957, Procter and Gamble was ordered to divest the recently acquired Clorox company in the **Clorox case.** The government argued that the Procter and Gamble acquisition had violated the **Clayton Antitrust Act** because of the company's power to make bulk television buys for media space. They said this reduced competition, and created a monopoly in the household liquid bleach industry. Procter and Gamble was able to buy over 30 percent more exposures than competitors because of their volume buying.

With the restriction of FTC powers to unfair competition by the courts, there were many advocates for changes in the powers of the FTC. These changes came in the **Wheeler-Lea Amendments of 1938.** The amendments put more teeth in the regulatory powers of the FTC by extending their power to "...false and deceptive advertising" for several product classes. In addition, deceptive practices were defined as unfair methods of competition, and the FTC was given more authority to seek restraining orders against business. But as a regulatory body, the FTC had to seek out and prove false and deceptive advertising claims on a case by case basis.

The **Lanham Act**, passed in 1947, was designed to protect slogans and brand names. The **Public Health Cigarette Smoking Act** in 1970, prohibited broadcast advertising for cigarettes. It also required specified warning copy to be displayed prominently in print advertisements.

In 1971, the FTC began a **substantiation program** which required advertisers to be able to support advertising claims if challenged by the FTC. Added power to create **trade regulation rules** was given to the FTC in the **Magnusson-Moss Warranty Federal Trade Commission Improvement Act of 1975.** Trade regulation rules allowed the FTC to control entire industries. Also included in the bill was the power to require **corrective advertising** to remedy **residual deception** in consumers caused by deceptive advertising.

Corrective advertising was first suggested by an activist group called **S.O.U.P.**, Students Opposed to Unfair Practices. This group reacted to the 1970 **Campbell Soup case**, where the advertiser had used marbles in the bottom of the soup to raise the ingredients out of the broth for photographic purposes. While the FTC found the practice deceptive, it didn't propose corrective advertising to get rid of residual deception, as the group had advocated.

In the **Pfizer Un-Burn case**, the FTC believed Pfizer ads had falsely implied that the Un-Burn ointment had been laboratory tested. In fact, only the active ingredient had been tested in other unrelated tests. The FTC lost this case because the court held that the ingredients had been tested previously.

A few of the early court cases provide insight into the effectiveness and practice of corrective advertising. In the **Profile Bread case**, ITT Continental Baking claimed Profile Bread was a diet bread. Actually, the slices had fewer calories because they were sliced thinner. The company was told to run corrective statements in advertisements equivalent to 25 percent of their advertising budget. The statements said the bread did not have fewer calories; it was sliced thinner. In this instance corrective advertising had little effect because the company withdrew brand advertising after a short time.

Broadcast commercials for **Ocean Spray** Cranberry Juice Cocktail had to correct a statement which said the juice had more "...food energy." The required remedial statement had to say, "Food energy means calories," because the difference was sugar content.

Perhaps the most famous corrective advertising example was the **Listerine case**. Warner Lambert claimed Listerine "prevented sore throats and colds." The FTC, after finding the claim deceptive, proposed corrective advertising to correct the claim. Warner Lambert disagreed, but the Supreme Court refused to hear the case, so the FTC action was upheld. After $11,000,000 of corrective advertising, research studies showed some correction of the deception. But, the survey results were certainly not as dramatic as the FTC would had hoped. Many people still believed Listerine was an effective remedy for sore throats and colds.

Congressional review of the FTC was guaranteed by the **1980 Federal Trade Commission Improvement Act**. The impact of this legislative change upon FTC policies hasn't been clear yet. By giving the legislature power over the FTC, the act provides at least an informal link between special interest groups, legislators, and FTC administrators.

Before we look at the major governmental issues, let's review the powers of the FTC. These powers were developed over time, and have been clarified through litigation. A **consent order** is an agreement between the FTC and an advertiser to stop a specific advertising practice. No guilt is admitted by the advertiser with this option. **Cease and desist orders** force an advertiser to stop a practice within a specified time frame. Again the advertiser doesn't have to admit deception in order to be regulated. **Substantiation** is a threat power of the FTC. Advertisers must be able to substantiate claims to the FTC and consumers. When the FTC requires **affirmative disclosure**, the FTC is trying to make important information about the product available to the consumer. As with Warner-Lambert and Listerine, **corrective advertising** can be required. **Injunctions** against an advertiser can be used when the FTC believes a deceptive practice will do harm to competition or to the consumer. **Restitution** may have to be made by an advertiser if there is evidence of damage to other parties or individuals. Finally, industry wide **trade regulation rules** can be written to regulate advertising practices common to an industry.

The Major Issues of Governmental Regulation

Deceptive advertising occurs when an advertising statement is false, or the net effect of an advertisement on consumer processing is misleading. Several questions quickly come to mind. How many, and what types of people have to be deceived in order to provoke governmental action? In the 1944 **Charles of the Ritz case**, the trademark "Rejuvenescence" was found to be misleading because it might be interpreted by the average consumer as a miracle life extender. In later cases, such as the **Gelb v. FTC case**, the FTC had claimed that a hair-coloring labeled "permanent" might be misinterpreted by a less educated consumer as permanently changing the color of hair at the roots. As in the case with "less educated consumers," the FTC has always been tougher on advertisements aimed at susceptible groups, like children. Aaker and Myers[3] pointed out that the advertising restrictions are more constricting than pornographic standards, because standards for pornography are based on the material being offensive to a majority of audience members. Advertisements can be challenged as deceptive if they have the potential to deceive a very small number of susceptible people.

In determining deception, the FTC examines the **general impression of an advertisement**, rather than the literal meaning of the advertising statements in it. Court cases have also determined that **ambiguous statements** may be deceptive if one of the interpretations of the statement is misleading. If an advertiser doesn't tell a complete enough story about his or her product, the FTC may require supplementary statements about the product. For example, many hair remedies must say baldness is hereditary and often untreatable.

Ads challenged as deceptive must contain a **material untruth** in order to be deceptive. This simply means the ad must contain material capable of affecting the purchase decision. Materiality was an issue in the "**mock-up cases.**" Use of mock-ups, or simulated products for television commercials have presented special problems. The **Rapid Shave case** is one example where materiality was found. Colgate-Palmolive wanted to demonstrate its razor on television, so it showed the razor shaving sandpaper. In fact, the razor was shaving sand on plexiglas. The courts believed this demonstration could lead to product purchase. Therefore, the practice was not allowed. Debates about television "mock-ups" followed. Mock-ups were permissible as long as the mock-up did not affect the purchase decision. Several cases known as the "**white jacket cases**" were heard in the 1960's. In several cases, actors and actresses wore white lab jackets in commercials and appeared to be doctors. Because consumers perceived the actors and actresses as doctors, the ads were considered to have material deception.

Two types of **puffery** have been examined by the FTC. One type reviews claims which are subjective evaluations of product quality, like "the best," "the greatest," etc. It's difficult to prove these types of statements false. Most have been supported as legitimate exaggerations by the FTC. A second type of puffery supported by court cases has been the spoof, or super-exaggeration. Characters like Joe Isuzu have been allowed because their claims are beyond the realm of believability for most consumers.

The second major issue which has raised important legal questions for government regulators is the **First Amendment** status of advertising messages. To what extent are advertising claims protected as freedom of expression by the Constitution? In 1942 with **Valentine v. Christensen**, the Supreme Court said First Amendment protection did not extend to commercial advertising. A decision in 1964, **The New York Times v. Sullivan case** gave some First Amendment protection to advertising.

---

[3]David A. Aaker and John G. Myers (1982), *Advertising Management* 2nd. Edition, (Englewood Cliffs, N.J.: Prentice-Hall, Inc.), 526-527.

Several decisions since 1964 have been made which support First Amendment protection for advertising messages. Protection by the First Amendment has been based on several factors, including the legality of the business activity, the amount of deception in the messages, and the public interest. One of the clearest examples might be the **Bolger v. Young Drug Products Corporation case** in 1983. The Supreme Court struck down state laws which prohibited direct mail advertising of contraceptive information. Since the campaign was directed at protecting consumers, the court said the beneficial effect was more important than the discomfort experienced by some consumers.

Issues of Self-regulation

There are several incentives for self-regulation in the advertising industry. As we said earlier, some self-regulation is an attempt to avert more direct control. In other situations, court cases have placed the responsibility for deception upon unexpected participants. The **Regimen case** in 1957 was important because it was the first time the advertising agency was held accountable for false advertising. Drug Research Corporation and its agency faked laboratory reports and starved models to sell Regimen weight loss tablets. Both the advertiser and agency were penalized.

Singer Pat Boone was forced to pay penalties for endorsing a product called **Acne-Satin**, when neither the advertiser nor endorser could provide substantiating documents. For advertisers and agencies protection from litigation is an important motivator.

The general arguments for and against self-regulation are not surprising. People in favor of self-regulation say it *reduces the FTC workload*. It *corrects advertising problems*, so it doesn't need to be punitive. They would also argue that *self-regulation has been effective*.

Those opposed believe self-regulation *doesn't punish offenders* sufficiently. Because of its biased perspective, they say, *public confidence in self-regulation will be low*. These critics also contend self-regulation *violates the rights of regulated businesses* because they can't conduct business freely.

Many advertising scholars believe self-regulation occurs at several levels. **Internal reviews** at the advertiser and agency would be the first level. Certainly this is a constraint upon advertising practice. Whether it should be called self-regulation is open to debate because the rules for internal review are not always outlined or stated. If it's considered self-regulatory, then it's an informal rather than formal constraint.

Trade associations for various product groups and for advertising organizations have more codified rules about advertising practices. **Media associations** and the **media** have also been important regulatory bodies. In print advertising, the Good Housekeeping Seal and subsequent tests by the magazine are designed to provide protection for the magazine's consumers. The National Association of Broadcasters had a code (**NAB code**) which specified commercial content and length, but the code was abandoned in 1982 after court challenges to it. Networks have assumed more review responsibility since the abandonment of the NAB code.

The primary self-regulatory body for advertising is the **National Advertising Review Board (NARB)**. This body acts in cooperation with the **National Advertising Division (NAD)** of the **Council of Better Business Bureaus**. The NAD examines national advertising and reviews complaints by competitors, consumers, and its own monitors. Once a complaint has been filed, the organization talks to the offender and seeks substantiation of its claim, and a resolution of the complaint. If no agreement can be made, the case is sent to a subset of members of the NARB which rules on the case. If no resolution can be reached at this level, the complaint can be sent to the FTC.

A majority of complaints to the NAD come from NAD monitors. About 30 percent come from competitors; about 10 percent from consumers. Very few complaints have been forwarded to the FTC. One third are substantiated. Another third of the advertisers modify their complaints. In the rest of the cases, the claims have been dropped for a variety of reasons. Results of NAD reviews are regularly published in *Advertising Age*, a weekly advertising trade publication. This publicity may be another deterrent to deceptive advertising.

Most scholars would say the NAD/NARB system has been an effective force in protecting the consumer from deceptive advertising claims. If there are weaknesses in the system, they are related to lack of scope in the self-regulatory review process. Local advertisements cannot be included in the review because of the large numbers of local ads. Most complaints reaching the NAD today are related to **comparative advertising** claims, where a competitor's product is mentioned or referred to in an ad. Requirements for accuracy and substantiation have been strongly enforced because the comparisons between products must be fair.

State Regulation and Control of Advertising

Most states attempt to control deceptive advertising through laws similar to the original Printer's Ink Model Statute. The original laws have been modified to make them more enforceable. But, an important regulatory issue was raised when the state of Florida imposed a tax on services, which included advertising space.

The **Florida ad tax**, as it was known in the industry, was enacted April 23, 1987. It went into effect July 1, 1987, and was repealed December 8, 1987. Under the bill advertising media buys were subject to a 5 percent sales tax . When Florida's law went into effect, several states drafted similar laws.

While the Florida governor and legislature saw the law as a way to increase state revenues, they didn't take into consideration the interdependency between advertising and the business environment. Because businesses pass costs to consumers, the tax resulted in double taxation.

Here's how. Advertisers raised their prices to meet the tax requirement; then sales taxes were levied on the newly-priced products. National advertisers withdrew advertising, so media revenues dropped. Convention business slowed because of the increased cost of doing business in Florida. Several lawsuits were filed against the tax, but dropped after its repeal. The governor's popularity in the polls fell. After review and re-consideration, the tax was removed. Legislative officials agreed to review the tax again in the future. A major controversy, the tax battle demonstrated an important interrelationship between advertising and the business economy.

Study Questions

❏ How did the FTC evolve over the years? What powers and constraints have been added?

❏ How have court cases altered or shaped regulation of advertising?

❏ What is the justification for corrective advertising? How effective has it been?

❏ What are the arguments for and against self-regulation by the advertising industry? Why is comparative advertising so important to self-regulators?

❏ What are the major regulatory issues faced by advertisers and agencies?

❏ What did Florida, and the advertising industry, learn from the Florida service tax on advertising?

Governmental Agencies Which Influence Advertising

Federal Trade Commission (FTC), Pennsylvania Avenue at Sixth St. NW, Washington, DC 20580.

Federal Communications Commission (FCC), 1919 M Street NW, Washington, DC 20554.

Food and Drug Administration (FDA), 5600 Fishers Lane, Rockville, MD 20857 (Dept. of Health and Human Services).

Bureau of Alcohol, Tobacco and Firearms (BTAF), 1200 Pennsylvania Avenue NW, Washington DC 20226 (Dept. of Treasury).

Advertisers, Media and Advertising Agencies

In order to understand the marketing system better, we need to examine the institutions of the advertising industry. The primary institutions are advertisers, advertising agencies, and media organizations. Other specialized organizations, like creative boutiques, sales promotion agencies, and public relations firms will also be discussed. Each type of organization has evolved to solve a specialized marketing problem so customers can be reached more effectively. First, we'll look at the organizations and see what they do. Then, we'll examine how they relate to one another.

The Organizations of Advertising

Advertisers produce, manufacture, and sell goods and services to customers. Many classifications of advertisers have been used in the past few years. But the most useful way to classify advertisers is by the scope of service or product delivered. If advertisers distribute products and services nationally, they are called **national advertisers**. Advertisers who focus on local distribution are known as **local advertisers**. This is a rather imprecise classification system because we could also talk about a middle group called regional advertisers. At one time, textbooks used to refer to the two groups as national and retail advertisers. Local advertiser is a better term than retail, because retail advertisers sell retail goods. Not all local advertisers sell products; some sell services.

 Advertising agencies are service organizations which assist the advertiser in developing plans and strategies to persuade customers to buy products. In their earliest days, advertising agencies bought space in magazines and sold it to clients. This was called "**brokering**" **space**. In the early 1900's, agencies began offering more services to their clients. Many performed several different functions, including consumer research, planning campaigns, creating advertisements and commercials, developing media strategy, buying media time and space, and evaluating campaign results. Agencies who perform this wide range of services are called "**full service**" **agencies**. Today, mergers between large agencies have attempted to combine advertising, sales promotion, public relations, and direct marketing functions in one huge advertising agency. Some agencies focus on business-to-business clients; others, called **creative boutiques**, offer only creative services.

Media organizations range from single weekly newspapers to large television networks. Organizations, like **cable television interconnects**, are marketing organizations for several different cable systems. Many media organizations serve very specialized audiences, others aim at a general mass audience. In all cases, the viability and profitability of a specific medium is tied to its ability to reach a known **audience**, and to deliver messages from advertisers to the audience. This is the reason media organizations are active in audience research, and why they use marketing techniques to build audiences. It's obvious this description of media applies only to those media which sell advertising time or space. If no time or space is sold, then the organization isn't important to the advertiser. The interrelationship between organizations can be seen more easily by looking at how advertisers organize their "marketing communications."

The Organization of Marketing Communications

Marketing communications is a phrase used to describe the relationship between communication elements in the promotional mix: personal selling, advertising, public relations, and sales promotion. In the attempt to communicate to customers and potential customers, advertisers generally use one of three organizational models. The model adopted, or some derivative, depends upon the nature of a company's product, and upon characteristics of its customers. Organizational type is also related to selected marketing strategies. These strategies will be examined in the next chapters. Figure 1 (page 32) provides a simple diagram of the most common models of organization.

When an advertiser has one or a few products, and only a few customers, a **direct communication** model describes the relationship quite well. Since there are a limited number of customers, media advertising would waste promotional money. So the company relies upon the sales force to carry information about the company. In this situation, the communication process may be managed by the sales manager, because the sales force is the primary communicator of company information. Sales promotion effort, if used, is expended on the sales force not the consumer. This type of organization is usually associated with companies which have very specialized products, and is more characteristic of local than national advertisers. It's hard to call an organization of this type an "advertiser" organization, because advertising plays such an insignificant role.

As the number of customers grow, it is impossible for the sales force to make contact with them all. Similarly, if the number of products produced by a company increases, more customers will appear. In this case, advertisers must use advertising to create interest in the products, and to generate sales leads for the sales force. Customers, in this case, tend to be a

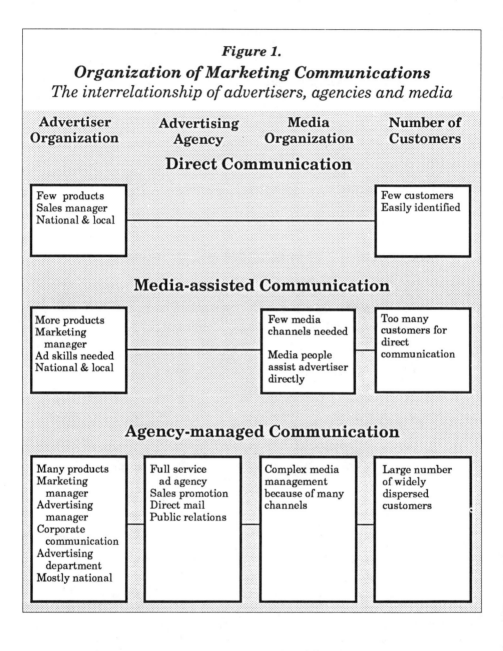

Figure 1.

Organization of Marketing Communications

The interrelationship of advertisers, agencies and media

Advertiser Organization	Advertising Agency	Media Organization	Number of Customers
Direct Communication			
Few products Sales manager National & local			Few customers Easily identified
Media-assisted Communication			
More products Marketing manager Ad skills needed National & local		Few media channels needed Media people assist advertiser directly	Too many customers for direct communication
Agency-managed Communication			

Many products
Marketing
  manager
Advertising
  manager
Corporate
  communication
Advertising
  department
Mostly national
	Full service
	  ad agency
	Sales promotion
	Direct mail
	Public relations
		Complex media
		management
		because of many
		channels
			Large number
			of widely
			dispersed
			customers

homogeneous group, like travel trailer dealers, or they will be concentrated in a geographic region. These customers can be reached using advertisements in a small number of media. Managing media buys is not a complex task for this type of advertiser. For this reason, the advertiser often seeks advertising help from the media rather than advertising agencies or consultants. This **media-assisted communication** model relies heavily on expertise from the media for success. The advertiser may hire a marketing manager to assist the sales manager and sales force. In these situations the marketing manager may supervise public relations activities for the company. Local advertisers who use this model usually contact media representatives directly to plan their advertising programs.

The most complex model is the **agency-managed communication** model. Here, a company has customers distributed nationally. There are usually different types of customers for several different products. Because of the geographic dispersion and dissimilarities between customers, many different types of media may be needed to carry the sales message. Increased complexity in media buying requires more sophisticated marketing planning. National advertisers and large retailers usually establish advertising and marketing departments to coordinate company activities. Advertising agencies are hired to provide creative input and to provide effective media management. There is an increased need for publicity and sales promotion help, so other firms who specialize in these activities may also be hired. Hardly any local advertisers organize their communication activities according to this model.

The three models discussed are oversimplifications. An example of a situation not described by the models could be found with moderately large retail advertisers, and some national advertisers. These advertisers need fast turnaround for production of ads because products change rapidly. Therefore, they may create an **in-house** or **house advertising agency**. The in-house agencies provide the same services as full service agencies, but service their advertiser as the primary client. Many scholars criticize this organization because they feel the creative product is too tightly controlled by corporate management. Others feel the in-house control yields financial rewards because there is closer fiscal monitoring of the advertising process.

Another reason retailers often use in-house agencies, or advertising departments, is related to the cost of advertising space. With most local advertising, no commission is paid to the advertising agency. Therefore, an outside agency would have to mark up its costs in order to make a profit. The costs of promotion would be higher. More detail about this relationship will be provided in the upcoming section about how advertising agencies work. First we'll examine how audiences are attracted, measured and sold by media organizations.

Advertising Media and Audiences

No concept in advertising is more important than "**audience**." Advertising rates are based on the number of people media can deliver. In terms of audiences, there are three characteristics which advertisers seek. **Substantiality** refers to the size of the audience delivered. A specific medium must be able to deliver enough potential customers to cover the investment in advertising, plus a return on the investment. An audience must be accessible to media. **Accessibility** is important because audience size means nothing if there is no way to efficiently deliver a message to it. **Measurability** is the third characteristic which advertisers want from an audience. In order to target messages more effectively, a medium must be able to supply characteristics of the people in its audience. What are their ages and incomes? What other media do they use regularly? What products do they use, and how frequently do they use them?

Advertisers are also concerned about the quality of audiences. Does a medium offer more high income, high frequency purchasers of a company's product than another? Because most media planners use multiple media in an advertising plan, they are especially sensitive to **duplication in audiences**. Duplication occurs when two media reach the same audience. Excessive duplication can result in less efficient media plans and wasted coverage.

There are several sources of audience data and planning information advertisers use when creating campaign strategy. *Standard Rate and Data* provides rate information and specifications for most advertising media. *Simmons Market Research Bureau (SMRB)* publishes an annual guide to markets and media reaching them. In the multi-volume research report are demographics for markets, and an analysis of print and broadcast use by people in the market. *Nielsen Television Index* and *Arbitron Ratings* provide regular estimates of broadcast advertising audiences. The **Audit Bureau of Circulation** and **Business Press Association** provide verification of audience size for many print media. A large number of organizations, including local newspapers, cable television systems, and television stations conduct research to determine characteristics of their audiences. These research reports supply data which can be used by the media representatives to sell advertising space and time. Once collected the research data is compiled and placed in **media packets** which are distributed to advertising media planners. The media packets are designed to attract advertisers by showing the size and quality of audience available from a specific medium. An **advertising rate card** is also included in the media packet.

Managers of radio stations, television stations, and the print media must market their media to two different groups. They've got to sell the audience characteristic to advertisers; but they're also got to sell the entertainment value of their medium to potential audience members. That's why radio stations change formats and use weekly promotions. That's why magazines use photo features, sensational stories and interesting covers. Competition for audiences is tough. Magazines like *People, Time* and *Newsweek,* spend considerable effort developing covers that sell well on the newsstand. Because shelf space is so competitive, many magazines offer retailers incentives for placing the magazine near the checkout counter.

Media selection for the advertising planner involves choosing the media, e.g. television, radio, outdoor, etc., then selecting individual **media vehicles**. Media vehicles are the specific magazines, specific television programs, and specific radio stations to be used in the media plan.

Many people have been concerned about **fragmentation of audiences** by the increasing number of media vehicles available. As more vehicles are created, media planning becomes a more difficult task, and audience size per vehicle shrinks. Fragmentation provides more choice for the consumer, but requires more promotion by a medium to hold its audience. Many media attempt to get power and audience size through sensationalism and self-promotion. Power actually comes from the acquisition of audience members, because media are really selling potential customers to advertisers through their advertising rates. Now, let's look at the role of the advertising agency in the interaction between advertisers and media.

How Advertising Agencies Work

Because of the huge expenditures on advertising, it's easy to overestimate the size of advertising agencies. Compared to multinational corporations, advertising agencies are relatively small. Several **advertising functions** are performed by full service agencies for their clients, including: consumer research, campaign planning, creative development, print and broadcast production, media planning and buying, and campaign evaluation. These functions are performed by an agency's most important resource—people.

Agency people might also be described by their functions. Account executives and other management personnel are responsible for coordinating operations between the client and the agency. The creative function is performed by writers, art directors, illustrators, designers, and creative administrators. The production staff may include broadcast producers and keyliners, but a key role is the traffic coordinator. This person monitors and oversees the production process from start to finish. A research staff may be separated by consumer and media function, but each has probably had experience in statistical analysis and research design. Media planners select media and develop strategy; media buyers place space and buy time in national and local media. While many people have stereotypic views of advertising people as wild and crazy creative types, many of the roles require traditional business training in financial analysis, planning, and management.

The advertising business has always been a turbulent one. Some client accounts move between agencies freely. Others have long term stable relationships. The advertising trade publication *Adweek* regularly rates agencies through their "Agency Report Card" criteria. Their indicators of successful agencies are high rates of client retention, substantial growth through new clients, growth from expansion of current clients, overall billings growth, creativity of the agency's output and management characteristics of the agency. Certainly the new business function in most agencies is one of the most critical areas of development because of client turnover. If unprofitable clients can't be replaced, then agency profitability will suffer.

Agency-client relationships have been the subject of debate and study for years. Clients often resent paying media commissions to agencies. Agency executives often resent having their creative hands tied by an overly conservative client. Several indicators of problems with the agency-client relationship appear to be, declining performance of a client's product and conflicts of interest between two or more of the agency's accounts. The problem of **conflicting accounts** has been an important consideration in the "mega-mergers" of large advertising agencies. Several advertisers have changed agencies because they would not tolerate the presence of a conflicting account at the same agency. Stagnation of the creative product dampens many long time relationships. Conflicting marketing philosophies and conflicts between personalities at the advertiser's organization and the advertising agency may also contribute to client turnover.

Agency compensation systems have changed over the years. After the brokering years of purchasing space, advertising agencies began operating under the **commission system**. Under this system, a 15 percent commission was returned to the agency by advertising media for all national advertising expenditures placed in a medium. Local advertising media varied in their acceptance of the commission system. Most local advertising media operate under a **dual-rate structure**. National advertisers pay a national rate with commission; local advertisers pay a lower rate which does not have a commission associated with it. The dual-rate structure of advertising rates in local media is one of the reasons many retail advertisers can't afford to hire advertising agencies. If no commission on space is returned to the agency, then the ad agency would have to charge a fee for their services to the retailer. Many local media offer advertising assistance to retailers at minimal rates, sometimes free.

Originally, the American Association of Advertising Agencies (AAAA) had rules which specified how an advertising agency could become eligible for commissions. This was called becoming a **"recognized agency."** These rules were disallowed because of a court challenge. The courts claimed the rules were violations of the Sherman Antitrust Act. They said any system of compensation could be negotiated.

While the commission system is less popular than it was previously, it still is used by many agencies because of its simplicity. The system pays agencies too much if an advertising program doesn't change very often. It underpays an agency when an advertiser has rapidly changing advertising requirements.

Another form of compensation for agencies is known as the **mark-up** or **fee for services**. Many agencies use this in combination with the commission system. For print production, research and other services which are not covered by the media commission, agencies mark-up their costs by 17.65 percent. Adding 17.65 percent to the agency cost for a service is mathematically equal to a 15 percent fee on the net cost to the client. For example, if keylining costs for a project were $250.00, the 17.65 percent added charge would be $44.13. Therefore, the client would be billed, $294.13. When the charge of $44.13 is divided by the total cost of $294.13, the result is 15 percent. Notice that this is the same commission returned by media to the agency.

The newest form of agency compensation system has been called the **"fee system."** Under this system the agency and client agree to a fee for advertising services. Media commissions are subtracted from this agreed upon fee. It's essentially a fee for a total advertising program. This is negotiated on the basis of administrative, production, and material costs. The effect of agency mergers has probably not been totally felt in the area of agency compensation systems, yet. Certainly one of the byproducts of mergers has been consolidation and streamlining of agency operations. Corporate managers have now been hired to look at the bottom line of agency operations. These changes may require further alteration of the compensation systems.

Study Questions

What variables determine how an advertiser organizes his or her marketing communications?

How are full service advertising agencies different from creative boutiques?

What characteristics determine the worth of an audience to an advertiser? What do the media do to make their audiences more attractive to advertisers?

Why are duplication and fragmentation important to advertising media planners?

How are agencies compensated for national media placement? For other services? What is the "fee system," and how does it work?

Advertising Agency Association Addresses

American Association of Advertising Agencies (AAAA), 666 Third Ave., 13th Floor, New York, NY 10017. A trade association designed to strengthen the advertising agency business. It has been active in industry public relations and professional development.

American Advertising Federation (AAF), 1400 K Street NW, Suite 1000, Washington, DC 20005. A broad based advertising trade association with many college chapters, interested in self-regulation. Sponsors national ADDY competitions.

Marketing Decisions

Understanding the relationship between marketing and advertising is essential for several reasons. This knowledge provides guidelines for the sequencing of marketing and advertising decisions. It also shows the domains controlled by the advertising manager and marketing manager. But the most important reason is to understand the relationship between marketing and advertising. If we stand back and look at the bigger picture, we can develop more effective and more coordinated marketing and advertising programs. While the focus in this section is marketing, the goal is to become a better advertising person as a result of more precise understanding of the marketing process.

Before we begin, we have to clarify some issues of terminology. You should realize the field of marketing is a very young one. In a few short years, it has evolved from the status of a trade or profession, to an academic discipline. One of the first steps in making this transition to an academic pursuit is defining terms and their meaning so they can be studied systematically. That's what has been happening in marketing. Advertising is an even younger discipline.

Many articles have been written debating the academic or professional status of marketing. Academics and researchers have attempted to develop and test theories of marketing. Shelby Hunt's *Marketing Theory: The Philosophy of Marketing Science*, has added scholarly rigor to marketing science and marketing theories. Many marketing textbooks began applying marketing science principles to management situations. Concepts in marketing are still being developed, defined and re-defined.

Early definitions described **marketing** as "...buying or selling in a market." While the definitions are still true, the early definitions were based on limited models of production in society. As soon as manufacturers were able to produce more goods than those demanded by consumers, the marketing process needed more definition. That's when the phrase, the **marketing concept** was developed. The marketing concept means adopting a customer orientation, or producing what customers need. This emphasis stimulated interest in the development of new markets and new products through consumer research. In recent years, marketers have talked about **broadening the marketing concept**. This "broadening" has been an attempt to extend the concepts of marketing products to the service and non-profit sectors of the economy.

Confusions in terminology have arisen because of the nature of advertising education. Most advertising education takes place in one of three units: the business school, a school of journalism, or an advertising department in a college of communication. Small discrepancies in language, such as "promotion mix" versus "promotional mix" occur because of the orientation of textbooks toward a business school or communication department audience. These differences are slight and shouldn't present too many problems.

A more important problem is a tendency to lose sight of the overall marketing process when one of its elements is discussed. In this chapter, we want to find out how the promotion mix differs when different marketing elements are manipulated by a manager. All of the elements in the marketing mix are connected to the promotion mix. Because of the interconnectedness it's difficult to assess the effect of one marketing element on the promotion mix.

Markets and Market-based Strategies

Because the marketing concept was based on consumer needs and wants, marketers began looking for groups of consumers who reacted similarly to a product or product class. These groups, or **market segments** as they have been called, allow more efficient marketing programs because members of the segment react similarly to persuasive appeals. They can usually be reached through similar advertising media. Programs directed toward these specialized consumers are more focused and precise, so they have been referred to as **target marketing**. Even though the target marketing idea implies "small and focused," it doesn't mean the potential audience is small. Some market segments are very large. Let's examine the requirements for target marketing more closely.

Four conditions must be present before target marketing makes sense as a marketing strategy. First, *market segments must exist.* Groups of consumers must possess a common set of characteristics which lead to similarities in the purchase of products. Another way of saying this same idea is consumer preferences must be clustered. In order to find these clusters or common characteristics, consumer researchers try to find good **bases for segmentation**. Another phrase used to describe the bases of segmentation is **segmenting dimension** of consumer behavior.

To find the most profitable market segments, marketing researchers correlate product purchase patterns with different variables or characteristics of consumers. These variables or characteristics become the "bases for segmentation" or "segmenting dimensions" when there is a high correlation to product purchasing.

There are several different types of segmenting variables which can be organized into groups. **Geographic variables**, like region of the country,

county size, or divisions of a metropolitan area sometimes provide
groups of consumers who have similar purchase patterns. **Demographic
characteristics** of the consumer, like age, sex, family size, family life cycle,
income, occupation, education, religion, race, and nationality have often
been used to segment markets. **Psychographic**, or social psychological
measurements of the consumer, like self-concept, lifestyle, and psychological needs attempt to go beyond demographic groups. Social psychological measures have been developed because some products, like sports
cars, play an important role in how a consumer views himself or herself.
The last group of segmenting variables are related to **product usage**.
Consumers can often be grouped on the basis of frequency of product usage,
quantities consumed, brand loyalty or similarities in where the consumer
purchases the product.

Before we move on to the other requirements for target marketing, the
selection of segmenting dimensions by a manager should be discussed. If a
marketing researcher wants to find a profitable market segment for a
product, he or she would conduct consumer research. This type of research
is an important part of the strategic planning process. Segmenting variables which may be important to the product are selected for study. Some
variables from the geographic, demographic, and psychographic groups are
included. Then, researcher judgment and statistical tests are used to
separate and define market segments. In most cases, the segments will be
defined by a combination of the variables studied, rather than a single
segmenting dimension or variable. There are several characteristics of
market segments which are important to researchers. These characteristics
happen to be the remaining requirements for target marketing.

The second requirement for targeting is that *characteristics of consumer
segments must be measurable.* If the characteristics and variables described
above can't be measured, then it doesn't make sense to talk about market
segments. For major marketers, **measurability** usually means standard
data about the segments must be readily available from syndicated research
firms, like Simmons Market Research Bureau.

Channels of communication must be able to reach the target segment, a
third requirement for targeting, has also been called **accessibility**. At the
most basic level, this requirement could be stated in a question, "Are there
media vehicles which reach the target market?" In larger marketing
programs, marketers ask more about the efficiency of media vehicles than
the existence of them. Characteristics of efficiency for media vehicles will
be discussed in the media chapters.

Market segments must be large enough to be profitable, is the fourth
requirement for targeting. Some people call this characteristic
substantiality. This means sales of the product to a specific segment
must produce enough revenue to justify the investment in marketing and
advertising. Marketers don't always look for the largest segment, because
competitors may be too powerful at marketing their products to the largest
segment. Sometimes specialized segments provide opportunities for entry

and growth in the marketplace, and provide the basis for more comprehensive strategies at a later time. Al Ries and Jack Trout used military analogies for these specialized strategies in their book *Marketing Warfare*. The strategies have also been described as **guerilla marketing** techniques and strategies.

Guerilla marketing is just one type of segmentation strategy. When most advertisers talk about segmentation strategies, they are referring to one of two general types. One type focuses the marketing effort on a single market segment and is called a **concentration strategy**. The other attempts to market products to more than one target segment and is called a **differentiation strategy**.

The decision to use a concentrated or differentiated strategy is often determined by the number of resources available and characteristics of the product. If a product can be adapted easily to different segments, then a differentiated strategy makes sense. Computer manufacturers have attempted to use differentiated strategies to market products to consumer and business markets. The efforts have been less successful than similar efforts by copier manufacturers, because fewer functions are performed by a copier.

Concentrated strategies are often used by companies where a single product or brand exists, or where marketing resources are limited. If resources are limited, then the use of different advertising media to reach different segments can dilute the total marketing effort. The effect of market segmentation, or targeting, on the promotion mix is determined by the strategy, and by the communication requirements for the target segment. In general, differentiated strategies will produce more complex advertising plans because there are different media requirements. Concentrated strategies will produce less complicated plans. But, other elements of the marketing mix, like the product and channel of distribution also have important effects on the promotion mix.

Product Characteristics and Product Strategies

Product development and product decisions are some of the most important for manufacturers and advertisers. Decisions about the product can mean success or failure for a company. These decisions determine whether a high profile national advertising campaign or a strong sales force is needed in the promotion mix. Let's look at the product from several different levels first.

Many people examine a product microscopically. They talk about its physical composition, and its chemical makeup. These physical characteristics can be very important for many products, including raw materials, industrial products, and medical products. In consumer products, the physical differences may not be as important as the perceived differences between products in the mind of consumers.

Realizing perceived differences exist, some advertising experts have defined products as a **bundle of attributes**. Others talk about **physical** and **psychological attributes** of the product. What they are saying is that an object, like a product, can have symbolic meaning. When the symbolic meaning, such as the sex appeal of a new sports car, is important, there may be changes in the importance of physical attributes. With sports cars cosmetic additions may be more important. With perfume or cologne, the actual physical differences may be less important than the perceived psychological differences. This is why the **branding** decision is so important to product developers. Let's use a cake mix example to illustrate.

Suppose we have a large plant capable of turning out huge volumes of cake mix. We can decide to market this product in bulk to the packagers of house brand cake mixes and generic products. We can also sell bulk packages to institutions. A different strategy would be to develop our own cake mix brand to compete with Betty Crocker and Duncan Hines. The decision is critical because with unbranded mixes we spend the promotion mix dollars on a highly trained sales force. Sales promotion dollars go to sales personnel, and customer price discounts. With the branded product, huge expenditures will have to be made in packaging and national advertising in order to create a brand franchise. Sales promotion dollars will still be spent on the sales force; but consumer introductions and repurchase promotions will demand large sales promotion expenditures.

The branding decision also requires careful consideration of a **brand name**. Branding requires national advertising exposure to establish the symbolic meaning for our brand name in the mind of the consumer. This established reputation and trust is especially important if we want to extend our product line to other products through **brand extensions**. Branding makes sense when we are trying to establish a family of products or product line of consumer goods, but has serious consequences for the promotion mix.

Before we examine product strategies, a couple of product typologies should be examined. One way to classify products is raw materials, industrial goods and consumer products. These groups require increasing emphasis on advertising in the promotion mix as we go from raw materials to industrial goods and consumer products.

Consumer products have often been classified according to three types, based on the consumer's purchase decisions. **Convenience** products, like bread, are often purchased at neighborhood stores as they are needed. If a favorite brand isn't available, substitution is readily made. **Shopping goods** stimulate some search in the consumer because product attributes, or the brand name is important. Consumers will expend more effort for these products, but will substitute if their regular brand is unavailable. **Specialty goods** represent those products consumers expend most energy to find. Consumers are least likely to buy substitutes for these brands. This typology parallels the type of retail outlet where the products are sold.

Brand name promotion is very important for specialty goods because consumers seek and prefer brand name products, regardless of the price.

The **price** element in the marketing mix has two dimensions. From a managerial standpoint, manufacturers must perform careful economic analyses of product pricing to achieve an optimum return on investment. Based on the discussion of brand names, and the typology of retail products, it's easy to see that price also has symbolic meaning to the consumer. Established **brand franchises**, or preferences for a brand, will cause consumers to pay more for a product. But, price is only one dimension in product-based marketing strategy.

In *Positioning: The Battle for Your Mind*, Al Ries and Jack Trout outlined the strategies of **product positioning** which they presented first in a 1972 *Advertising Age* series called, "The Positioning Era." Product positioning, according to Ries and Trout, requires finding holes in the marketplace by examining how consumers perceive products. In a consumer's head are perceptions of products which can be altered through simplified advertising messages. For an advertiser, knowing the relative positions of competitive products is extremely important for success. Once the structure is known, the job of an advertiser is to *position his or her product in a new niche* which is more favorable, and profitable for the company. The Avis line, "We're number two," and "...we try harder," is a classic example of repositioning a service. Positioning places increased emphasis on consumer research to find the existing positions of products in the consumer's mind. It also speaks more to the content of advertising messages than it does to differences in the promotion mix.

Another product-oriented strategy also relates more to message content than differences in the elements of the promotion mix. This is the decision to use primary or selective demand strategy. **Primary demand strategies** sell and promote an entire product class. **Selective demand strategies** sell individual brands of the products. While selective demand strategies are most common, products which are unique in their product class often require primary demand strategies. The Mazda automobile with its rotary Wankel engine was one example of a primary demand campaign. Attributes of the Wankel engine had to be sold, before the car could be promoted. Message content was altered by the strategy, but the promotion mix was less affected. As we'll see in the next section, the promotion mix is more dramatically changed by differences in the channel strategy employed by a marketer.

Distribution and Channel Strategy

Advertising managers don't usually think about the effect of distribution strategy on promotion because of their isolated positions. Most companies have ways of distributing their products which have been in existence for long periods of time. It's only when new channels are created that managers become more aware of the promotional needs and requirements of the new channels. Let's examine a couple of methods of distribution to see differences in the promotion mix.

There are basically two methods of distribution, **direct** to the consumer, and **indirect** through wholesalers, jobbers, retailers or other intermediaries. Direct distribution has received much more emphasis recently because of the increased sophistication of **direct marketing**. Retail stores, like Lands' End, have developed large customer bases through direct channels. These direct marketing efforts require support from national advertising to generate sales leads and to stimulate product purchases. Once purchases are made, careful analysis of geographic, demographic, and product purchase information makes it possible to sell more products to the customer. Indirect methods of distribution are more complicated than this.

In the indirect chain of distribution there are varying amounts of cooperation received and control exerted over product distributors by the manufacturer. For example, some products go from manufacturer to independent distributors. Here, cooperation is not guaranteed, and the manufacturer has little or no control over product quality or advertising exposure. Enticement to buy company products through promotional offers and discounting is often necessary to move the product through the distribution channel.

For some products, the distributor may be chosen by a manufacturer to carry products based on purchasing power. Contractual agreements may exist, as they do with many national franchises . As the power of the manufacturer increases over the distributor, more cooperation in marketing exists. Control over product distribution also increases quality control to the consumer.

Push or **pull strategies** are promotion strategies tied specifically to product distribution. In push strategies, the promotional effort is an attempt to get wholesalers and retailers to stock the product. These strategies are heavy in sales promotion to wholesalers and dealers. Pull strategies attempt to stimulate consumer demand through national advertising. Once demand by the consumer is established, the advertiser assumes distributors will order more of the product to meet consumer demand. As the level of cooperation and control increases in the distribution network, pull strategies are used more frequently.

One of the classic examples of changes in promotional effort as a result of channel strategy was the introduction of L'eggs pantyhose. While many characteristics of the product were revolutionary, the distribution of hosiery in supermarkets and drugstores was a dramatic difference in distribution. Previously, hosiery were sold in boxes at millinery stores. These changes required more emphasis on national advertising and consumer promotion than the previous methods of distribution.

Manipulating the marketing mix does produce important changes in elements of the promotion mix. Promotion decisions are all related to the product, the method of distribution and marketing strategy. In the next chapter we'll find out how marketers use marketing analysis to discover opportunities for their products.

Study Questions

❏ What are the justifications and requirements for target marketing? Why would a marketer target, rather than market to the masses?

❏ What are bases of segmentation and why are they important?

❏ Why is branding so important? What is a brand franchise? How does branding affect the promotion mix?

❏ How does product positioning differ from market segmentation?

❏ What effect do cooperation by distributors and control by manufacturers in a distribution chain have on promotional strategy? How do these factors affect composition of the promotion mix?

Brand Name Selection Articles

Bruce G. Vanden Bergh, Keith Adler, and Lauren Oliver (1987), "Linguistic distinction among top brand names," *Journal of Advertising Research*, 27 (August/September), 39-44.

John Murphy (1987), "Branding: the game of the name," *Marketing* (UK), 29 (April 23), 32-33.

Bruce Campbell (1986), "Rechristening the company," *Working Woman*, 11 (September), 134-135, 187.

Lorna Opatow (1985), "Creating brand names that work," *Journal of Product Innovation Management*, 2 (December), 254-258.

Walter A. Woods (1983), "Gravy Train has it, Drive doesn't -- How to measure the 'impact' of brand-name candidates," *Marketing News*, 17 (September 16, Section 2), 10, 13.

Walter Stern (1983), "A good name could mean a brand of fame," *Advertising Age*, 54 (January 17), M53-M54.

Ira Schloss (1981), "Chickens and pickles: choosing a brand name," *Journal of Advertising Research*, 21 (December), 47-49.

Marketing Analysis

Two important information skills are needed for **marketing analysis**. An advertiser has to be able to *gather and organize information* about the market, the consumer, the environment, the product, and the company. He or she has to be able to *use the information gathered to gain an advantage in the marketplace.* Gathering information is the reason **marketing information systems** have been established in companies. The widespread availability of **electronic databases** with marketing information has made these systems more timely and efficient today. Gaining an advantage through the use of the information requires knowledge of marketing strategy, good judgment, and insight into where the market is headed.

You might wonder where marketing analysis fits in the total promotion picture. The analysis described here occurs in several places. One obvious place is in the preparation of new advertising campaigns. **Situation analysis** is a formally prepared statement of analysis which precedes the development of new marketing and advertising strategy—a first step in campaign planning. Many people use the situation analysis to describe marketing **problems and opportunities** for a firm. But if we only think about problems and opportunities, it's easy to focus on negative aspects of the product rather than the entire marketing program. A second application of marketing analysis is in **feasibility studies** for the introduction of new products.

The marketing analysis described here will be divided into four areas: market characteristics and product performance, corporate marketing strategy and practices, environmental surveillance and prediction, and strategic arguments. Before we start let's look at how information should be presented for the analysis.

In marketing analysis, we find information and state conclusions, predictions and recommendations. Each statement must be supported by **good reasons** or **justifications**, and by evidence or facts. These reasons and evidence are parts of an argument. Each conclusion, prediction or recommendation is a **claim**. **Evidence** is a factual statement of information which supports the claim. Good reasons have been called **warrants** in an argument, because they tell how the facts are related to the claims. Regardless of what we call them, each conclusion, prediction or recommendation in a marketing analysis must be supported by justification and evidence. Now, let's look at each of the categories more closely.

Market Characteristics and Product Performance

In order to study the market and our product's performance in it, we need to contrast changes in the market with our product's performance. We need to know the historical development of the market. In the comparison, we may find that our product is growing faster than the market. Or, we may find the market has outpaced a stagnating product. This information is essential for marketing planning.

Market growth and development can be studied most effectively through a **historical analysis** of the product class, market segments, and consumer trends. **Market size** and changes in size are a critical parts of this historical background. Changes in consumer attitudes toward the product are important for modification of existing products, or for the introduction of new products.

Since we want to contrast our product's development with market development, we need a historical record of product performance and sales. While most companies should keep sales statistics according to market segments, many don't. Sales data by segment may have to be estimated from other sources.

A historical study of the product will also give clues about the **product life cycle**. The product life cycle is a description of product growth and decline through four stages: introduction, growth, maturity, and decline. Each of the stages requires a different type of promotional strategy.

Product analysis also requires a description of the major competitors by company and brand. If we were doing the marketing analysis for a retail store, then competitive stores would be the focus, rather than competitive brands. Typical statistics which might be compiled are **market share** for a brand, or share of customers for a retail market. Consumer awareness or **share of mind** for a company or brand has often been measured to find out what brands consumers think or know about.

How do we accumulate such detailed information about an industry, market segments, and the competition? Let's talk about three classification systems for information, first. A step-by-step information gathering example will be presented at the end of this chapter. The first classification system examines primary versus secondary information. **Secondary research information** is information gathered from existing sources, like library references, research reports, and journal articles. This is contrasted with **primary information** which is obtained from research studies we conduct. An example would be a survey of consumer attitudes toward a product.

The second classification system separates information as internal or external data. **Internal data** is information routinely collected inside a company or organization, such as sales data. **External data** refers to data accumulated from sources outside the company. As you can see, the first two classification systems have overlap in their categories.

The third type of classification system is used to organize information in electronic databases. Electronic databases generally contain two types of information, **textual** or **bibliographic information,** and **numerical** data. If we're looking for article abstracts in a database we're searching for bibliographic information. Census information is one type of numerical information available in electronic databases.

All of the information we find will be used as evidence to support our conclusions and recommendations for marketing action. The contrast between market structure and product performance requires conclusions about: a) the size of the market; b) the number and size of consumer segments in the market; c) important changes that have occurred in the market with their influencing factors; d) market share for the company's product; and e) growth or decline in product sales over time. Each of these conclusions requires evidence from accepted sources.

Since each section of the marketing analysis will require some integration of information from electronic, standard reference, and corporate sources, the step-by-step example will show how different types of information are related. Let's examine corporate marketing strategy and practices next.

Corporate Marketing Strategy and Practices

Advertising managers sometimes overanalyze the marketing practices of a firm. Marketing decisions critically impact advertising, so they should be examined. But marketing decisions don't depend on advertising decisions. Advertising decisions are determined by the marketing strategy and plans. There may be a better way for an advertising manager to look at marketing decisions. Let's look at an analogy from biology.

In agriculture, scientists describe a **law of limiting factors.** Stated simply, it says plant growth occurs at a rate determined by the most limiting growth factor. If the limiting factor is sunlight, then increasing the light intensity with supplemental lighting can produce faster growth. The principle has been used to produce larger roses by raising the plants in a greenhouse with high carbon dioxide content. Think how this might apply to marketing practices in a company.

Marketing factors can also be limiting. Production of products may be slowed by a few distant suppliers. Knowing this limitation provides a clue to the solution of the problem. The other elements of the marketing mix can also be analyzed this way. In analyzing corporate marketing practices we are trying to find product and product development factors that slow down product purchasing in the market. We are looking for price factors in the product which slow sales to various segments. We are looking for distribution characteristics which slow down the spread or repurchase of products. And, we are looking for promotional factors which inhibit growth of our brand. Almost all managers say the amount of money allocated for promotion is the most limiting factor. But increases in promotional expenditures do not necessarily result in proportional increases in product purchasing. The limiting factor approach is valuable because the conclusions reached are constructive, rather than negative. Each criticism suggests ways to improve the marketing system.

The conclusions developed about corporate marketing practices depend upon good internal information about operations and marketing decision-making. Conclusions are only necessary when limiting factors can be identified. When limiting factors exist conclusions in the marketing analysis will be about: a) product factors which limit acceptance by the market; b) pricing factors which may be important to the expansion of markets; c) distribution factors which may limit the effectiveness of promotions, or product purchasing in the market; and d) promotional factors which might slow the growth of the product. Of course each conclusion must be supported by good reasoning and facts. The next analysis, environmental surveillance, depends almost entirely on external information.

Environmental Surveillance

An environment is made up of **uncontrollable variables,** or variables that can't be controlled by the marketer. The decision to monitor specific environmental variables may be determined by: increased political and legislative action, economic fluctuations which influence consumer purchases, changing social norms or heavy competitive activity. In monitoring the environment advertisers are trying to anticipate changes that will result in more or less demand for their products. At the same time, contingency plans can be developed for unexpected events.

Political, legal and social changes can be monitored through electronic databases quite easily. Competitive activity is more difficult. Industry references, like *Leading National Advertisers* or special issues of *Advertising Age*, provide some estimates of competitive activity for national brands. Many research organizations regularly monitor broadcast television advertising. The Nielsen company, from TV rating fame, performs shelf audits to determine the movement of products. Local advertisers have fewer resources to monitor competitive activity before planning advertising campaigns.

Monitoring local advertising is easy for print advertising. It's more difficult for broadcast. For print advertising an advertiser can build a clipping file of competitive ads from all print media in the market. Once collected, the ads can be critically examined for weaknesses. One way to examine the ads is to start broadly by searching for marketing strategy strengths or weaknesses. For example, was the best possible market segment selected? Next, look for errors in advertising strategy. Do the ads talk to the target market selected in the marketing strategy? Are the sales appeals to the target segment strong enough to sell the product? Finally, look at each ad to find flaws in the way the strategy was executed. What graphic illustration or copy statements in the ad reduce the effectiveness of the message? By looking at a couple of the ads together, you can tell whether the ads have a consistent graphic layout. A competitive campaign is stronger if the ads are consistent.

Local broadcast ads are more difficult to monitor because they are aired at many different times. There are a couple of guidelines for determining whether competitive ads are strong or not. First, try to remember if you've heard any competitive ads. Do you remember what the competitor was selling? Ask several friends if they remember ads from your competitor. If they don't remember, then the ads may not have been appealing. Or, the ads may not have been aired enough.

From the environmental surveillance, advertisers will make predictions about the importance of legal, political or social factors which will influence product sales in the future. Ways to reduce any negative effects may be suggested. The general marketing and advertising strategies should be developed with environmental constraints in mind. Evidence is also needed to support the predictions that are made.

From observations and reports of competitive activity, an advertiser can make predictions about: a) relative competitor strength in the market; b) amount of competitive activity; and c) number of competitive products in the marketplace. All of the evidence and conclusions become background for the strategic arguments which attempt to outline market opportunities.

Strategic Arguments

In our strategic arguments the goal is to demonstrate where opportunities for growth exist. It isn't necessary to develop complete strategies. Instead, possible strategies are developed for market openings. The phrase **"strategic arguments"** was selected because it implies more reasoning than the previous analyses. There is also a major difference between the strategic arguments and the arguments or conclusions made about market structure, corporate strategy and the environment. When the previous conclusions and predictions were made they were based upon existing facts.

Strategic arguments require new evidence based on primary information. Here's why. Because strategic arguments are attempt to propose new marketing alternatives, there has to be some evidence that the new strategy will work.

One example of a strategic argument could be developed from the history of franchise hair salons. Before franchise salons were popular, the use of salons by teenagers was negligible. If we had done a market structure analysis of the hair salon industry, the absence of teenagers as salon users would have been apparent. We would have concluded that there was a market opening for the teenage market because no one was adequately reaching it. When we say, "...teenagers represent a new opportunity for our franchise operation," we have to provide some evidence that teenagers can be persuaded to use franchise salons. This new evidence, if acquired, will give support to the new marketing strategy.

Primary information is needed to support our suggestions for new directions. Secondary information will still be examined first. In the hair salon example, we would try to find secondary information about how teenagers select and use hair care services. But some primary information is necessary to show that teenagers can be persuaded to come into franchise salons.

What kind of primary information is needed? The primary information obtained in the situation or marketing analysis is a preliminary form of strategic planning research. One type of research is a qualitative group interview, called a **focus group**. Simple surveys may be performed to find out consumer attitudes and intentions. When huge expenditures are at stake, more sophisticated **test market** studies will be performed to explore different marketing techniques. These studies in isolated test markets are actually more related to strategic research, rather than to marketing analysis. But this is one area where the borders between marketing activities blur.

Effective strategic arguments are the ultimate goal for any marketing analysis. The historical factors, corporate philosophies and environmental concerns provide a background; but marketing history can be made by making great strategic choices.

A Few Rules for Gathering Information

There are several simple rules which will be helpful in deciding what types of information to gather and use in a marketing analysis. As you might expect, you should *use secondary information before trying to gather primary information.* The research has already been done. Unfortunately, because another person's research was not done to solve your marketing problem it may not provide enough insight into your specific marketing situation. Several sources of secondary information may be necessary in order to construct a picture of what's going on in the marketplace.

When no information exists about the markets you are interested in, *national sales data and segment information should be scaled down* to provide rough estimates of market size.

Use electronic information retrieval, rather than library methods. Gathering information through computer networks in much faster, and it's easier to organize.

Companies should routinely collect and examine sales data by market segment. If no system exists, a manager should establish a system. It is not unusual for a company to not know demographics of their customers; but it's a tragic mistake because the information is so readily available. If no sales data exist, then this portion of the marketing analysis becomes a history of the product class and competition.

Primary information should only be used when no other information exists. The most common type of primary information gathered during the marketing analysis is a consumer survey to determine how much awareness there is of the company's brand, and competitive brands. Attitudes toward the product class and company offerings may also be measured.

In general, *it's easier to understand an industry and a marketing problem if the industry-wide historical data is gathered first.* A general overview lets you contrast your company's data to the industry data.

Study Questions

❏ In what situations is it important to perform a marketing analysis?

❏ What characteristics of the market are most important? By what criteria do we measure the "goodness" of a market segment?

❏ What is product life cycle, and why is it important?

❏ Think of examples of secondary research information, primary research information, internal data, and external data.

❏ How does the law of limiting factors apply to an analysis of marketing strategy in a corporation?

❏ How can competitive activity be monitored?

Costs for Electronic Database Research

Here's how database costs are distributed. When you sit down at your computer, you'll need a **modem**. This device lets you connect your computer to the telephone line and transmit and receive messages. You'll need a piece of **communication software** to send and receive messages. Costs vary depending on the speed of transmission for the modem, and the software complexity.

With your modem and software, you'll connect to an information service, like Dialog. The local number you dial is a **node** on a national **communication network**. You'll type in the **information service address**. To log-on, you'll type in your **password**. Charges for using the communication network are included with your database account.

Once connected to the information service, you can usually search **files** in different databases. Databases are maintained by different database suppliers. Each database has a per/hour connect fee. Each database also has a per item charge for printing information you find. Connect fees usually range from $50 to $500 per hour; printing charges range from $.15 to $1.00, or more depending on the length of the data record. Typical searches range from $20 to $50. Compare these costs to library search efforts.

Using Electronic Databases for Marketing Analysis

Computers have revolutionized the information business. In past years, a researcher would spend hours in a library looking for market and industry information and statistics. Today the most comprehensive research can be done from a computer terminal or personal computer. Information services charge customers to access information; but the cost must be weighed against the time spent searching in a library. Library searches may take weeks; computer searches take minutes. Because computer time is expensive, we have to develop strategies for searching which minimize the costs. For the example here, a strategy will be developed using Dialog® databases. Dialog Information Services, Inc. is a subsidiary of the Lockheed Corporation which operates one of the largest and oldest information services. Dialog provides access to hundreds of databases.

There are less expensive alternatives to Dialog; but Dialog was selected for several reasons. The breadth of marketing and business resources is most visible when thumbing through the *Dialog Database Catalog*. From a user's perspective, there are probably more self-instructional materials and seminars about Dialog use than other information services. Common search procedures across the databases make it easier to study information from different sources. Dialog also has some lower priced alternatives to the full search service. One of these is called the Business Connection, and provides access to major business databases. There are also computer programs which monitor on-line costs; Dialog produces one of them called Dialoglink™.

An Information Gathering Strategy

The most important way to make information retrieval more economical is through effective information gathering strategies and efficient search strategies. The information gathering strategies must be designed to select appropriate databases and information sources. Search strategies are designed to speed up search within a database. The following example of an information gathering strategy for a marketing analysis will integrate computer search procedures with standard references.

Step 1. Perform a comprehensive survey of the industry. Bibliographic information and abstracts which survey an industry will provide information about industry history and growth, competitive product introductions, legal issues and constraints, and other important marketing issues. Several databases from Dialog provide this type of information: (Numbers in parentheses are Dialog file numbers.)

> PTS PROMT (16)—(Provider, Predicasts) abstracts thousands of periodicals, magazines, trade newspapers, and journals. A good general business reference.
> PTS MARS (570)—(Provider, Predicasts) contains information about the marketing and advertising of consumer goods and products.

PTS NEW PRODUCT ANNOUNCEMENTS/PLUS (621)—(Provider, Predicasts) contains complete text of new product news releases which can be accessed on-line.

FINDEX REPORTS AND STUDIES (196)—(Provider, National Standards Association) indexes and describes all industry and market research reports, studies, and surveys which are commercially available.

A historical overview and a summary of environmental factors can be developed from these abstracts and articles. Some market data will be reported in these articles; but more extensive searching is necessary for numerical data about the market.

Step 2. Compile market statistics and projections. Dialog does not provide the most comprehensive market statistics by product. But, demographic and geographic information can be compiled by searching the following two databases:

CENTATA™ (580)—(Provider, U.S. Bureau of the Census) contains Census-related statistical data and information available from the Federal government.

D&B DONNELLEY DEMOGRAPHICS (575)—(Provider, Donnelley Marketing Services) includes census data from the 1980 census, and proprietary estimates develped by Donnelley Marketing Information Services. Information can be accessed using standard advertising research organization designations.

To supplement Dialog search procedures, market data can be compiled from standard trade publications and syndicated sources. *Sales & Marketing Management Survey of Buying Power* provides demographic information by retail markets. Simmon's Market Research Bureau provides the comprehensive market information in their reports. Simmon's data is also available on-line. Some information found in Step 1 will also help in developing a market profile.

Step 3. Find out about competitors. If your business is local or regional, you'll find little information available about competitors in an on-line database. In local and regional marketing situations regular monitoring will provide the best information. For national advertisers, *Leading National Advertisers* will provide a list of competitor companies. Once a list of competitors has been developed, Dialog can be used for **corporate intelligence**. Several databases provide information about public companies and corporations. A sampling of these databases would be:

DISCLOSURE® (100)—(Provider, Disclosure Information Group) contains financial information about companies from SEC reports.

MOODY'S® CORPORATE PROFILES (555)—(Provider, Moody's Investor Services, Inc.) has descriptive and financial information about publicly-held U.S. companies. Some historical data is available.

PTS ANNUAL REPORTS ABSTRACTS (17)—(Provider, Predicasts) indexes annual reports for many publicly-held companies. CORPORATE AFFILIATIONS (513)—(Provider, National Register Publishing Company) can be used to trace company connections between parent and subsidiaries.

While the corporate information in Dialog is interesting and current, it is less likely to be directly related to advertising and marketing strategy. The exceptions are annual reports which list corporate expenditures on advertising.

Step 4. Compiling and presenting information. Electronic information retrieval will result in large amounts of information for the advertising planner. This makes organization of the material even more important for a marketing analysis. After reviewing the information, an advertising manager should construct strategic arguments, as described earlier. These arguments will incorporate the bibliographic information as evidence for specific marketing and advertising approaches.

This four step procedure provides a simple process for compiling industry information from a variety of sources. As we said earlier, you also need a search strategy for selecting items from within the database.

Developing an Efficient Search Strategy

An efficient method of searching is important because typical rates for on-line services range between $60 and $150 per hour. In addition, each record you print or type at the terminal may cost between .30 and $1.00. Telephone connect charges are also added to the cost of the connect time; but these are quite reasonable because of nationwide telecommunication networks. The costs shouldn't alarm you. A typical search may last five to ten minutes. Off-line printout may contain 30 to 50 references with abstracts. In order to see how to search more effectively, we need to know a little about how database searching works.

A database supplier abstracts magazine, newspaper or journal articles and sends in a computer tape with complete information. This information is used to update information in the database, which is managed by Dialog. When you search, you use keywords, called concepts, to find articles and abstracts of interest. In this example, we are not going to use the computer commands to find words. Instead, the example will provide a general method of **building sets** of keywords. For the example, let's say we want to find information about sponsors who use event promotions, like rock concerts, to market their products.

The first step is to separate the concepts we're looking for. In our case we want to know about "sponsors" and "event promotions". It's not enough to search just for these two terms, because related terms exist. In searching for information, you have an advantage over the librarian doing the search because you have specialized knowledge. You have to provide synonyms for each of the concepts you're looking for.

To build one set we ask the computer to select "sponsors" **or** "sponsorship". To build the other set, we may ask for "event promotions" **or** "event marketing" **or** "special event." *The "or" includes the synonyms in the sets we are building, so it makes each of the two sets larger than it would have been using just one term.* In most database procedures sets with two word phrases like event marketing can be constructed using simpler procedures. For now, just remember the "or" is what we use to build the largest sets for our concepts. While we want the sets to start out large, it's important to be precise in the words we select. The computer will tell how many articles are included in each set.

After building our two sets for sponsors and event promotion, we combine them. This is done by asking the computer to select articles which have sponsors **and** event promotion in them. As we ask the computer to combine the sets with the "and" command, we check the number of articles selected. If there are too many to pay for, we ask it to narrow the selection even further by doing another "and" operation. In the event promotion example, we might narrow the selection by asking the computer to combine "concert" and "sponsors" and "event promotion."

If you have trouble finding synonyms for advertising terms, you may want to use one of the popular dictionaries of terms, like the *Barron's Dictionary of Advertising and Direct Mail Terms.* Searching takes practice; but it's not difficult.

Sources of Database Information

Dialog Information Services, Inc., Marketing Department, 3460 Hillview Avenue, Palo Alto, CA 94304. Information about access, publications and catalog available. Knowledge Index and Business Connection are simpler versions of the main system.

BRS Information Technologies, 1200 Route 7, Latham, NY 12110. BRS is an less expensive alternative to Dialog, with fewer databases. BRS also offers an advance purchase plan.

Advertising & Marketing Intelligence, Mead Data Central, P. O. Box 933, Dayton, OH 45401. Newspapers and advertising/marketing publications are indexed as part of the Nexis system.

Interactive Market Systems, 55 Fifth Avenue, New York, NY 10003. Offers a wide range of media planning services, including software programs which access SMRB, Arbitron and Nielsen. Business is divided by marketing and media categories, and microcomputing services.

10
Marketing and Promotional Strategy

Advertisers have always been fascinated with the idea of strategy. Whether its marketing strategy, advertising strategy, or promotional strategy, advertisers can't resist arguing over how to demolish and demoralize their competitors. Military analogies can be found in most advertising books, and advertising people have a natural affinity for competition. Brilliant strategy can turn paupers into millionaires, and vice versa. Yet, strategy continues to be one of the most misunderstood concepts in advertising. As you'll see from this discussion, strategy is easy to understand; it's much more difficult to execute. To begin, we need to clarify some of the terms used in discussions of strategy.

Strategy and Tactics: A Military Analogy

One of the first distinctions to be made is the distinction between *strategy* and *tactics*. This is one of the military analogies which has also been applied to athletics. In football, you could think of strategy as the decision to rely on a strong passing offense to win a game. The tactics would be the set of passing plays to be used during the game. Winning is the goal. The same principles apply in other areas. A weight reduction strategy might be designed to reduce caloric intake and increase physical exercise. Meal plans and menus and the exercise regimen are the tactics that would be used. In advertising, a strategy may be designed to position your product as a low priced alternative to the top brand. Tactics might include using comparative advertisements in the three most popular magazines.

As you can see, **strategy** is a *general statement of the plan to reach a stated or implied goal*. In football, it was winning the game. In weight reduction, it was reaching a certain weight. In advertising, it was gaining market share. **Tactics** is the term given to the *complete set of specific methods and techniques used to achieve the goal*.

Notice the ways strategy and tactics can fail. A bad strategy is a plan that doesn't lead to the chosen goal. In other words, if a manager believes certain tactics are necessary to reach a goal, and they aren't; failure is certain. A weight reduction plan with too many carbohydrates may not lead to weight loss. A passing attack in football may not win a game. Tactics can be bad for two reasons. The set of tactics used may not necessarily lead to the intended goal, as we just suggested. In addition, the tactics chosen may not reflect the strategy selected. For example, a person who selects national television spots as a tactic for a regional target market is obviously making a mistake. Evaluating the fit between the strategy and tactics isn't always this easy. The possibility for failure means a manager has to be sure to select a proper goal, the best strategy, and suitable tactics for reaching the goal. What makes strategy decisions more difficult is the fact that two different strategies may be equally effective in reaching a goal. In these cases, it probably doesn't matter which strategy is selected, as long as the tactics selected match the strategy. The distinctions between strategy and tactics are important because they show how critics will attack your marketing and advertising strategy. They also show how you can defend your strategy.

If there is agreement on your advertising and marketing goal, then there are only three criticisms that can be made about your strategy: a) the strategy can be criticized because it will not lead to the intended goal; b) the tactics chosen can be challenged because they don't match your strategy, and c) some critics might argue that the set of tactics you've chosen are not powerful enough to reach the intended goal.

To defend your strategy you have to provide arguments and support for the strategy selected. And, it means you have to provide support for the selection of tactics to reach the goal. This is exactly what you'd have to write or state in any **strategy presentation** . You state your goal, telling how it was selected. Then, you describe your strategy, and provide support for it. Finally, you outline the set of tactics you believe are needed to reach the goal. Tactics need to be supported by good reasons and justifications. There may be several different types of support, including a company's previous experience with a product, or secondary research data.

Once again, **strategic arguments** are important. Strategy and tactics are just one way of looking at those arguments from another perspective. The idea of "objectives" was introduced to provide more effective evaluations of strategy. Let's look at objectives in general, before we look at advertising objectives.

Why and How "Actionable" Objectives are Important

Behaviorism in psychology stimulated interest in overt, or observable, behavior. Rather than focus upon mental imagery or cognitive concepts, the behaviorists wanted to orient psychology to behavior that could be observed and counted. This focus resulted in widespread interest in "objectives." Teachers were required to set behavioral objectives for each student; instructional objectives were designed as plans of action for an entire classroom. Business writers began talking about **management by objectives**, or **MBO**. In all cases, writing objectives forced psychologists, teachers, and managers to state their goals in terms of *observable changes in behavior*. The reasons for preparing objectives are as important today as they were when they were first introduced.

Writing objectives is important for two reasons. *Objectives reduce vague goal statements to a set of sentences which outline a **specific plan of action***. At the same time, these sentences which outline the plan of action *become the **evaluation standard** to measure success in reaching the goal*. For example, if we said one instructional objective was "...to have 25 students memorize the spelling of 10 words within one week," we could easily determine whether the goal was reached or not. To determine if we were successful, we would give a spelling test after one week. The results would be compared to the statement of our objective. Since the behavior we focus on in the objectives has to be changeable, some authors have called them **"actionable objectives."** Objectives in marketing and advertising are used for the same two reasons: to outline a specific plan of action for reaching a goal, and to provide the standard of evaluation to measure success in reaching the goal.

Objective Setting in Organizations

Since objectives can be used by all managers in an organization, there may be several levels of objectives. For example, a corporation may have a long term plan of action which is stated in corporate objectives. Marketing objectives would have to consider the overall corporate objectives. A marketing plan may have written objectives for channel, pricing, or promotion strategy. An advertising manager may write objectives for the overall advertising plan, for the creative strategy, and for the media strategy. In all cases, objectives must be supported with strategic arguments.

The responsibility for writing objectives should lie in the hands of those who develop and state the strategy. Regardless of level in a corporation, objectives should be stated in terms which are measurable and which provide an adequate basis for evaluation.

Writing Realistic Advertising Objectives

Russell Colley wrote the major book about advertising objectives in his ***Defining Advertising Goals for Measured Advertising Results***, known by most advertising people as **DAGMAR**. The book was sponsored and published by the Association of National Advertisers and introduced several important issues for the use of objectives in advertising planning. Colley suggested that advertising objectives were made up of three parts, *a) a **communication goal** which represented the advertising effect; b) a **specification of the target market** to whom the advertising was directed; and c) a **time frame** for the completion of the advertising process*. As we'll see in the discussion later, some of Colley's work has been changed a little; but the principles are still being used by advertisers.

Colley required a communication goal for an advertising objective because of problems in using sales as an indicator of advertising effectiveness. While sales figures meet the requirement for measurability in objectives, they are influenced by many other factors. There are too many **intervening variables** between advertising and sales which can cause sales figures to fluctuate. This makes it impossible to separate the individual effect of advertising on sales. Sales may be affected by point of purchase displays, personal selling incentives, and many other marketing and communication variables.

The only time sales or sales-related variables are important in advertising objectives is with **direct response advertising objectives**. Intervening variables do not play a major role in direct response advertising. Instead, a direct response advertisement is the exclusive vehicle for communication between manufacturer and consumer. Yet even with direct response advertising, many managers prefer to state objectives in terms of "response to ads," rather than sales.

In general, sales is not used in an advertising objective because the presence of intervening variables confuses any evaluation of advertising made from sales data. A good question would be, "What are appropriate communication goals for advertising?"

Remembering the discussion of objectives, we know the communication goals have to be measurable and observable. Colley referred to a **hierarchy of effects** model of communication in his book. With this approach, he believed consumers moved through stages of *unawareness, awareness, comprehension, conviction and action*, so his communication goals were associated with these stages. Many similar hierarchical models of communication have been described. One talks about *awareness, interest, desire and action*, known as the **AIDA** model. The use of the hierarchical models have also resulted in the strongest criticism against Colley's work. Researchers, like Michael Ray[3], have pointed out that at least two other types of hierarchies must be considered in advertising.

Ray calls the type of hierarchy used by Colley a **learning hierarchy**, or the **learn-feel-do hierarchy**. He believes this hierarchy provides an adequate description of how consumers behave when they are interested in a product. A **dissonance-attribution hierarchy** has been found in consumers where the consumers act first, then change their attitudes toward and knowledge of the product. This is called the **do-feel-learn hierarchy**. This type of behavior occurs when a consumer has a strong desire for the product; but criteria for choice among alternatives are not clear. The last hierarchy described by Ray was the **low involvement hierarchy**. Called the **learn-do-feel hierarchy**, the low involvement hierarchy seems to describe consumer behavior best when products are not

---

Michael Ray, Advertising and Communication Management, (Englewood Cliffs, New Jersey, Prentice-Hall, 1982), pp. 184-188.

very important and the differences between brands are minimal. The different hierarchies are important for understanding consumers; but objectives can easily be written from what we've learned so far.

Several communication goals can be written from the hierarchies described above. An advertising manager might want to: a) increase awareness; b) increase comprehension of sales points; c) increase preference for a brand; or d) increase direct response to an advertisement as measured by returned coupons. These are measurable communication goals which could be written for any advertising campaign. Other communication goals could be written, as long as they meet the criteria of measurability.

Specialized types of advertising have specialized goals. For a **retail advertising objective**, increasing store traffic has been a primary objective. **Promotion objectives** have ranged from increasing attendance at special events to increasing coupon redemptions for declining products. **Corporate advertising objectives** often focus upon improving the general attitudes of consumers toward a corporation.

Within an advertising campaign, creative and media strategists can formulate and write creative objectives and media objectives. **Creative objectives** use communication goals, like increasing comprehension of sales points, to show how the advertising is supposed to work. **Media objectives** make precise specifications of how often and how many people will be exposed to the advertising. Creative and media objectives will be examined in detail in later chapters.

Colley's requirement for specification of the target market makes sense because of the popularity of target marketing. Since most campaigns are targeted to specific markets, the evaluation of a campaign must also be done using members of the target market. Target markets which are described in advertising objectives should be specified using categories from syndicated data sources, like Simmons Market Research Bureau. By using SMRB demographic categories to describe a target market, comparisons can be made between your market and syndicated national data.

Time frames for objectives depend upon the planning time. Long range objectives may use one to several years as the time frame. Most campaigns write objectives which match the length of the campaign. This may range from the four weeks of a media run to the six months of a retail campaign.

Advertising objectives are written as single sentences which describe the desired change in the communication goal, the target market and the time frame for attainment of the goal. But one of the most difficult parts of objective writing is determining how much change should be expected. In the learning hierarchy, we know it gets progressively more difficult to get changes. For example, through intensive media schedules, we can change awareness in a target market from 40 to 60 percent. If 60 percent of our market is aware of the product, then a significantly smaller proportion will know what the advertised sales points are for the product. This may be around 25 to 30 percent. Similarly, 8 to 10 percent of the target market may say they prefer our brand when asked which brand they prefer. Action or purchase may only be made by one to three percent of the target market. Using these estimates, it's easy to see that an objective which said its goal was to increase comprehension from 10 percent to 75 percent would be unreasonable. The change proposed is simply too great.

There are a couple of methods of estimating how much change can be expected in a target market because of advertising. One way would be to conduct a **test market study** where we try advertising and measure the change. Another is to make conservative estimates from past research data or previous campaign experience. Since objectives are one way of evaluating advertising campaigns, its important to trace the change in awarness and comprehension. **Tracking studies** have often been used to continually monitor changes in consumer variables like awareness and recall. At best, changes predicted in the statement of objectives are only estimates. Great campaigns will surpass all expected communication goals; poor ones will surpass nothing.

Study Questions

❑ What is the difference between strategy and tactics?

❑ What is the purpose of objectives? What are Colley's requirements for an advertising objective?

❑ What effect does a model of communication have on how we state objectives?

❑ Why is sales not usually a good goal for the statement of an advertising objective?

❑ How is evaluation of an advertisement or campaign related to the campaign objectives?

A Quick Review of Objectives!

An advertising objective must specify a directly measurable goal, usually a communication goal rather than a sales goal. The goal must be realistic. The objective must describe the target market using standard categories which have been previously measured. A time frame for completing the goal should be included; it's usually used to designate the length of time for a campaign. Look at the following objectives to see different levels of precision for the goals, the target markets and time frames.

Goal-setting example. XYZ Corporation would like to *educate* 25 percent of men between 25 and 55 *about our new new method of hair replacement* during the next four months.

PROBLEM. *To educate* is a very abstract goal. It can't be measured effectively because there are many different types of education. Do we mean ability to recognize our product's differences, or what? *About our new method of hair replacement* is not precise enough because it doesn't say what product features you want the target market to remember.

SOLUTION. Select a new objective *to create awareness of the XYZ hairweaving method of hair replacement.* To measure the effectiveness, you would have to decide whether a target market member would have to be aware of the technique only, or the association of the technique with XYZ Corporation. Also, you would have to decide whether evaluation would require unaided memory or aided memory of the advertising message. Achieving awareness is considerably easier than "educating." Notice that a goal could be stated as achieving awareness *in 25 percent of the target market,* or it could be stated as a change in awareness, such as, *to increase awareness by 25 percent in the target market.* Both goals assume a knowledge of present awareness; but the second goal has a difficulty. When you state an *increase awareness by 25 percent goal* you have to remember there's a difference in difficulty depending on how much awareness already exists.

Target market example. XYZ Corporation wants an increase recall of the brand and corporate name for Splash Guard by 30 percent, in *men who buy new cars*, within the 4-week television campaign period.

PROBLEM. *Men who buy new cars* is a very imprecise target market because it doesn't separate rich from poor. It doesn't give an age specification. As it stands, the objective could include those who bought once, but are now too old to buy another. *Men who buy new cars* is not a typical segmentation category.

SOLUTION. Why not describe this target market as *men between the ages of 18 and 55, who have incomes above $20,000 per year.* Adding the age restriction points to the optimum car-purchasing ages. The income restriction would focus on those who have enough money to buy a new car. Specificity helps focus on the right segment.

Time frame example. XYZ Corporation wants to create awareness of the speed-drying feature of the Max-L Hairdryer, in 50 percent of women between the ages of 18 and 45, *within the next year.*

PROBLEM. One year is a long time for an advertising objective.

SOLUTION. We might separate an objective into short and long term objectives. In this case, the time period may be for the *first quarter of 1989*, and a reduced percent of awareness. It might say, XYZ Corporation wants to create awareness of the speed-drying feature of the Max-L Hairdryer, in 20 percent of women between the ages of 18 and 45, during the first quarter of 1989. And, a long term objective would have a statement of the complete goal, "...increase awareness in 50 percent of women...during 1989..."

11

Advertising Campaigns

When people think of advertising campaigns, they usually visualize the
television intensive fast food advertising of McDonald's, Burger King or
Wendy's. When asked, consumers can sing jingles and recite dialogue from
many of the commercials in these campaigns. If they can't , then advertising managers should ask why not. Millions of dollars are spent trying to
get information recall and sales from the targeted consumer groups.

Advertising campaigns are *sets of ads and commercials* which
usually have a *common theme and visual continuity.* Many people associate
advertising campaigns with large advertisers. They shouldn't be. Every
advertiser would have more effective advertising if he or she thought of an
advertisement or commercial as part of a larger advertising campaign.
Here's why.

When consumers read advertisements or see commercials, a learning
process takes place. Consumers have to learn brand names, company
names, and retail locations, as well as features of the product. Not every
consumer sees every ad. Consumers never remember everything they see.
So each advertisement or commercial has to build from past images of the
product or the company. If there is enough visual and copy similarity, the
consumer won't have to relearn brand names or try to figure out who's
doing the advertising. Instead, there will be a greater possibility of the
consumer remembering sales points. So, *using a campaign approach aids
consumer recognition and learning.*

*Thinking about advertising as a campaign planning process will also
result in more effective strategy.* The **advertising campaign planning
process**, described in Figure 2, forces consistency between marketing and
advertising strategy decisions. It addresses elements of the promotion mix
from the advertiser's perspective. And the process illustrates how tactics
are connected to strategy. The campaign planning process will be discussed
in the next section.

Advertising Campaign Decisions and Outputs

Planning advertising campaigns has always been one of the most exciting
parts of the advertising industry. New ideas, new approaches and new
challenges stimulate the creative juices of most advertising people. But in

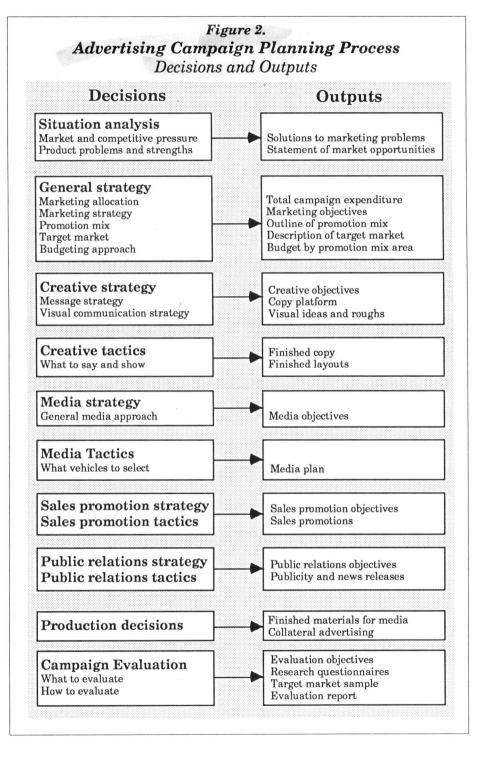

Figure 2.
Advertising Campaign Planning Process
Decisions and Outputs

Decisions

Situation analysis
Market and competitive pressure
Product problems and strengths

General strategy
Marketing allocation
Marketing strategy
Promotion mix
Target market
Budgeting approach

Creative strategy
Message strategy
Visual communication strategy

Creative tactics
What to say and show

Media strategy
General media approach

Media Tactics
What vehicles to select

Sales promotion strategy
Sales promotion tactics

Public relations strategy
Public relations tactics

Production decisions

Campaign Evaluation
What to evaluate
How to evaluate

Outputs

Solutions to marketing problems
Statement of market opportunities

Total campaign expenditure
Marketing objectives
Outline of promotion mix
Description of target market
Budget by promotion mix area

Creative objectives
Copy platform
Visual ideas and roughs

Finished copy
Finished layouts

Media objectives

Media plan

Sales promotion objectives
Sales promotions

Public relations objectives
Publicity and news releases

Finished materials for media
Collateral advertising

Evaluation objectives
Research questionnaires
Target market sample
Evaluation report

the excitement, it's easy to confuse debates over strategy with the goals of the debate. For this reason, Figure 2 separates the campaign planning process into **campaign decisions** and **campaign outputs**. As you can see, the outputs are the written results of the decision-making process. Each step in the process will be briefly examined.

Situation analysis. From previous discussion, we know the situation analysis was designed to evaluate the problems in marketing which might hinder an advertising campaign. Decisions debated in a situation analysis may require extensive consumer or product research, and corporate reorganization. But the output from the decision-making process will be solutions to the internal marketing problems and a statement of realistic market opportunities.

General strategy decisions. General strategy decisions indicate the major interface between marketing and advertising. The **marketing allocation** is a decision about how much will be spent marketing a product or service. The result from this decision will be the total promotion expenditure and total **campaign expenditure**. Marketing strategy decisions will also lead to written marketing objectives. One of the most important strategy decisions for an advertising planner is the determination of the relative importance of elements in the promotion mix. This decision will produce an estimate of the **relative weights for each promotion element**. Later these weights can be combined with the total promotion expenditure to produce a **budget for each promotion mix element**. Target market discussions will determine the target market strategy to be employed. A description of the resulting target market or target markets will be produced.

Creative strategy and tactics. Debates over creative strategy will establish creative objectives for the campaign, a **copy platform**, and the first visual images for a campaign. The copy platform is a statement of the concept to be communicated, and the approach to be used in advertising. Client approval of these initial strategy decisions is important before finished copy and layouts can be produced. The finished copy and layouts, or finished commercials, are the creative tactics for the campaign.

Media strategy and tactics. Strategy discussions for media are related to creative strategy, because the media selected must be capable of conveying the appropriate message. Once the media have been selected, then scheduling of media becomes an important issue. As a result of the strategy discussions, an advertiser will state media objectives, and select type of media. Media tactics require selection of individual media vehicles, and writing schedules for the vehicles in the **media plan**. The media plan may include efficiency data about each vehicle.

Sales promotion strategy and tactics. First discussions of sales promotion strategy will attempt to decide whether incentives should be offered to purchasers or to sellers of the product. In some cases, promotions will be offered to the sales force, the purchasers, and the consumers. Tactics of sales promotion are the actual devices to be used, whether they are cents-off coupons, rebates, or contests.

Public relations strategy and tactics. Public relations programs can be designed to promote the corporation, the corporation's products, or both. For small companies, like retailers, too little emphasis is placed upon developing adequate public relations programs. News releases, news conferences, brochures, public service activities and customer relations departments are the tactics of public relations.

Campaign evaluation. Whether a formal evaluation should be done or not is the first decision an advertiser has to make. In some cases, the total budget may not be large enough to warrant a formal evaluation of an advertising campaign. If evaluation is proposed, then decisions have to be made about the method of evaluation. These must be linked to campaign objectives. Evaluation tactics are the evaluation objectives, research questionnaires, the target market sample, and the evaluation report.

This has been a brief overview of campaign planning decisions and written outputs produced during an advertising campaign. The number of decisions and outputs made vary according to the size of the advertiser, and according to the complexity of the product. Complexities in the market often make strategy decisions more difficult; but a systematic way of examining the decisions makes it easier to study their effectiveness.

Budgeting for Advertising Campaigns

The question most often asked about advertising is, *"How much should I spend on advertising?"* The answer is, nobody really knows. We can all make guesses, and there are a few good guidelines; but there is no right or wrong answer. Part of the problem lies in the terminology surrounding the budgeting decision.

Marketing allocation is the total amount of money spent on marketing for a product. This includes product development and research, and many other factors distantly related to advertising. The **promotion expenditure** may include commissions and promotions to the sales force, so it too can misrepresent the advertising expenditure. **Total advertising expenditure** has been used by some authors to talk about the amount of money spent on advertising. The **advertising appropriation** has been used similarly.

The word "budget" usually means how the total expenditure is divided up between categories. So, an advertising budget would describe how much is spent on media, production and administration of advertising programs. Sales promotion and public relations expenditures may or may not appear in the advertising budget, depending upon the type of company or product. A useful way to talk about a total expenditure is to look at the promotion budget by elements of the promotion mix, with one qualification. That qualification would be to eliminate the personal selling costs from the budget. Regardless of the qualifications, *any discussion of expenditures and budgeting must state specifically what is or is not included in the budget.*

Once the ground rules have been stated, there are several general principles that apply. For overall expenditures on promotion or advertising there are factors which require more money. New product introductions can increase the needed expenditures by 50 to 100 percent. Heavy competition will increase promotion costs. Market dominance tends to reduce promotion costs. Building a new corporate image requires support for the new messages.

Many managers would say spend what you did last year, plus an increment for increased industry costs. That's only a guideline. Industry figures are available which provide **advertising to sales ratios**. For example, advertising cosmetics may require an expenditure equal to 20 percent of sales. Industrial products may require less than one percent of sales. The National Retail Merchant's Association distributes yearly expenditures on promotion by product class, and by month for retailers. These national estimates weighed against campaign objectives, such as a new product introduction, can produce the best rule-of-thumb estimate of expenditures.

The categories for determining advertising expenditures found in most books about advertising are based on what managers and store owners actually do. They have no relation to what is reasonable or defensible. For example, the **"all you can afford"** method means exactly that. We certainly won't spend more than we can afford; but we often spend more than we have to. **"Go for broke"** means mortgage your house and gamble on your new product. It's great if you get lucky; but it usually is a stupid strategy. The **"mail-order"** method means keep spending on advertising as long as returns from sales will pay for the advertising. A return on investment model would make a little more sense.

Some authors are more academic. They talk about the limitations of fixed methods, like **unit of sale**. Here an advertiser puts back a promotional amount for every item sold. **Percent of sale** is another way of doing the same thing. **Competitive parity** means spending what your competitors spend. The limitations of these methods is that they don't consider your company's actual need to advertise. New companies have to spend more. Heavy competition and complex products require more. To compensate for these limitations, authors endorse the **objective/task method** of determining expenditures.

The objective/task method is supposed to look at campaign objectives, or the advertising task, and spend what is needed for the task. Unfortunately, making that assessment is as subjective as saying spend all you can afford. The difference is that the objective/task method requires an argument, or good reasons, to spend money on advertising. It's unfortunate that the name of this method has the word "objective" in it, since it's related to advertising objectives, not objectivity.

In recent years, some companies have turned to a **return on investment** model (ROI) to determine advertising expenditures. This method requires either an extreme confidence in a company's ability to separate the influence of advertising from other sales influences, or disregard for the effects of good advertising. Other companies employ complicated financial models to determine the expenditure.

To budget advertising expenditures, there are three simple guidelines. First, *determine how important elements of the promotion mix are to your objectives and strategy.* Use a percent measure to divide expenditures between advertising, sales promotion, and public relations. Second, for any advertising campaign *spend the maximum amount of money possible on message delivery.* In other words, maximize media expenditures within any budget. Don't overspend on production. People have to be exposed to an advertisement or commercial before they can respond to it. Finally, *it's cheaper, and often more effective, to out-think competitors than to outspend them.*

Study Questions

❑ What is an advertising campaign?

❑ Why is thinking in terms of campaigns more important than thinking in terms of single advertisements or commercials?

❑ Describe the advertising campaign planning process.

❑ Why is the promotion mix decision so important to strategy, and to budgeting?

❑ How should advertising budgets be established?

The Importance of Campaign Themes

A promotional theme for an advertising campaign should be like an umbrella. The theme should allow many different kinds of advertisements and commercials. Long running campaigns, like the Miller Lite beer campaign, used a single idea, "Tastes Great, Less Filling," to create a highly successful series of commercials using retired athletes in humorous situations.

Strong campaign themes help for several reasons. With the same theme, several new commercials can be added for freshness. The overall theme provides longevity for the message. Strong themes also provide a good background for promotions, both sales and event, and public relations activities. Maintaining a theme protects the advertising investment that has been made in creating recall for the theme. Once a theme is well known and established, it costs a great amount of money to change consumer memory of themes and slogans.

Advertisements and commercials must demonstrate their connection to an overall campaign theme. This may be done in a tagline, a graphic symbol, or in the copy for a commercial or print advertisement.

12

Understanding Consumers
and the Advertising Process

If we know nothing about how consumers make buying decisions, then every advertising decision we make is a guess. Unfortunately, guessing in advertising is extremely expensive. That's why advertisers study **consumer behavior**. At universities the study of consumer behavior has stimulated interdisciplinary research between business schools, and departments of psychology, sociology, and communication. For social scientists, the business environment has provided a laboratory for testing psychological, sociological or communication theories. From this starting point, it's easy to see why modifications of social science theories can be found in marketing and advertising.

The practical question is, "'How can an advertiser get the consumer to choose and buy his or her product, instead of a competitor's product?" The question can get very complicated. First, not all product decisions are the same. We act differently depending upon the importance of the product, or our involvement with it. Second, not all consumers make similar decisions about the same product. We may have different reasons and motivations for purchasing the product. Third, an individual consumer may have different reasons for purchasing a product at different times. In order to make generalizations about consumers, we usually have to find out how the average consumer processes information to choose between products. Some advertisers use strategic consumer research; others rely on intuition.

This chapter will attempt to sort out variables which influence consumer behavior by examining the role of the product, the social scientific background, and the impact of the variable on the advertising process. Decision-making will be examined first.

Consumer, Shopping and Buyer Decision-making

There are several ways to look at decision-making. Each perspective has its own terminology and variables associated with it. One useful way to classify and talk about decision-making is by the *number of people involved with the decision-making process*. A similar system might study the *number of people for whom a product is purchased*. Both frameworks organize decision-making from **individual decision-making** by single consumers, to **joint decision-making** in families, to decisions made by purchasing agents or purchasing committees in large corporations. **Buyer decision-making** is the term given to institutional purchasers of products. As the number of people involved in a purchase decision increases, the buying process becomes more complex, and the decision more subject to negotiation.

At least three types of individual consumer decision-making have been described by researchers. **Complex decision-making** has been the most studied form of decision-making. When faced with a need or desire for a product, the consumer begins a search process for information. Once sufficient information has been accumulated, the consumer evaluates the alternatives and makes a decision. Once the product is purchased, an ongoing evaluation of the decision provides **feedback** for future reference. The decision is deliberate, calculated and conscious. Advertising and personal selling play important information roles for this consumer. Yet, some products are purchased without deliberation.

Two types of consumer decision-making occur without deliberation, **habitual decision-making** and **low involvement decision-making**. Both are related to the amount of risk a consumer is willing to take in a product decision. Habit formation in purchasing is one way of avoiding risk in making a decision. Once we've found a product that satisfies our need, it's much less risky to repurchase the same product. We don't need to perform an information search or go through a deliberative process. **Habitual behavior** in consumers, like habitual behavior in psychology, has been associated with **classical conditioning**. **Brand loyalty** is one form of habitual behavior. In order to counter the effects of brand loyalty the advertiser has to offer incentives, usually through sales promotion, to stimulate **brand-switching**. Since habitual behavior is not risk free, the disappearance of a favorite brand may initiate a return to complex decision-making in order to find a substitute brand.

Low involvement decision-making is low risk decision-making. When consumers have low involvement with a product, brands are substitutable. Selection criteria are not constant, and consumers often try new brands in an attempt to seek variety. Some marketers believe it's possible to move consumers from a low involvement state to a higher involvement state. They think this can be done by linking a low involvement product to a situation, attribute or benefit that is more involving. Researchers have also attempted to separate and define several different types of involvement, including ego involvement, issue involvement, product involvement, product importance, and brand commitment. Whether promotional dollars should be spent on consumers with low involvement is open to debate. In many cases, a more involved target market would be preferable.

In order to anticipate consumer response to advertising, it's necessary to separate the decision to purchase within a **product class** from **brand selection**. Once a decision has been made to purchase a product from a specific product class, such as an automobile, a refrigerator or a hairpiece, the consumer must select between brands. Consumer researchers describe the consumer's set of possible alternatives as the **evoked set**. Knowing the evoked set is important because it can provide valuable information about consumer knowledge, awareness of competitive products, and criteria for selection between brands.

For retailers, consumers may also have an *evoked set for stores* where they would shop for a certain product class. Selecting a location for shopping is only one part of the shopping decision. **Shopping behavior** is not necessarily purchase behavior. In fact, we know there are many reasons people shop from store to store. Consumers may shop for entertainment, to gather information about future product purchases, or as a social activity. Certain types of stores have evolved around the type of shopping behavior exhibited by consumers. For example, entertainment shoppers don't shop convenience stores for entertainment. Grocery store shopping is often guided by necessity, rather than enjoyment.

Regardless of the complexity of the purchase decision, or type of behavior used by a consumer, the advertiser must use what he or she knows about the consumer to develop a marketing advantage. The next section will look at the interface between consumer behavior and the advertising process.

Knowledge of the Consumer and Advertising Effectiveness

Two pieces of information about consumers are extremely important for effective advertising strategy. To be successful the advertiser has to know: a) what consumers should be exposed to an advertising message; and b) what to say in order to get a favorable response to advertising from consumers.

Accessibility, or the potential for exposure, is one criterion used for selecting target markets. More precisely, an advertiser wants to know the relative importance of **target audiences**. Target audiences are selected from statistics about the audiences available from different media vehicles, whether they're print or broadcast. Target audiences are designed to match target markets; but they are always smaller than target markets. No advertising media vehicle can reach 100 percent of the target market. Because exposure to the message is so important, and expensive, planning research is almost always used to examine media usage by the target market. Examples of questionnaire items which measure this usage can be found at the end of the next chapter.

Individual consumer characteristics also influence what needs to be shown or said for advertising to be effective. Consumers can't attend to every print advertisement or broadcast commercial they see. We call this **selective perception**. Members of a target market or a target audience are more likely to attend to advertising if a headline mentions that audience or market. Individual messages will be more persuasive if they speak the language, and use the logic of target market members.

The purpose of consumer behavior theories is to find groups of consumers who behave alike. When sizeable groups are found, we use them for target markets. In the next section, we will examine the bases for segmentation which advertisers use to discover profitable market segments. A connection will be established between the segmentation techniques and popular consumer behavior theories.

Segmentation and Consumer Behavior Variables

Geographic segmentation is based on the premise that people who live close to each other will exhibit similarities in purchase patterns. In major metropolitan areas, regions of the country and neighborhoods, we know there are three types of consumer influence which explain similarities in purchase patterns for these geographic segments. **Cultural** and **subcultural** regularities exist in ethnic regions and neighborhoods. If media can be found which reach these neighborhoods, then this segment-ation technique can be effective. Knowledge of the individual cultures also provides the advertiser with the sensitivity needed to write effective adver-tising copy.

Sociological similarities can be found in geographic segments when one separates city dwellers from rural inhabitants. The norms and atti-tudes of rural consumers will be more similar to each other than to their metropolitan counterparts. Knowledge of the differences in norms and language can also make advertising messages more persuasive for geo-graphic segments.

One of the most powerful explanations of purchase regularities in geographic segments is **situational** or environmental influence. People who live in geographic areas travel the same highways, see the same bill-boards, usually have similar incomes and occupations, and have many other characteristics in common with their neighbors. In order to use these simi-larities for advertising copy, further research has to be done to determine the similarities in attitudes toward an advertiser's products.

Purchase regularities in *demographic segmentation* are indirectly related to sociological, psychological and economic influences on behavior. Similarities in education, income, and occupation are related to **social class** or social status. Consumers who are at the same stage in their **family life cycle** can be expected to have similar attitudes about products, especially those relevant to the family. Families with new children will have similar attitudes about family life and products associated with it.

In addition to its connection with social class, income is also an **economic** variable which explains some purchase consistencies. Major pleasure purchases require discretionary income. People with limited income and restricted budgets may have similar purchase patterns. Those consumers not so restricted seem to want similar kinds of products, as "symbols" of their economic purchasing power.

With demographic segmentation, like geographic segmentation, an advertiser must do additional research to profit from consumer purchase regularities. Advertising copy cannot be written without some idea about how the members of the segment are similar.

Psychographic segmentation has ties to psychology, sociology and anthropology. In recent years, psychographic segmentation has been coupled to the measurement of consumer **lifestyle**. This coupling was due in part to William D. Wells' discussion in *Lifestyle and Psychographics*. Also, the Arnold Mitchell book, *The Nine American Lifestyles*, and the Stanford Research Institute Value and Life Style Program (**VALS**™), contributed to interest in psychographic research by major ad agencies. The psychographic measurement technique has four major divisions: outer-directed, inner-directed, need-driven, and integrated. Within the four divisions, the VALS program identifies nine associated lifestyles including: Integrated, Achievers, Emulators, Belongers, Sustainers, Survivors, Societally Conscious, Experiential, I-Am-Me.

Psychographic measurement attempts to find regularities in psychological characteristics of the consumer, like self-perceptions of personal activity. VALS attempts to identify cultural values which are similar across segments. Since psychographic statements may be generated by the product and marketing situation, there is some question about whether psychographic measurements can be tied directly to media vehicle selection. The success in constructing media plans, or writing copy, based on psychographic research is determined by the relative power of psychographic characteristics on product purchases.

Behavioristic segmentation strategies measure product usage and rates of product usage. Product usage rates may be influenced by **psychological conditioning**, but have limited application to media selection or to copywriting. Media scheduling is more directly related to psychological conditioning when one views an advertisement as reinforcement of a message.

Conflicting Perspectives

While the study of consumer behavior has provided valuable information about how consumers decide, choose and buy, there have been a few problems. Complex consumer behavior models must be tested across different marketing situations. Most have many variables to monitor. Models have to be complex in order to account for behavioral complexity. But, for the individual advertiser or marketer, narrowly focused strategic research may furnish more answers than general consumer behavior approaches. Rather than study all aspects of the decision-making process, the individual advertiser can study the "dominant" influence on the behavior of his or her customers.

Study Questions

❑ Outline the differences between consumer behavior, buyer behavior and shopping behavior.

❑ How is complex decision-making behavior different from habitual or low involvement decision-making behavior?

❑ How is brand loyalty related to classical conditioning?

❑ Why is the evoked set so important for an advertiser?

❑ What are the underlying consumer models for geographic, demographic, psychographic and behavioristic segmentation?

❑ What is VALS? How does it relate to market segmentation and models of consumer behavior?

The Seven Most Important Consumer Questions for Successful Advertising!

Why do consumers use the product? Sometimes, consumers can't tell you why they use a product. You need to know what attributes or features interest consumers most.

When do consumers use the product? Are there fixed seasonal periods for using the product? Are there regular periods of product use?

When do consumers buy the product? Are there peak periods of purchasing? Do they wait for promotions and special prices? Do they purchase the product for someone else?

Where do consumers get information about the product? Do they read specific media to find out product information?

Where do consumers purchase the product? Do they buy from discount sellers? Do they purchase direct from the company?

What enticement will get consumers to purchase a different brand of this product? What is their brand loyalty? How likely are they to switch?

How frequently do consumers read or watch advertising about the product? Is viewing or watching accidental or planned?

13

Strategic Advertising Research

Advertising research is not a neutral topic. Advocates preach it. Skeptics curse it. Popular writers try to expose it. More people use it than understand it. But simply put, advertising research is research. It's *a tool which trys to find answers by providing systematic methods for removing bias.* In advertising, there are two periods when research is important. **Strategic research** is done early in the planning stage of a campaign to provide information about the product, the market, competition or advertising messages. The answers are the basis for strategy development. **Evaluation research** is used after advertising has been placed to determine its effectiveness. Evaluation research will be discussed in a later chapter.

A description of common misuses of advertising research shows why it's important to view research as an objective tool. Advertising agencies and advertisers have often tried to use research to "prove" their strategies. While objective research information does become evidence for strategic arguments; the evidence must come *before* the argument. End of year money may be spent on advertising research. Here the objective is to spend money, not necessarily to find answers. Sometimes research is done simply because a company has a research department, or because a manager thinks research is an important part of every project. This is not true. Because research costs are high, there may be times when the cost of doing research is not justified by the potential return from an advertising campaign. There must be good reasons for making a decision to do research. And once the decision has been made, the research has to be done well.

"Doing good research" means a manager understands the **research process,** and is willing to play the game according to the rules of science. The research process, illustrated in Figure 3, can actually be described as a series of research decisions. Like many other descriptions of research and problem solving, this is a social science version of the "scientific method" found in the natural sciences. It's a good way of analyzing the decisions made by an advertising researcher.

Research Decisions

When to Do Research

If we use the word research to describe any method of getting information about a product or market, then research should always be done. Every advertising manager or account executive must find information about new products or new markets. In order to advertise a product, the manager, art director and copywriter should experience it. Where possible, he or she should try the product, and witness the purchasing system first hand. Of course this works better for fruit juices and hamburgers than it does for bulldozers. Every advertiser should also try to find as much secondary data as possible about a product or market. These two steps in advertising research are necessary regardless of whether any other primary research is going to be done. For this discussion of research, the question "Should research be done?" could be restated as, "Should *primary research* be done?"

The answer to the "primary research" question is sometimes yes, sometimes no. Primary research should be done when the cost of research will result in more effective marketing or advertising. Improvement in sales must be strong enough to pay back the research costs. Many marketing research texts provide formulas which estimate the **value of information** received from research. These formulas are subjective, rather than objective, estimates of value.

When would we decide not to do primary research? The most obvious time is when our promotion budget is very small. Primary research is a luxury we sometimes can't afford. There are also times when the research question we ask has an obvious answer. For example, attempting to find out awareness for a product that hasn't been advertised doesn't make much sense. It's easier to say, "just a few," than to find out precisely how many consumers are aware. In any case, there has to be a good reason, or good return, from the research process.

Research Questions

Once a manager decides research is necessary, the objectives for research are written. Like other objectives, the objectives for research must be "actionable." Most researchers would like to see a list of decisions to be made on the basis of research results, before research begins. This usually doesn't happen. The reason researchers like to see the list before, is because negative results are often discounted by managers when the results disagree with favorite strategies. If research is not strong enough to be tied to decision-making, then there's a question of whether it's worth doing at all.

The **research question** is a single question which expresses the purpose of the research project. It focuses the project so the procedures don't become too broadly defined to answer. In addition to focusing, there

Figure 3.
The Research Process
Major Decision Points

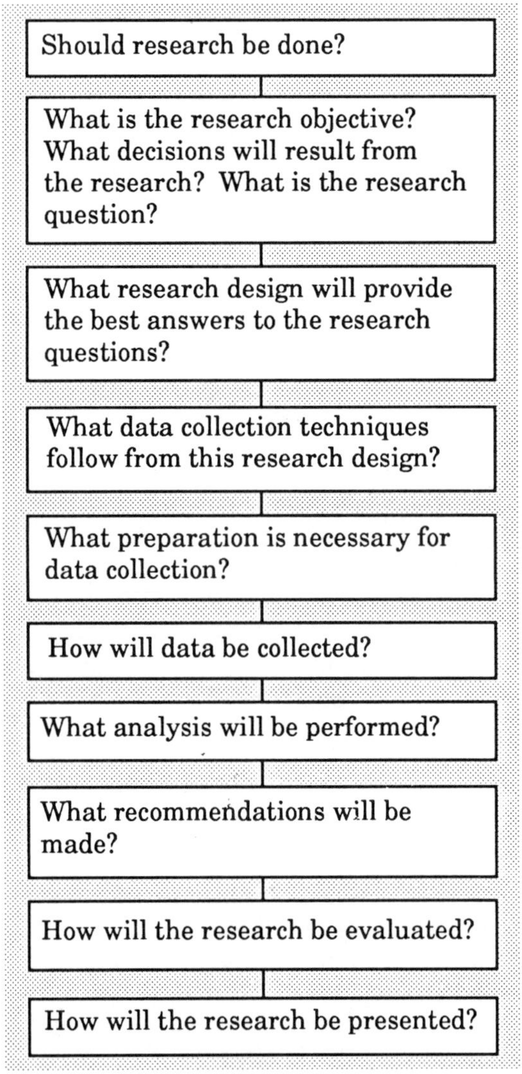

Should research be done?

What is the research objective?
What decisions will result from
the research? What is the research
question?

What research design will provide
the best answers to the research
questions?

What data collection techniques
follow from this research design?

What preparation is necessary for
data collection?

How will data be collected?

What analysis will be performed?

What recommendations will be
made?

How will the research be evaluated?

How will the research be presented?

are several other characteristics of good research questions. 1) For good research questions, *finding reasons is as important as finding answers*. For example, rather than ask, "Do consumers like or dislike product *X*," a researcher could ask, "Why do consumers like or dislike product *X*?" Without reasons, the research question doesn't provide enough support for a managerial decision. 2) *Negative research results are as interesting as positive results* when good questions are used to guide research. Using a question like the one above may find consumers who don't like your product. But the reasons they don't like it will provide valuable insights into changing your marketing or promotion strategy. 3) Good research questions *anticipate future research needs*. A company could ask "What does the adjective 'soft' in a brand name mean to members of the target market?" A better question would be, "What adjectives in a brand name for our product provide more recall by members of our target market?" The second question would provide answers useful for other product introductions.

The research question decision shapes and controls the entire research process. Three approaches to advertising research follow directly from the type of research question asked. Let's examine the three approaches, and the three types of research questions.

When no information is available, and we need ideas, we use *explore why* questions. "Why do consumers like or dislike our new condom commercials?" For this question, we have no existing information about likes and dislikes. We can't compare these likes or dislikes to anything. We can't prove anything from the research. We're looking for possible reasons from consumers. *Explore why* questions lead to an **exploratory** research approach. The goal of exploratory research is to look for as many *potential solutions* to a marketing problem as possible. Exploratory research is not designed to provide a specific answer to our problem.

What is questions are more specific and try to describe what exists in the marketplace. For example, "How many heavy, moderate, light and non-users are there in the Atlantic states?" Notice that this question is based on the researcher having more information about the product, market and consumers. Categories of heavy, moderate and light have been established. The market has also been divided into regions. If we have breakdowns of national data for the Atlantic region, we can also compare our product to the national norms. *What is* questions look for specific answers about what exists. They lead to a **descriptive** research approach.

Sometimes we need more precise information about why one advertising technique is better than another. Or we may need to know exactly what factor influences consumer preferences. To find these answers, the researcher has to use more control in his or her research procedures. In these instances, the researcher asks *prove what or why* questions. *Prove what or why* questions attempt to isolate and establish the cause of differences in consumer response. This has been called a **causal** research approach.

Research Designs

Research designs are related to the research approach. Three research designs will be examined in this section: qualitative designs, survey designs, and experimental designs. The choice of a research design is determined by two factors: 1) the amount of control over outside influences the researcher wants to have in the research process, and 2) how much similarity the researcher wants between the research setting and the market environment. These two factors are related to **validity** in the research process. Unfortunately, as the researcher exerts more control, the research setting gets more artificial.

Validity refers to the ability of the research process to provide "correct" answers to research problems. There are many types of validity based on different characteristics of the research process. A researcher must be able to argue for the validity of his or her research study. Three types of validity will be described here.

If a research project makes intuitive or "gut" sense, we say the project has **face validity**. There are no tests, or ways to test, face validity. It's a belief that reasonable researchers would agree the approach is acceptable.

Internal and external validity are most relevant to the choice of research designs. As the researcher controls outside influences he or she is increasing the **internal validity**. *Increasing internal validity attempts to guarantee a "correct" conclusion by ruling out other influencing variables.* Researcher control over outside influences may include bringing research participants to a theater in order to expose them to different messages. But bringing the people into a theater is not a normal viewing situation. This artificiality is related to **external validity**. As the research setting becomes more natural, we are increasing the external validity. *External validity is the ability to reach "correct" conclusions about the marketplace, based on the smaller sample of people we study.* If the situation or group studied is artificial, the conclusions may be open to debate. Furthermore, since "other influences" are actually part of the environment, it may be unwise to attempt to control them in a research study. Let's look at the three research designs, and compare their validity.

Qualitative research designs are used to describe methods of research which rely on participants to provide qualitative information about products or themselves. Traditionally, not as many participants are used in these designs; findings can't be generalized to a larger target market. Since these exploratory designs attempt to provide avenues for later research, it's probably not appropriate to enforce internal or external validity standards for them. Because the research is exploratory, internal validity is non-existent. Depending upon the research setting, qualitative studies will have varying levels of external validity.

Surveys are the most common type of design used in descriptive approaches to research. Because they attempt to answer *what is* research questions, they must try to question participants in natural settings. For this reason, surveys are high in external validity. Since the researcher exerts only minimal control in the research setting, surveys are low in internal validity. In addition, in order to provide maximum generalizability survey researchers have sophisticated ways of selecting participants called **sampling**.

Experimental designs attempt to *prove what or why* some factor influences another, so control is heavily exerted. Researchers try to control all outside influences. Therefore, experimental designs have higher internal validity than surveys; but they have lower external validity. One attempt to achieve a balance between internal and external validity has been the **field experiment**. Field experiments are experiments carried out in natural settings. There is still manipulation of important variables, but these variables are measured in the natural environment. In terms of validity, it's a good compromise; but higher costs usually favor other designs.

Data Collection Techniques

In deciding what data collection technique to choose, the researcher has to match research approach, research design, and economics of the study. Only the most common **data collection techniques** will be reviewed. In qualitative studies, the focus group is the most common procedure. For descriptive research, observational methods, telephone and mail surveys are generally chosen. Causal studies use lab experiments with various types of measurement, including a few observational methods. Let's examine each briefly.

Focus groups are groups of 6 to 12 people and a moderator who talk about a specific topic for one to two hours. Discussions are usually audiotaped; sometimes they're videotaped. Transcripts are processed for each focus group. While selection procedures for participants are not as stringent as they are for other types of research, participants must be from targeted groups. Bias is controlled in focus groups by the neutrality and nondirective leadership of the moderator. Focus groups were developed as a less expensive replacement for personal interviews. Many research suppliers offer slight variations in the technique.

Observational methods of data collection are often among the most accurate and precise measurements. Scanner data and electronic methods of monitoring television audiences are the newest techniques being used. In the past, the most severe limitation of observational methods was their inability of producing information about consumer attitudes and beliefs. As with scanner data, product information could not be linked to specific consumers. Syndicated research and media research firms have now developed ways of coupling observational data to specific consumers.

Telephone and mail surveys use telephone interviews and mail questionnaires to obtain information. Telephone interviews, because of their integration of computers, can tabulate and report data much faster.

Mail questionnaires are limited by the speed of mail delivery in two directions. Mail questionnaires also take more effort on the part of the respondent. Choice between the two techniques should be determined by the target market, and the likelihood of completion.

Laboratory experiments often expose different groups of consumers to different copy techniques or approaches, then administer questionnaires. Serious consideration of the materials presented to participants must be given in order to control outside influences. For example, if we want to test recall of brand names, we have to use techniques to control order effects on recall, and many other variables.

Figure 4 was designed to show the influence of research approach, research design and data collection method on three types of advertising research. Three common data collection techniques are represented: focus groups, telephone surveys, and lab experiments. Figure 4 shows the steps in each of the research processes.

Data Collection: Preparation and Completion

The researcher must determine what types of materials are needed to collect data. Questionnaires must be designed, tested and printed. Experimental materials for lab experiments have to be developed, tested and produced. Protocols, or topic lists, have to be prepared for focus group moderators. Let's examine what it takes to develop a questionnaire for research in the field or in the laboratory.

Almost everyone has filled out a **questionnaire** at one time or another. To **design a questionnaire**, the researcher has to systematically develop the questions. Some questions are easy, like demographic questions "How old are you?" Routine income, age, sex and education questions can be taken from existing questionnaires. The only difference in wording is the difference between a mail questionnaire and a questionnaire used by telephone interviewers. Spoken language style must be used on the telephone questionnaire; the mail questionnaire must be self-explanatory.

Some items, or questions, on a questionnaire are called **scales**, because they are used to measure attitudes or values. For example a scaling item may ask, "On a scale from 1 to 10, where 10 is very important, how important is the decision to purchase a new car this year?" Scaling questions are designed to measure some product or consumer attribute. In the case above, we wanted to know how important the decision to purchase a new car was to the consumer. Consumer attitude scales have become popular in recent years, because some of the scales offer different ways of segmenting markets. As we said earlier, the Stanford Research Institute developed the **VALS**, Values and Life Styles measuring system for consumer attitudes. Here's how scales are developed.

Several different questions are put in a pool of questions and given to research participants. The researcher looks for bad wording and style mistakes. In addition, the researcher is looking for certain characteristics

Figure 4.
Three Research Approaches

Research Question		
What problems do consumers see in our new commercials for aspirin? *WHY?* (handwritten)	What proportion of the target market prefers scented deodorant to non-scented deodorant? *WHAT IS?* (handwritten)	What copy statement is the strongest in convincing consumers to purchase our brand, instead of the major competitive brand?

Research Approach		
Exploratory	Descriptive	*PROVE WHY* Causal *OK WHAT!* (handwritten)

Research Design		
Qualitative	Survey	Experimental

Research Objective		
To find initial consumer reactions to new aspirin commercials.	To find how many target market members prefer scented to non-scented deodorant.	To find out which of three copy statements is the strongest at getting consumers to switch to our brand from the primary competitor's brand.

Data Collection Method and Procedures		
FOCUS GROUP	**TELEPHONE SURVEY**	**LAB EXPERIMENT**
Write a protocol for the moderator. Select participants from the target market, randomizing isn't necessary. Select a moderator or research supplier. Prepare any needed materials. Conduct the focus group. Transcribe conversations.	Write a first questionnaire. Pretest questionnaire on a small sample of target market members. Revise questions and re-test, if questions are unclear. Use standard categories if they are available. Prepare questionnaires. Select participants. Get a random sample from a research supplier. Train interviewers or hire a research supplier. Conduct the survey. Code questionnaires and tabulate.	Select your copy manipulations. Prepare stimulus materials. Pretest stimulus materials and questionnaires for measurement. Revise, if necessary. Select participants from target market. Random selection less important, because copy manipulations will be random. Select appropriate lab setting. Conduct the experiment. Code questionnaires, and analyze data.

Conclusions		
Can only compare what is said in the transcript to the research objectives. There is no way to test conclusions.	In the survey, we can find out how many prefer products; but we have no way to test why they prefer specific ones. Survey data can also be compared to national data.	If done right, the experiment can tell us which copy statement is most effective because it is subjected to a statistical test.

Strengths and Limitations		
Good at generating ideas and hunches. Information can be very distorted by the small groups of 8-12 participants.	Quality of data is as good as the sample. Data is collected in the actual environment. One of the most used research techniques. Many dislike the lack of control.	Excellent control of experimental manipulations. But the laboratory setting is very artificial. For some problems these settings are ideal.

of the scale. The scale must be related to some particular consumer behavior or decision. Scales must possess a characteristic known as **reliability**. Reliability is the ability of a scale to produce similar results when administered again. Once reliability is established, the researcher combines all questions into the final questionnaire and gives it to the main research participants. Scale development is called **pretesting a questionnaire**, or pretesting the instrument. **Instrument** means questionnaire, because of its similarity to other measuring processes.

Deciding who will collect the data is also important. Internal data collection by a company can result in poor quality data. Other job responsibilities may interfere with the speed of data collection. Higher overall costs may not justify data collection by a research supplier. Once collected, the data have to be put into a form suitable for analysis.

Data Analysis and Conclusions

The analysis and conclusions from each of the three types of advertising research are restricted by the type of questions asked. In qualitative research, where the goal is to *explore why*, information acquired from research can only be compared to the objectives. In focus groups, this means citing passages and quotations as evidence of support for the study's objectives. Descriptive studies describe, so their primary analytic techniques are descriptive statistics. Researchers compare means and frequency distributions to national data. One of the most frequently used statistical techniques is **cross tabulation** or **crosstabs**, where data is organized in tables by categories. Higher level statistics are used in causal studies to study causality. For these causal studies, like lab experiments, the researcher can test the strength of certain variables.

Selecting Approaches to Research

While selecting a research approach seems like an important choice, it is often determined for you. If you have no information, you have to select a qualitative, exploratory design. If you have information about a product or market, you can use descriptive studies. Causal studies usually require much more information about a product, consumers and the market.

The Domain of Strategic Advertising Research

Purists might assign different roles to advertising and marketing researchers. Under a separation system, marketing researchers might be assigned all product and market research. Advertising researchers would be asked to study competitive advertising activity, the influence of messages on target market members, copy and concept research, and audience research as it relates to advertising strategy. The borderlines are not that distinct.

It's true advertising researchers spend most of their time doing **copy testing** and **concept testing**. In addition, **media research** is done to assist media planners in developing effective media strategies. As indicated earlier, advertising researchers rely on syndicated studies for media information. Both message and media researchers include marketing-oriented questions on their research questionnaires.

Strategic copy research attempts to study concepts for advertising before the copy is developed. For **concept tests**, statements of the general message idea are usually placed on cards and evaluated by study participants. **Copy tests** expose research participants to specific wording of the advertisements. Concept tests occur at an earlier stage of research than copy tests.

A Quantitative Research Postscript

Business school graduates swear by the doctrine of empirical research. They study numbers. They try to convert everything into numbers. They feel helpless without numbers. Yet studies have shown that when research data is presented, many managers seem to act on the first hunch they get. Upper-level management, and the public, places a great deal of credibility in research data, regardless of its quality. An effective manager has to know what it takes to get good research data. Good information must be acted upon in order to get a clear strategic advantage.

Study Questions

❑ What are the steps in the research process?

❑ How does a research question affect the research design and data collection method for a research study?

❑ What characteristics are important in a research question?

❑ Evaluate the internal and external validity of qualitative designs, survey designs, and experimental designs. How does a field experiment compare to the other three designs?

❑ What is observation? What have been the major limitations of using observation as a data collection method?

❑ Distinguish between a questionnaire and a survey.

❑ How should we determine whether primary research is needed or not?

Writing Simple Questionnaires

Everyone ought to write at least two questionnaires. The first would provide an appreciation for the difficulty of the task. The second would allow the writer to sharpen his or her writing skills. Questionnaire writing is important because questionnaires can be used to extract information from the consumer's mind. All advertisers, including retailers and noncommercial advertisers can benefit from systematic monitoring of consumer purchase patterns or attitude change.

If questionnaires are written well, marketing and advertising opportunities may emerge from the findings. If they're written poorly, there are two possibilities. Co-workers may notice how poorly the questionnaires are written and suggest redoing a project. If the poor quality goes unnoticed, bad decisions may be made on the basis of poor questionnaire data.

The purpose of this section is to provide basic questionnaire writing skills for simple marketing questionnaires. In addition to looking at sample questions, suggestions for questionnaire organization and design will be provided.

What You Need to Know About Questions Before You Start Writing Them

There should be two guiding principles for questions on every questionnaire, *focus* and *clarity*. Here's why these principles are so important. Whether you're writing a very short intercept questionnaire, or a longer mail questionnaire, *you can never ask every question you'd like to ask.* As questionnaires get longer, survey participants get more tired and less likely to answer your questions. Focus, in questionnaire writing, means getting the most important information from participants.

Questionnaire writers can stay focused by writing objectives for questionnaire research. Statements of objectives answer the question, what information do you intend to get from the questionnaires? These objectives might be as simple as, "We want participants to give us a list of reasons why they like or dislike our store location." Another way to keep focused on getting the best information is to set priorities for pieces of information. This will aid in knowing which questions have to be omitted.

Clarity, for the questionnaire writer, means *asking questions participants understand.* They should be clear and unambiguous. Preferred answers should not be suggested by the question. Questionnaire writers can guarantee clarity by going through a process of writing, pretesting, and rewriting questions on the basis of pretest results. Here's how it works. You write a number of questions. These questions are given to two groups of pretest participants. The first group is asked to tell what he or she thinks you're looking for in each question. This is a qualitative pretest.

A second group of participants, usually 20 to 30 is asked to fill out or answer the questions. For mail questionnaires, participants should work with written questions. For telephone questionnaires, participants should have questions read to them. From these participants, you want to find out if there are any problems in how people answer the questions. Before beginning the second part of the pretest, participants should be told to ask any questions necessary in order to answer the questions. The following two references give many helpful hints about making questions clear so they evoke precise answers from participants. The first is a classic book about asking questions; the second is a newer guide oriented to social science research.

Stanley L. Payne (1951), *The Art of Asking Questions*, (Princeton, New Jersey: Princeton University Press).

Seymour Sudman and Norman M. Bradburn (1983), *Asking Questions: A Practical Guide to Questionnaire Design*, (San Francisco: Jossey-Bass Publishers).

Selecting the best question type is an important decision for many reasons. Simpler questions can be answered faster. This cuts the time spent with each survey participant. Analysis of the results can proceed much faster, because less individual coding or tabulating of results will be needed. Simpler questions may allow you to get more information from survey participants because more questions can be added to the questionnaire. Difficult questions often result in more unfinished questionnaires. This adds to the administration cost of research. But, longer, more involved questions can provide very important marketing information; even though follow-up analysis is more complicated. If processing time is important, then the questioning process should be less complicated. Let's look at a couple of question types.

One way of classifying questions looks at how much freedom a person has to answer the question. These will be referred to as **open and closed questions**. Other names for the same classification system are: open-ended and closed-ended, and open and closed response. Open questions place fewer restrictions on the person answering. With this question, "What do you like about bicycling?" a person is free to say anything. He or she could give a one word answer, like "Nothing!" Or, the person could give a 15-minute discourse on why he or she liked bicycling. Problems arise when a manager or store owner tries to summarize the results of an open question. Each answer must be examined separately and put into categories. If 400 people answer the bicycling question, 400 individual answers must be categorized. This takes time, and costs money.

A closed question for bicycling might be, "Do you like bicycling?" This yes or no question allows only three possible answers: yes, no or sometimes. Notice how this particular closed question tells little about reasons, and reasons are important for marketing strategy decisions. It may seem like the decision between open and closed questions is a no-win situation. It really isn't. What researchers do is compromise.

For open questions, researchers have several alternatives. Here are a couple. Typically, open questions require asking a person for more information, rather than trying to stop a person from talking. When more information is needed, the person doing the interview is told to **probe** for more information. **Probing questions** are questions like, "*Is there anything else...?*" "*Any other reasons you can think of...?*" When a questionnaire pretest indicates research participants talk too much, the interviewer must shorten answers. On written questionnaires, this is done by drawing boxes for answers. Boxes suggest an appropriate amount of information to be supplied by the research participant. In personal or telephone interviews, the researcher may add restrictions to the question, such as *"In a few sentences..."* or *"What are the three most important reasons..."*

Here's another approach. Open questions are included on a pretest questionnaire which is given to 50 or 60 people. From the answers given, the researcher develops categories of responses. Instead of using the open question on the final questionnaire, written questionnaires have a closed question with the most popular categories. Most questions like this also use an "other" category where the survey participant writes in responses which don't fit the categories. This approach actually converts an open question to a closed question.

Closed questions can be made more open. The yes-no bicycling question could have included a **follow-up question** like, "What do you like [or dislike] about bicycling?" If time was important, closed responses could be tabulated immediately; follow-up responses could be tabulated later.

Open and closed questions are just one type of question. Sometimes it's important to know how much more important one product attribute is than another. When measuring differences is important, researchers use **scaling questions**. Scaling questions measure degrees of difference in survey participants. Let's look at three types of scaling questions, each measures satisfaction with a new car in different ways.

1. *How satisfied are you with your new car? (Check one)*
   _____ *Very satisfied*
   _____ *Somewhat satisfied*
   _____ *Neutral*
   _____ *Somewhat dissatisfied*
   _____ *Very dissatisfied*

2. *On a scale from 1 to 10 where 10 is Very Satisfied, tell me how satisfied you are with your new car? _____*

3. *If the best car you ever owned was 50 on a satisfaction scale, how would you rate your satisfaction with your new car? _____*

In question 1, categories of satisfaction are very broadly defined. Question 2 gives us a numerical rating of satisfaction. If we used this type of scaling question on several different products, we could compare the results numerically. Question 3 has an actual zero point which shows when a person is not satisfied at all. This type of scaling question could easily be used on different products. Several considerations should be given when selecting a scaling type of question.

As you progress from question 1 to question 3, the task of answering the question becomes more difficult for the participant. It requires more effort to make a judgment; therefore more time and effort will be required. Finer distinctions are made in question 3, than in questions 1 and 2. This is called the **precision** of a scaling question. From question 1 to question 3, the questions become more precise. Precision is important to the statistical analysis of questionnaire information. For many simple questionnaires, increasing the precision of questions is not as important as making it easier for participants to answer the questions.

Questionnaire Types and Questionnaire Organization

A **survey** is a study which attempts to collect information from a **sample** of participants using one of several data collection methods. The three most common data collection methods for a survey are: **telephone interviews, mail questionnaires**, and **intercept interviews**. All three of these data collection methods use questionnaires; but, there are some important differences which affect how questions should be written. Questionnaires used by telephone or intercept interviewers are read to participants. Mail questionnaires are sent to participants. An interviewer can explain any question the participant doesn't understand. Questions in mail questionnaires must be self-explanatory. There are also differences in wording because we don't talk like we read or write. Questions for telephone and intercept interviews must be more conversational in tone. In the sample questions to be included, written and spoken versions will be indicated.

Another difference between the three data collection methods is the time frame for answering questions. Intercept interviews, which are often done in shopping malls, must be shorter than the other methods. Typical intercept interviews last 5 to 10 minutes. Telephone interviews probably average 10 to 12 minutes. Mail questionnaires may take 15 or 20 minutes to be filled out by a research participant. As the time available for answering questions get shorter, questions must be made simpler and easier to answer. As an advertiser or researcher, you can extend the length of interviews by either hiring professional interviewers, or by offering incentives to survey participants.

In recent years, many companies have used phoney survey research techniques as a disguise for telemarketing programs. These attempts to deceive consumers cause considerable damage. The techniques are unethical, and contribute to consumer distrust. It's important to consider negative reactions to telemarketing approaches when offering incentives for filling out a question-naire. A coupon offer in your retail store will probably increase participation. A "sales pitch" for an incentive may sound like a telemarketing offer, rather than a genuine research survey to the potential participant. Now, let's examine questionnaire organization.

Questionnaires which are used in a mail survey, telephone interview or intercept interview have the same organization. The most important design principles is: *if a questionnaire is simple, more people will fill it out and fewer mistakes will be made.* When you write a questionnaire you're usually commun-icating to at least three different people. Each questionnaire asks questions for the survey participant to answer. But, it must also provide instructions for an interviewer, and instructions for the person who tabulates the information, usually the data processor. Effective organization of a questionnaire considers the needs of each group of questionnaire readers. Let's see how information is organized for each group of readers.

The main purpose of a questionnaire is to gather data from survey participants. To do this, each questionnaire has four parts: a) the introduction tells the participant the purpose of the study and asks for cooperation; b) screening questions put you in touch with the right survey participant; c) central questions of the survey are asked in the middle section; d) demographic and media usage questions are asked last. Since intercept interviews are shorter than telephone interviews, some of the central questions and some demographic questions must be eliminated from the questionnaire.

Interviewer instructions are included on telephone and intercept questionnaires. This information tells the interviewer how to record participant answers, and provides a roadmap for the questionning process. To distinguish interviewer instructions from questions for survey participants, instructions are often typed in a different type style. See Figure 5 for an example of how interviewer instructions are included on a telephone questionnaire. Figure 6 shows the dialogue between the interviewer and survey participant.

Computer tabulation of questionnaire data will be more effective if the questionnaires include information for the data processor. This information is called **"coding information."** Coding information is a number, or text, which is typed into a computer for each answer given by a participant. Figure 7 shows the data processor coding information for the telephone questionnaire. Before a project begins, a researcher may prepare a list of questions, with their coding information. This list is called a **codebook**. Now we'll examine the entire questionnaire writing process.

Questionnaire Writing from Objectives to Codebook

The writing process begins with the survey objectives. Descriptions of the other steps are listed in their order of appearance on a questionnaire. Actual question writing may be done in any order you prefer. Example screening, scaling, media usage, and demographic questions have been included in this section.

Step 1. Write the survey objective. Just like advertising objectives, research objectives must describe observable behaviors to be studied in a survey. For example, we might say, *"We want to do a telephone survey to determine awareness and recall of fast food advertising by different demographic groups in Northeastern Detroit suburbs."* This objective suggests that awareness and recall would be central questions for the survey; demographic questions would provide a standard of comparison for demographic groups.

For a smaller retailer, we might propose the following objective. *"Intercept interviews with store customers will be performed to determine frequency of shopping at the store, types of products purchased, and general satisfaction, by demographic group."* In order to improve advertising, we might specify a study which, *"...will perform intercept interviews with store customers to measure shopping frequency, perceived competition, suggestions for improvement, by demographic and media usage groups."* Notice how the data collection method and the group to be studied have been included in the objective. For more effective data analysis, a marketing research text, or consultant, should be used to determine the best way to select participants in the survey. This is called **sampling**. A brief description can be found in Chapter 13.

Step 2. Write the introduction. Since time is limited, the introduction should be a short statement about why you're doing research, such as, "...to determine new ways to serve your customers," or "...to find out what people in our school district think about the millage issue." Try to make the introduction straight forward, and not deceptive. Give your name, and ask politely for help. You may also say you'd be happy to call back at a more convenient time, many researchers do. Don't provide so much information that participants know exactly what you're looking for. Participants will go out of their way to give you the answer you want. You should want their honest and unbiased opinions. Again, the simpler the statement, the better the response. Here's a general sample.

SPOKEN. Hello, my name is (your name). I'm working for (your company), and we're trying to find out what people think about (product or issue). Could you give me about 5 to 10 minutes of your time to answer a few questions. It's very important. [If participant hesitates] If this is an inconvenient time, I'd be happy to call back. What time would be convenient for you?

WRITTEN. This questionnaire has been written to find out what you think about (product or issue). Your feelings and opinions are very important to (your company), because once we know how you feel we can produce better products for you (or other goal of research). Would you please go through each question carefully. There are instructions next to each question. Thank you very much for your help. As soon as we receive your completed questionnaire, you will receive (incentive) in the mail.

Step 3. Write the screening question. From the statement of whom you're talking to in the survey objective, write a question which selects that group. This question can be added immediately after the introduction. For example, you might say, *"We need to talk to mothers of children between the ages of 7 and 10, do you have children between those ages?"* Another screening question might be, *"Could I speak to the person who purchases paper towels for your family?"* Screening questions are designed to find people in your target market. If the questions are too narrow, you will waste considerable effort and money performing short interviews to find target market members.

Step 4. Write as many of the central questions as you can. To write the central questions in the questionnaire, you need to know what you want to measure, or ask about. Do you need scaling questions? Or, do you need closed-ended questions? Are there open questions needed to explore new opportunities? If so, there shouldn't be too many. Here are a few types of attitude questions for written and interview questionnaires.

SPOKEN. As I read each of the next five statements to you, would you tell me how you feel. Do you strongly agree, agree, neither agree nor disagree, disagree, or strongly disagree.

Figure 5.
Telephone Questionnaire
Interviewer Instructions

MSU CONDOM ADVERTISING STUDY
Interviewer Name _____
Date _____
Time _____
Telephone Number called _____
Respondent Number _____

INTERVIEWER INSTRUCTIONS
Conduct this telephone interview using the telephone number provided. As you go through this questionnaire, read only the information in BOLD type. Follow instructions carefully. When asked to fill in OTHER categories, or to write out the participant's comments, record as much information as possible. Please be courteous, and try not to offend the respondent, since this is a sensitive topic. Practice administering this questionnaire with a friend before performing the telephone interviews. Begin the interview.

1. Hello, I'm _____, a student in the Department of Advertising at Michigan State University. As part of a class project, we are trying to determine attitudes toward condom advertising on Detroit television stations. The interview will only take five to ten minutes. For the purpose of this study, I need to talk to someone in your house who is eighteen or older. Would that be you?

Continue <- - - - - - - - - -	Yes	1
Ask to speak to <- - - - - -	No	2
the appropriate person.		
Terminate <- - - - - - - - -	Don't Know	8
	Refused	9

2. In the past few weeks, some Detroit area television stations have begun advertising condoms. Have you heard that condoms were being advertised on television?

Continue <- - - - - - - - - -	Yes	1
	No	2
Skip to Question 3 <- - - -	Don't Know	8
	Refused	9

Figure 6.
Telephone Questionnaire
Dialogue with Survey Participant

MSU CONDOM ADVERTISING STUDY
Interviewer Name _____
Date _____
Time _____
Telephone Number called _____
Respondent Number _____

INTERVIEWER INSTRUCTIONS
Conduct this telephone interview with using the telephone number provided. As you go through this questionnaire, read only the information in BOLD type. Follow instructions carefully. When asked to fill in OTHER categories, or two write out the participant's comments, record as much information as possible. Please be courteous, and try not to offend the respondent, since this is a sensitive topic. Practice administering this questionnaire with a friend before performing the telephone interviews. Begin the interview.

1. **Hello, I'm _____, a student in the Department of Advertising at Michigan State University. As part of a class project, we are trying to determine attitudes toward condom advertising on Detroit television stations. The interview will only take five to ten minutes. For the purpose of this study, I need to talk to someone in your house who is eighteen or older. Would that be you?**

Continue <----------- Yes 1
Ask to speak to <------ No 2
   the appropriate person.
Terminate <---------- Don't Know 8
              Refused 9

2. **In the past few weeks, some Detroit area television stations have begun advertising condoms. Have you heard that condoms were being advertised on television?**

Continue <------------ Yes..........................1
              No..........................2
Skip to Question 3 <---- Don't Know 8
              Refused 9

Figure 7.

Telephone Questionnaire
Data Processor Instructions

MSU CONDOM ADVERTISING STUDY
Interviewer Name _____
Date _____
Time _____
Telephone Number called _____
Respondent Number _____

INTERVIEWER INSTRUCTIONS

Conduct this telephone interview with using the telephone number provided. As you go through this questionnaire, read only the information in BOLD type. Follow instructions carefully. When asked to fill in OTHER categories, or two write out the participant's comments, record as much information as possible. Please be courteous, and try not to offend the respondent, since this is a sensitive topic. Practice administering this questionnaire with a friend before performing the telephone interviews. Begin the interview.

— —

1. Hello, I'm _____, a student in the Department of Advertising at Michigan State University. As part of a class project, we are trying to determine attitudes toward condom advertising on Detroit television stations. The interview will only take five to ten minutes. For the purpose of this study, I need to talk to someone in your house who is eighteen or older. Would that be you?

Continue <- - - - - - - - - - Yes 1
Ask to speak to <- - - - - - No 2
  the appropriate person.
Terminate <- - - - - - - - - Don't Know 8
                              Refused 9

2. In the past few weeks, some Detroit area television stations have begun advertising condoms. Have you heard that condoms were being advertised on television?

Continue <- - - - - - - - - - Yes........................... 1
                              No...............................2
Skip to Question 3 <- - - - Don't Know 8
                              Refused 9

SPOKEN. Let me ask you about the service from our service department. Would you say you are very satisfied, satisfied, dissatisfied, or very dissatisfied with our service.

SPOKEN. On a scale from 0 to 100, where 100 is very important, how would you rate the importance of the following features in an automobile? Powerful engine. Leather upholstery. Etc.

WRITTEN. Check the response below which indicates how important locker room service is to you at the Welsun Health Club.
> _____Very Important
> _____ Important
> _____ Unimportant

WRITTEN. Please put a check mark (✔) in the blank that describes your feelings about the cereal advertising you have just seen.

> *EXCITING* _____ : _____ : _____ : _____ : _____ *BORING*
> *INNOVATIVE* _____ : _____ : _____ : _____ : _____ *TRADITIONAL*
> *PERSONAL* _____ : _____ : _____ : _____ : _____ *IMPERSONAL*

For this type of question the adjectives have to be tested, and the position (left or right) determined by a flip of a coin. Order of appearance should also be assigned randomly.

Step 5. Pretest all the central questions. Ask participants in the pretest to tell you what the questions mean. Test any numerical questions with a larger group of participants.

Step 6. Select the best central questions for the questionnaire. Remove or rewrite questions with ambiguities. Choose questions which give you the most interesting and most complete information related to your survey objective.

Step 7. Select the most appropriate demographic and media usage questions.

AGE.
How old are you? _____

Please put a check by your age group.
> _____ 18-24
> _____ 25-34
> _____ 35-44
> _____ 45-54
> _____ 55-64
> _____ 65 or Older

SEX.
(On interviews) Have the interviewer code the participant male or female.

Please put a check by your sex.
   _____ *Male*
   _____ *Female*

EDUCATION.
What is the last year or grade in school that you completed?
   _____ *College graduate*
   _____ *Attended college*
   _____ *Graduated high school*
   _____ *Did not graduate high school*

MARITAL STATUS.
Please indicate your marital status below.
   _____ *Single*
   _____ *Married*
   _____ *Divorced / separated / widowed*

EMPLOYMENT STATUS.
What is your current employment status?
   _____ *Employed full time*
   _____ *Employed part time*
   _____ *Unemployed*

RACE.
(Interview) *What is your race? Are you...*
   White _____
   Black _____
   Hispanic _____
   Oriental _____
   or some other race? _____

INCOME.
What was your family's total income last year? _____

Please mark the income category below which indicates your total family income for 1987.
   _____ *Under $10,000*
   _____ *$10,000 to $14,999*
   _____ *$15,000 to $19,999*
   _____ *$20,000 to $24,999*
   _____ *$25,000 to $29,999*
   _____ *$30,000 to $39,999*
   _____ *$40,000 to $49,999*
   _____ *$50,000 or more*

MEDIA USAGE (NEWSPAPER).
Newspaper usage is very important for retailers. That's why the last three questions are open questions.

How many days a week do you read a daily newspaper?
Do you read more than one daily newspaper? (Circle one) YES   NO

Please list the names of the newspapers you read during the week.

Please list the names of newspapers you read on Sunday.

Which shopping guides or weekly newspapers do you read?

MEDIA USAGE (RADIO).
Radio usage is difficult to measure because people remember call slogans, D.J. names, and numbers on the dial; but never consistently. For interviews, and for written questionnaires, the alternatives have to have the AM or FM number, the call letter sequence, the slogan and any other identifying information possible.

How many hours a day do you listen to radio?
What are your favorite radio stations? (Code responses)

MEDIA USAGE (CABLE TELEVISION).
Do you subscribe to cable television? Yes No
What kinds of programs do you watch on cable? (Must be coded later)

MEDIA USAGE (NETWORK TELEVISION).
On an average day, how many hours during the day do you watch television?

On an average day, how many hours during the evening do you watch television?

What are your favorite television programs?

PRODUCT USAGE.
About how often do you purchase (product) for your own use? (Categories must be developed from a pretest, or product information.)
    _____ *Once a day*
    _____ *Once a week*
    _____ *Once every two weeks*
    _____ *Once every month*
    _____ *Once every three months*
    _____ *Once every six months*
    _____ *Once a year*

About how much do you spend on (product) purchases during an average (week)?

EVOKED SET/BRAND USAGE.
If you had to purchase a new (product) today, at what stores would you shop for a new one?

What brand of (product) do you use?

If your brand was no longer available, what other brands would you consider purchasing?

Please list as many brands of (product) as you can.

Step 8. Make a rough questionnaire with all the questions. In the rough questionnaire, you want to combine the central questions with demographic, product, and media usage questions. Now, test the questionnaire on a few individuals. Time the questionnaire to make sure it's not too long.

Step 9. Write instructions for the questionnaire. In mail questionnaires this means communicating directly to the person filling out the questionnaires. Make the directions simple and straightforward. For telephone and intercept interviews, the instructions have to tell the interviewer how to administer the questionnaire. They also have to be told what to do when survey participants have questions.

Step 10. (optional) Put data processing information on the questionnaire and write a codebook. Coding information can be added later. It's much better if you can add it at this point; but coding requires a little knowledge of computer operation. Figure 8 shows a simple codebook organized by questions. Some researchers add other information for data analysis; but this simple codebook will speed coding and tabulation.

Step 11. Decide on a design for the questionnaire. Look at questionnaires you've received. Look at marketing textbooks. Look at the Telephone Questionnaire example in Figure 5. Make the design simple and easy to use for interviewers. Good design in a mail questionnaire makes it appear to be short, whether it is or not.

Step 12. Do one last test before having the questionnaire printed. Ask an innocent person to try to fill out, or to try and administer the questionnaire to someone. If he or she has problems, make the necessary revisions.

14

Creative Strategy in Advertising

No topic in advertising generates more argument and debate than the development and implementation of **creative strategy**. Creative strategy is responsible for translating marketing strategy into a plan for talking about and visualizing the product or service to be advertised. Like all strategies, creative strategy is a plan of action which has its own set of **creative objectives**. These objectives provide one way of evaluating a creative plan. Before we talk about developing creative strategy, let's look more closely at some of the controversies that emerge when the topic of creative strategy is discussed by advertising people.

Common Creative Debates in Advertising

The word "creative" causes much of the problem. In art or science, the word creative is usually linked to new ideas, new perspectives, or new ways of looking at something. So, one definition of creative would be a novel, new or innovative idea.

Creative may also be used as an attribute for an individual. A creative individual would be a person who, on the average, has more new ideas or ways of looking at a problem, than other individuals. This doesn't mean every idea is new and original, only that the person has a history of producing new ideas. Actually, every person can alter their ability to generate new ideas to some extent. That's why popular psychologists offer seminars and strategies for improving a person's creative output. Some of the most popular guides to creative thinking are Roger Von Oech's, *Whack on the Side of the Head*, and it's sequel, *Kick in the Seat of the Pants*. Edward De Bono gave us *Lateral Thinking*, and several others, including the *Six Thinking Hats*. Other authors, like Robert Weisberg, in *Creativity, Genius and Other Myths*, take a more skeptical approach to the topic of creative thinking. All of these popular authors provide entertaining and practical suggestions for developing creative skills, but the creative problem in advertising is more complex.

For years, writers, art directors, and production people in advertising have been labelled "**creatives**". Since many people view the ultimate goal of advertising as the production of new selling ideas, hiring creative people is an important task for advertising executives. In most advertising agencies, people who work on the creative product, writers, art directors, and designers, are located in the **"Creative Department"**.

Unfortunately, the label creative leads to further problems. Since the **creative product**, or advertising message, is the most visible part of an advertising program, there is considerable ego-involvement for the people who develop a successful advertising campaign. That's why advertising people like to claim responsibility for successful campaigns. Sometimes even those not responsible for the success claim they were key individuals. Almost no one in advertising wants to claim responsibility for a flop. That's not unusual.

The creative department label tends to establish new ideas as the domain of the creative department. But, new and effective ideas can be generated from any creative individual in an organization. Sometimes naive people discover them because they don't view a problem in traditional ways. Since creative ideas can come from many sources, the interchange between key marketing and creative personnel should be open and unrestricted, so valuable ideas and strategies are not lost.

Creative ideas can also be lost when a company over-controls the creative product. In these situations, management personnel are usually reluctant to delegate responsibility for the production of creative advertising messages to specialists in the creative department. Unwarranted management control can lead to mediocre messages. The most negative result can be the demoralization of creative professionals. When this occurs, high turnover rates and lack of productivity usually follow.

Competitive tension over advertising is unavoidable, and necessary, for the production of high quality messages. When the debates are based on evidence, sound reasoning and facts, the resulting messages can be more effectively developed and monitored. William Marstellar's book, *Creative Management*, provides a discussion of management techniques for creative environments.

Creative people also have a few complaints about their work environment. Many feel an over dependence on research and evaluation takes the excitement and spontaneity out of advertising messages. While management by objectives is a systematic approach, these people question its effect on the production of thrilling, spectacular and dynamic messages.

Managers complain that creatives don't know how to "sell" the product. While advertising messages may be new and entertaining, they frequently miss the major selling points of the product. This may cause problems in the marketplace.

If you talk to any copywriter, art director or account executive in an advertising agency, you'll find comments which reflect these debates. The creative process demands teamwork because the creative strategy must provide an effective translation of marketing strategy into verbal and visual messages.

What is Creative Strategy?

Traditionally, creative strategy is a plan which tells how the marketing strategy is carried out in copy appeals and visualizations. Many books combine discussions of creative strategy with discussions of the target market and product positioning. While these targeting and positioning decisions are important, the creative strategy should be a unique plan of its own, with objectives and actions that can be evaluated.

Several concepts have been included as part of the creative strategy. The most common is the **copy platform**, which gives the essence of the message to be conveyed by advertising plus some other information. Other information often included is a description of product features, an outline of the audience, and a sketch of the typical consumer. Both verbal and visual messages are often included in the copy platform. If both are not included in the platform, then there should be an accompanying statement of visual communication strategy.

Several problems exist with traditional creative strategies. They are often defined by conflicting marketing concepts because they originate from different corporate levels. Approaches may have been initiated by the creative department, an advertising manager or a brand manager.

Discussions of creative strategy in advertising have not always included **strategic arguments** to justify the copy approach or visual treatment of the product. In several instances, authors of creative books for advertising have focused on creative strategies to the exclusion of integrated marketing concepts. Because of these deficiencies, the next section of this book will introduce a new concept for building advertising and marketing strategy. This method will provide systematic guidelines for strategy building. The technique will provide more effective campaign evaluation and adjustment, and will force integration of promotional programs. Because the new process of strategy building is integrated, consistent messages will be produced for all promotional areas, including: advertising, sales promotion, public relations and personal selling.

Study Questions

❏ How does the word "creative" interfere with the development of creative ideas in advertising?

❏ Why is there so much confusion over creative strategy in organizations?

❏ What is a copy platform and why is it important?

❏ How do strategic arguments fit into a creative strategy?

❏ What goals could be used in a "creative" objective for advertising?

How to Build *Structured Strategies* for Promotion

This section will provide a method for constructing strategies for marketing, sales promotion, advertising, product-oriented public relations and personal selling. Using this hierarchical technique, you'll see how marketing strategy and objectives can be effectively translated into specific plans for sales promotions, advertising copywriting, the production of advertising visuals, advertising media planning, and publicity dissemination. Before we find out how to build *structured strategies*, let's see why we need a new method for strategy development.

Problems with Existing Promotional Strategies

Several problems make strategy development difficult. In corporations and on the street, everyone thinks he or she is a strategy expert. Very few are. Unfortunately, conflicting marketing and advertising strategies may contribute more to poor advertising performance than any single marketing factor. Often, marketing-based strategies focus on one specific technique, like product positioning or market segmentation in order to build response to commercials and advertisements. In some cases, these singular approaches don't consider enough marketing factors to be effective. In almost all cases, the techniques don't provide enough guidance about what should be communicated in advertising copy and visuals. Nor do the singular approaches offer guidelines for advertising media planners, or other promotion functions like sales promotion and public relations. Because of the separation of job functions in many organizations, sales promotion and public relations plans often emerge as unrelated and unintegrated corporate activities. New attempts have recently been made to coordinate promotional activities more completely in many companies.

Biases in the organizational superstructure of a corporation may contribute to the confusions in marketing strategy. Many managers believe there is only one "right" marketing strategy that leads to profitability. Actually, many different strategies will work; but they must be executed well. Strategic trademarks, or **creative philosophies**, have been associated with several legendary figures in the advertising industry. Bill Bernbach was noted for his emotional appeals and creative insight. Leo Burnett developed campaigns based on the "inherent drama" of the product and a Midwestern slice-of-life presentation style. David Ogilvy has often been characterized by his reliance on strong research foundations, and a focus on brand image building. Each style and creative philosophy developed from experiences with a different set of products. But if the clients were shuffled between agencies (as is often the case in advertising), each of these advertising men could have developed successful campaigns without abandoning his personal style.

Great advertising and promotion strategy requires a great idea, flawless execution, and consistency in the presentation of messages to consumers. This doesn't mean great advertisers can't fail. Advertising and marketing are dynamic processes. Products, consumer perceptions of products, competitors and markets change. Every strategic choice is a well-informed guess, until feedback about product sales arrives from the marketplace. All strategies must be monitored and fine tuned to meet changing dynamics in the market.

Three Interdependent Decisions: The Foundation for *Structured Strategies*

Conventional approaches to strategy might start by examining the marketing mix, consumer product preferences, and existing market segments. Some of these concepts will reappear in this discussion of *structured strategies*; but there are fundamental differences. A *structured strategy* will be based on the **interdependence** of three key marketing decisions. The assumption of interdependence means the consequences of each decision must be evaluated simultaneously with the other two decisions in order to develop effective strategies. The three key decisions are: 1) choosing a **product identity**; b) determining a suitable **competitive distance** from major competitors; and c) selecting an appropriate **market segment**. To defend his or her choices, an advertiser or marketer must provide strategic arguments, or reasons for believing a strategy will be effective. The set of strategic arguments for the entire marketing program will be called the **strategic framework**. This framework, not individual advertising or marketing decisions, should be the focal point for debates about strategy in an organization. In the discussion to follow, we'll first look at the critical decisions; then, we'll see how and why the decisions are interdependent. The descriptions in this section apply the strategy building technique to existing products. Extension to new products is straightforward.

Product Identity

There are two relevant questions. How is my product or service presently perceived by purchasers? How would I like my product or service to be perceived by purchasers? Broadening the questions makes them more strategically important, and demonstrates their interdependence with other decisions. How is my product perceived by purchasers, relevant to competitive products in the product class? And, how is my product perceived by different market segments?

There are some obvious ways to illustrate differences in product perceptions. For example, consider "blue jeans" as a product class. A simple classification might divide the market into two segments, users and nonusers. From a marketing perspective, the user category would be more informative if it was separated into subgroups of purchasers, such as: generic or house brand jean purchasers, brand name jean purchasers, and designer brand jean purchasers. These categories reflect different perceptions of jeans by purchasers. They also reflect different degrees of financial commitment to the purchase of jeans. Because of the differences in financial commitment, the market could also be divided or segmented by income levels. A study of these income segments would probably mirror the segment categories created earlier.

If we wanted to introduce a new jean product, we would have to decide on a product identity for our marketing efforts. Two types of product identities can be created. a) An **attribute/benefit identity** attempts to differentiate a product using physical attributes of the product, or consumer benefits derived from the product. b) An **associative identity** couples a **product sign,** like a brand name, to a selling concept, a person, or an experience. This **symbolic association** requires advertising support to establish a new symbolic meaning for the product name in the mind of the consumer.

An example of associative identities can be seen in the jeans market. Lee jeans attempted to couple their brand name to fit. By repeating a theme like, "Lee jeans fit," a product identity was established. Of course, establishing one identity rules out other identities for your product. Designer jeans, like Calvin Klein and Guess, also use a brand name for promotion; but they couple their identities to psychological attributes or romantic consumer experiences. As brands proliferate in a product class, each brand must establish a **position** for itself against other brands.

The first step in creating a profitable position is determining how your product is perceived by various market segments, today. But, the key step for a new strategy is determining where to go and how to get there. To make these choices, you have to evaluate which product identity will best meet corporate objectives. Initial research can provide some guidance. You must find out what product features or consumer benefits are most important to consumers the segments you want to reach. You also need to know the relative strength of competitive products on the product features and benefits of interest to your target market. If your product doesn't compare well with the competition, or has features which don't interest the target market, you'll have to change strategies.

For jeans, a decision to introduce a generic or house brand product must consider the competitive offerings, and features important to the generic or house brand segment. Introducing a brand name product forces a decision about what characteristic should be coupled to the brand name. Similarly, a designer jean introduction would also have to consider existing products and positions. To support a decision to identify your product in a specific way, you must have good reasons for selecting the product identity. The best reasons will depend on weighing the relative positions of competitors, and segment preferences.

Competitive Distance

Recent concern over **"me-too" marketing strategies** and **"knock-off" products** demonstrates one dimension of competitive distance. By imitating competitive advertising styles or product packaging, some marketers reduce the distance between themselves and the competition in order to build fringe markets, or to create brand switching. Competitive distance, achieved through marketing communication, is similar to the Ries and Trout definition of product positioning. Not too many people like to admit they have chosen a "me-too" positioning strategy.

In the Hertz and Avis rental car campaigns, the Avis position was, "We try harder because we're number 2." Many other companies were close to Avis initially; but Avis used advertising to create a closeness with the leader. With this strategy, they outdistanced the companies that were close to them.

Competitive distance must be communicated in advertising creative executions. To cut through advertising clutter, you must also provide a **contrast** between your advertising and competitive messages. Both competitive distance and contrast can be established verbally and visually. Selecting the right distance is also related to product identity. In the jeans example, a new creative look and style may be necessary to develop new associations for an existing brand name.

Segment Selection

Every existing product has a **purchaser profile**. This profile represents the market segments which are attracted to your product. Sometimes the segments are clear and visible. Other times segments are almost indistinguishable. The important question for market growth is whether there is a "better" segment to reach for your product. A better segment may be larger, or it may have more high frequency purchasers. Early beer drinking research showed that 80 percent of the beer was purchased by the heavy-drinking segment.

Another criteria for selecting segments is whether your major competitors are weak in certain segments. Most small manufacturers and retailers begin their growth by attacking the weaknesses of their major competitors. This was described earlier as guerilla marketing.

Notice how the search for better segments may alter your choice of a product identity. The product identity communicated must be the best identity for the market segment you are attempting to reach.

Altering product identities and segments can create new problems. If existing product purchasers don't like the new positioning or advertising messages, they may switch products. Organizations which build memberships frequently have internal problems with their membership when they offer incentives or promotions to new members. Strategies like these fail to recognize the importance of building from a stable customer base. In order to prevent these problems all new strategies should be evaluated with existing and potential purchasers of the product.

The three key, interdependent decisions—product identity, competitive distance and segment selection—must be made on the basis of existing knowledge and good judgment. Strategic research should try to determine what the existing product identity is. It should assess the existing competitive distance between your product and market contenders. Research should profile existing product purchasers by segment. Changes in identity, distance and segment selection should be supported by sound reasoning and research evidence where possible. After the three marketing decisions are made, *structured strategies* can be developed for creative messages, media planning, sales promotion, product publicity and personal selling.

Building a *Structured Strategy*

The phrase *structured strategy* is used to indicate the interlocking, coordinated plans which extend from initial marketing decisions through all promotional programs. Let's briefly review the marketing choices (See Figure 8). Product identities may range from a simple attribute/benefit focus to more complex associative identities where brand names must be established. Possible competitive distances may range from complete similarity or dissimilarity with all products, to a set of mixed similarities and dissimilarities, depending upon the competitive product. Segments selected may be the same as those selected

Figure 8.
Building Structured Promotional Strategies

	PRODUCT IDENTITY	COMPETITIVE DISTANCE	SEGMENT SELECTION
Marketing Strategy	*Attribute/ Benefit* U.S.P. *Associative* Branding	*Similar Dissimilar Mixed*	*Existing Wider Narrower New*
Sales Promotion Strategy	How does the sales promotion device or event reinforce the desired identity of the product?	How does the sales promotion device or event create or maintain the competitive distance between competitors?	How does the sales promotion device or event meet the response objectives for the market segment?
Advertising Copy Strategy	How does the persuasive message reinforce the desired product identity?	How does the style and content of the advertising message establish or maintain the competitive distance?	How does the copy technique or style account for the language require- ments of the target segment?
Advertising Visual Strategy	How do the campaign visuals create and maintain the desired product identity?	How do the campaign visuals contrast with competitive visualizations, and how do they main- tain the compet- itive distance?	How are the campaign visuals relevant to the perceptual experiences of the selected segment?
Advertising Media Strategy	How does the editorial environ- ment of the media and media vehicles selected complement the desired product identity?	How do the ads or commercials, or schedules, create or maintain the com- petitive distance?	How does the media schedule accomplish the reach and freq- uency objectives for the segment?
Public Relations Strategy	How does the content of publicity and media channels selected promote the desired product identity?	How do public relations messages maintain the desired distance between compet- itors?	How effectively do the channels of distribution cover the media of selected market segments?

in past promotional programs. They may be wider, narrower or totally new segments. Multiple segments may also be selected.

The principle of *structured strategies* was designed to guarantee consistency of message and promotional strategies, given a starting point of three marketing choices. Elements of the promotion mix are also examined in Figure 8. While some of the elements of the promotion mix discussed in Figure 8 have not been described in prior sections of this book, they will be examined in later chapters. The *structured strategy* approach was introduced at this point because it will help illuminate upcoming discussions of copywriting, visual communication strategy and media planning. Now we'll look at the individual elements of the promotion mix.

Sales promotion is commonly used to stimulate immediate product purchases. If your target market is wholesalers, then you're using a **push strategy**. A push strategy encourages wholesalers to stock up. Wholesalers will then encourage or "push" retailers to buy more products. Consumer sales promotions create a demand at the retail store level. If stores don't have the product, they will ask wholesalers to order it. This strategy is called a **pull strategy** because consumer demand "pulls" products through the distribution chain.

Consumer sales promotions have many purposes. They are used to **induce trial** for new users, or to **create sales** for a new product. **Repeat purchasing** or **shelf-stocking** are other goals for sales promotions. Even in giveaways, contests or sweepstakes, the product identity should be reflected in the giveaway item or contest procedures. **Event promotions** should also consider the product identity and market segment. Like popular soft drink campaigns, the celebrities selected for product endorsements should create a favorable association with the brand name. This is the reason celebrity endorser contracts are often terminated after a celebrity endorser has received bad publicity. Competitive distance can be created by selecting a different sales promotion than competitors, or by using sales promotions more or less frequently.

Advertising strategy includes creative strategy, with guidelines for copywriting and campaign visualizations, and media strategy, with its resulting media plan. The persuasive messages in a copy strategy or copy platform must create and reinforce the product identity. At the same time, differences in style and content of advertising copy can be used to establish a competitive distance between available advertising messages. The language of advertising copy must be understandable and persuasive for the selected target market.

Visualizations and visual communication strategy have similar requirements. Visual images must create and reinforce the product identity. The images must be selected to establish the desired competitive distances, and must have meaning for the target market.

Notice how this method of *structuring strategies* does not restrict the creative freedom of designers and copywriters. Different writing styles or visual techniques can be used to establish an identity or create competitive distance. The only requirement is that evidence, or a strategic argument, be used to support the creative approach. It does not tell copywriters what to write, nor does it tell art directors what to show in advertising. Any restrictions lie in the marketing decisions about which identity is appropriate, how much competitive distance is necessary, and who the selected segment should be. Because of the interrelationship of the critical marketing decisions, creative personnel should be involved early in the marketing planning process. During these early stages, creative personnel can indicate how identities and competitive distances can be communicated most efficiently.

Advertising media planners can supplement and extend the marketing strategy by selecting media vehicles which match the identity and market requirements for your product Competitive media strengths and weaknesses must be considered in the media planning process. Vehicle selection should also integrate the marketing choices by selecting media where the editorial environment complements the desired product identity. Effectiveness of the media plan must be measured by its ability to reach the target segments. But, this has always been a criteria for effective media planning.

Public relations for products or services is designed to supplement other promotional efforts. **Product publicity** and public relations is an attempt to get editorial coverage of a product in the media. Expert practitioners can build publicity programs which stimulate added interest among product purchasers and nonpurchasers.

Because of the product or service focus for this discussion, **publicity releases**, or **news releases**, delivered to the media must reflect the product identity. The content of all messages must reinforce the product identity and competitive distance through media channels. All publicity sent out, or being used by media, must be evaluated by its ability to reach the target market.

Figure 8 provides a set of questions for evaluating strategic elements of the promotion mix. Similar constraints could have been written for personal selling. Sales pitches, and message appeals should support the identity of the product, the competitive distance, and the target market. Structuring is one method of making strategies more consistent. While consistency in strategy will go far in making advertising and promotion programs more effective, the three primary choices are most important.

The "art" of marketing strategy is selecting a promotable and affordable identity, determining how a product must relate to various competitive products, and adjusting the target market to achieve more marketing success. Advantages in the marketplace are often created by exploiting the weaknesses of competitors. These weaknesses may force narrower segmentation strategies. Bold competitive moves, like the Avis rental car campaigns against Hertz, required careful positioning...and guts. Regardless of the strategy selected, the total marketing and promotion program will be more effective when all elements have consistent messages. Building **structured strategies** will result in increased marketing efficiency.

Since the foundation for effective strategies is research, Figure 9 shows what research information is optimal for a manager. These informational goals will never be fully reached; but the information acquired does provide a foundation for strategic decisions.

Figure 9.
Optimal Information for
Structured Promotional Strategies

	PRODUCT IDENTITY	COMPETITIVE DISTANCE	SEGMENT SELECTION
Marketing Strategy	How is the product perceived by existing and new segments?	How is the product perceived relative to competitive products?	Who is the current product purchaser or user?
Sales Promotion Strategy	How effective has sales promtion been for this product and this product class?	How have competitors used sales promotion in their marketing programs?	Are there differences in response to sales promotion for different market segments?
Advertising Copy Strategy	What message appeal associated with the desired product identity is most persuasive?	What message appeals are being used by competitors?	How have competitive products been promoted to target market segments?
Advertising Visual Strategy	What form and content of visual images conveys the desired product identity?	How do competitors use visual images in their promotional programs?	What visual images are most persuasive or interesting to your targeted segments?
Advertising Media Strategy	What media and vehicles have editorial content which enhances the desired product identity?	What media vehicles and scheduling patterns do competitors use in their advertising program?	What media vehicles and scheduling will provide the best coverage of the targeted segments?
Public Relations Strategy	What forms of publicity and media channels will provide the most appropriate information about the product? What media channels are most accessible?	How do competitors use publicity and public relations in their marketing program?	What media do the targeted segments use most frequently? What media offer the most complete coverage or the product and product class?

15

Copy Decisions and Platforms

Effective advertising copy is shaped before the writing begins. This chapter will look at what copy choices have to be made in order to produce powerful and consistent advertising messages. You'll see how to write a **copy platform**. The copy platform is a one-page document which summarizes the copy concept, identifies the copy concept's strength against the competition, and shows the relevance of copy appeals to the target market. It also establishes a link to past advertising in order to build on the consumer's past recognition and recall of messages. The copy platform will also demonstrate how the copy concept can be extended and developed. One of the first copy choices is the selection of an advertising medium. Media choice affects both content and style of advertising copy.

Which Media?

In the early stages of campaign planning media choices will be made. The choices should consider the unique qualities of the product, competitive advertising, and the media habits of the target market. From a creative angle, the advantages of certain media are common sense. Television is a visual medium where demonstrations work well. Visual fantasies and spectacular events can also be effectively created in the television medium.

From a copy perspective, radio has been called a fantasy medium because verbal copy can stimulate an infinite number of images in the minds of consumers. It has been called the "theater of the mind."

Newspaper and magazine advertisements tell stories well. They also provide space for explanations of complex products, and allow illustration of multiple product benefits. Outdoor boards supply last minute punch when consumers are headed for the store. They can also remind consumers of brand associations. Point-of-purchase materials offer a final inducement before the sale.

Consumers can't read and re-read broadcast advertising messages. So, transient radio and television spots can only focus on the product or store name, and a single copy theme. Because of their fleeting nature, radio and television messages sometimes direct consumers to more detailed promotional copy in newspapers, supplements or magazines.

Consumers spend more time reading newspaper and magazine ads, when they are interested in the product. That's why more product appeals can be used in the print media. Direct mail advertising, because of its highly selected audience, provides a forum for a complete sales pitch. Since direct mail isn't constrained by newspaper and magazine formats, direct mail can also offer exciting graphical layouts in an interesting package.

Most advertising campaigns use multiple media. The challenge for the copywriter is to convey a consistent sales message across media, while operating within the constraints of each medium. A print campaign which focuses on several different product advantages requires a creative refocusing in order to sell the same story on an outdoor board. This is only one of the challenges copywriters face every day. Determining the copy concept is another decision that will direct the copywriting process.

What Copy Concept?

Like other strategic decisions, the decision about what to say must be made with the critical marketing decisions. Some traditional advertising textbooks begin the campaign process with an analysis of the **problems and opportunities**. There are a couple of problems with this approach, even though the analysis does provide some campaign direction. A marketer or advertiser who tries to analyze the problem of poor sales performance may find more problems than he or she wants to find. Ineffective corporate policies, bad market climate, and poor advertising may all contribute to the newly discovered problems. Returning to the three critical marketing decisions will help resolve the disadvantages of a "problems and opportunities" approach.

There can be only two problems with a product identity. Either we don't have a product identity, or we don't like the one we have. A similar situation exists with competitive distance. If there is a problem, it is that we haven't created the best competitive distance between our product and competing products in the minds of the consumer. Market segmentation problems could be a little more complex. We may not appeal to a specific segment. We may not appeal to the "best" segment for our product, or for our corporate methods of production and distribution. All of the problems associated with the critical marketing decisions are related to promotion. Even better, they can all be solved through changes in promotional strategy.

The **copy concept**, or what we plan to say in our advertising, should be a simple statement which outlines the "core" message to the target market. This core message should describe the strongest appeals for our target market, and it should tell how the messages will meet our requirements for product identity and competitive distance.

A major consideration is the relative importance of verbal and visual elements in our advertising messages. The decision to accentuate either the visual or verbal may be the result of a unique product identity which requires more visual than verbal treatment. Competitive approaches may force us to emphasize verbal over visual messages, in order to establish competitive distance. Limitations of our target market may also be crucial. The relative emphasis on verbal and visual elements should be described in the copy concept. A concept test may be performed to find out which copy concept is best for our market situation.

To Test or Not to Test Concepts?

Concept testing has been criticized by almost everyone in advertising. Yet, it's almost always done. Sometimes concepts are tested using formal research procedures. Creative directors and copywriters test concepts against their experience, and they often solicit reactions from other creative personnel. Formal testing procedures may or may not be needed.

Major expenditures on an advertising campaign warrant spending money on a concept test. The test should determine how well received the concept is by target market members. Strength against existing competitive messages should also be estimated. The most frequent type of concept test is a focus group. More controlled and extensive tests may be performed in shopping mall interviews, or in a laboratory setting. Concept test participants, who should be members of the desired target market, are usually asked which concept would be most convincing to them. Once the best concept has been discovered, advertising managers and creative personnel summarize the copy decisions in a copy platform.

How to Write a Copy Platform

You don't have to write a copy platform to have effective advertising. The majority of national ads and commercials you see did come from a copy platform. This platform may have been written formally, or it may be the result of verbal agreements about what to say in advertising. The platform provides a quick review of the decision-making process. It also provides a reference which can be used to evaluate advertising copy which is to appear throughout an advertising campaign.

The copy platform should include: a) the **product name** and model; b) a statement describing the **product identity** to be created and reinforced through advertising; c) a short description of the desired **competitive distance**; d) a summary of the **target market** characteristics using standard categories for defining the target segments; e) the **copy concept** should be written as it was described in the previous section, including the description of how the copy will establish the product identity, how the copy will establish and maintain the desired competitive distance, and how the copy will appeal to the selected segment. If copy adjustments are needed to meet the requirements of different media, they should be briefly noted.

Copy platforms are useful guides for establishing continuity in an advertising program. When advertising programs are complex, copy platforms help coordinate team production of advertising messages.

Study Questions

❑ Through what mechanisms are marketing decisions transferred to advertising copywriting?

❑ What effect does an advertising medium have on copywriting?

❑ What are the relative advantages of print media over broadcast media, and vice versa?

❑ What is a copy platform and why is it used?

❑ Explain what concept testing is, and how it is usually performed.

❑ Outline the parts of a copy platform.

Concept Testing and Copy Testing: The Differences

With concept testing, you're trying to find out what aspect or dimension of the product has the most selling power for your target market. In copy testing, you're trying to evaluate ways of talking about a single concept. For example, suppose our product is recreational vehicles. Four different concepts might be tested: construction quality, road performance, convenience features, and comfort features.

In order to perform a concept test, four paragraphs describing each concept would be prepared. Members of the target market would be asked to evaluate the importance of each concept for their decision to pick a specific recreational vehicle. They might also be asked to rank the importance of each concept. When such a concept test was actually done, men ranked road performance first, construction second. Women ranked convenience first, comfort second. Since the decision to purchase a recreational vehicle was a joint decision both sets of concepts had to be used.

Copy tests were performed with each concept. Road performance will be used to illustrate. Three different copy statements were written about recreational vehicle performance. One was a testimonial about road performance by a respected columnist. One was a narrative description of the product performance features and their benefits. The third was a description of the company's automotive experience and their ability to design performance vehicles.

When men in the target market were asked which of the copy statements were most believable, the majority indicated the endorsement by the automotive columnist. So, part of the national campaign associated a small picture of the columnist, with his statement of roadability for the vehicle. Any number of copy statements could have been tested. In this case, three statements were enough.

16

Advertising Copywriting

This chapter could have been titled, "How to get advertising results using average writing skills." It's not as negative as it sounds. There are three reasons for centering the discussion on the average writer. This is an introductory book about advertising, not a copywriting text. Most people have average writing skills, so the techniques should be useful for a majority of readers. People with superb writing skills can still benefit from advertising fundamentals. You can teach fundamentals; you can't really teach talent. Finally, great results from advertising don't always come from great writing. Effectiveness is the result of clear communication to a target audience, with enough **media exposure** to make a difference. In many local advertising campaigns, it's impossible to tell whether the advertising copy was effective because not enough money was spent on media.

To dramatically illustrate the types of people who write advertising copy, let's look at several types of copywriters.

The *uninformed and foolish copywriter* is the person who thinks he or she knows how to write copy for all media. This person can often be seen dressed in funny costumes, delivering copy in funny voices. Fifty percent of these commercials use buckets of water to get a laugh.

Uninformed and practiced copywriters have to write ads every week; but because of inconsistency and lack of training, advertising efforts are only hit or miss.

An *informed and practiced copywriter* writes ads every week, even though it's not his or her job. This person often reads about advertising, or seeks help from professionals. Ads from this writer usually perform fairly well.

Among the non-professionals, the *informed, practiced and talented copywriter* is the business owner who knows the business and how to communicate it to customers. He or she is a rarity.

Next, is the *professional and practiced copywriter*. This writer writes advertising copy for a living; but may not be the most effective writer. Copywriting is a job, not an exciting experience.

Professional, practiced and talented copywriters consistently produce effective advertisements and commercials. Their life is writing. They can produce exciting messages in many different media.

The last group of writers is worth mentioning because they are the *professional, practiced, talented and lucky copywriters.* These people write the right copy at the right time, for the right client. These are the advertising award winners.

People who foolishly become ego-involved with advertising probably can't be helped by copywriting principles. But, the uninformed can be informed, and the unpracticed can become practiced. Writers can improve through practice and training. Let's see what a copywriter must know before he or she writes a word of advertising copy.

Before the Writing Begins

When discussing strategy, we said copy strategy had to translate the appropriate product identity, establish a suitable competitive distance and provide relevance for the target market. The copywriter's specialty is words and language. In order to produce effective messages, the copywriter has to know the language of the product, the messages of the competitors, and how consumers understand the product.

All products have a language associated with them. Technical products have a more technical language than mass-marketed consumer products. By learning the descriptions, names and features of the product, the copywriter can establish his or her credibility with the consumer—and the advertiser. Copywriters should immerse themselves in the product. They should purchase it, study it and experience it. Much of this experience should come as a naive observer because copywriters can often judge consumer knowledge better by experiencing the product first hand.

Copywriters must also know how competitors talk about their products. Knowledge of competitive appeals and competitive product features is necessary in order to create the desired competitive distance. This knowledge also provides a better perspective of the entire product class.

Copywriters should talk to target market members and product users about the product. He or she should develop an understanding about how the target market members talk about the product, their language. Copywriters should also try to find out what appeals to this group of purchasers? In order to provide product explanations, copywriters should know the level of product understanding in consumers.

As a last step, the copywriter should review the creative strategy to clarify the product identity desired, to review the competitive distance to be achieved, and to characterize target market members. The next step is writing.

Writing

After reviewing the copy platform, writing begins. Write headlines for print ads, write body copy, write television or radio spots which convey the ideas in the copy concept. Don't worry about how the copy looks or sounds, yet.

At this stage, it's better to write too much, than too little. There's always time to edit and rewrite. Most copywriters don't write and rewrite enough. Generate as many unique copy executions, written ads or spots, as you can.

During the next phase of copywriting, we'll refine the message. Before we do, let's examine some general copy principles that are almost universal.

1. *Get your target market's attention.* In headlines, or through graphic content, indicate who should read or listen to your advertising messages. For example, the following headline signals golfers. "Golfers. The new Midway Course is open!"

2. *Sell your promotion first.* Sales promotions are designed and tested for immediate action. An audience listens and responds to these promotions. Describe sales promotions first.

3. *Use simple messages to sell better.* Clarity sells products. Consumers will understand and remember simple claims and appeals about your product. Short tight writing styles are more effective.

4. *Sell benefits, not product features.* It's not a P4D Converter, that's important. It's the fact that a P4D Converter protects your family from electrical shocks which sells the product. "Sell the sizzle, not the steak," is the old advertising adage.

5. *Use your strongest appeals first.* There are order effects in advertising recall. Say what's most important first, repeat it at the end.

6. *Use the active voice when you talk to the audience.* Advertising promises happen today. They're now! The active voice is more interesting and engaging.

7. *Tell the audience what you want them to do.* People do what they're told. Make sure you ask them to buy your product, visit your store, or change their attitude.

8. *Don't let technique spoil your message.* Fancy graphics and illustration techniques, and unusual humor may distract from the sales message. You'd rather create a product purchase than a laugh. Great graphics and humor work *with* great copy, not against it.

9. *Say the product or store name several times in your advertising.* Repetition creates recall and learning. Learning will lead to more purchases.

10. *Match your style to media requirements.* For print ads, make your ads read from top to bottom. Subheads should express product benefits. If possible put them in the headline, too. Readers should be able to get the sales idea by reading the headline and subheads. Don't be afraid to use copy. That's the strength of print advertising. Make sentences and paragraphs short.

In broadcast commercials, copy has to sound like spoken, rather than written, language. Use attention-getting sounds and visuals. Make dialogue realistic and persuasive. Sell one idea and the product name in broadcast advertising. Use models, actors and actresses who typify the target market.

Outdoor boards need seven or fewer words. Use the product name and primary feature. In many cases, this is store location.

Direct mail copy should tell a complete sales story. Use short sentences and paragraphs. Get help from direct mail advertising books in order to prepare a complete mailing package. A good starter is *Successful Direct Marketing Methods*, by Bob Stone.

Editing and rewriting

Rewrite the copy several times. Take out all unnecessary, non-selling words. Proofread your copy well. Build continuity through a consistent style. If your company is research-oriented, three or four copy approaches should be tested on target market members. Specific copytesting techniques will be described in the campaign evaluation chapter.

Study Questions

❑ What characteristics of copy should be used in broadcast to make it interesting and believable?

❑ What kinds of information must the copywriter know about the product, the competition, and the target market before writing begins?

❑ What do we mean by a product language? Give an example.

❑ Why should promotional copy appear first?

❑ Think of some examples of "selling sizzle," rather than selling the "steaks."

Don't Forget the Detail Copy!

In every advertisement, and some commercials, there are small pieces of copy which are crucial for effective selling. Coupon copy has to be written so consumers can fill out the information correctly, and easily. Small type disclaimers have to be tightly written, so they don't occupy too much space in the ads.

Addresses have to be clear. Phone numbers need to be larger if consumers are supposed to order by phone. Telling people to call early, soon or now, may evoke an immediate response.

Small print regulatory copy, for banks and specialized products, must meet the specifications required by regulatory agencies. Rules for sweepstakes must be written carefully. All of this specialized copy must be proofread carefully.

Small print copy must sell as well as large print copy. Mistakes in the small print copy can have the most important legal consequences.

Copywriting Books

There are many things a young writer can do to improve his or her copywriting skills, not the least of which is practice. But reading about copywriting, and reading good writing develops a knowledge of techniques which can be a valuable asset in honing a personal style of writing. It also gives the writer a chance to experience, and experiment with different writing styles.

The following sampling of copywriting books was selected as a starting point for developing copywriters. Several points are worth noting. Many books are old books that are out of print, which means some searching in libraries will be necessary in order to find them. Writing hasn't changed much in the fifty years since Bedell's copy book was written. But media have changed , so some of the books have been included to provide guidelines for specialized types of advertising, like broadcast, retail and direct mail. A sampling of good writing books have also been included in the list. One trend that has occurred is titling a book as a writing book, then talking about general advertising principles, rather than talking exclusively about how to write advertising copy.

Copywriting Classics

ISBN Numbers indicate that a title is currently in print; out-of-print books do not have these numbers.

Hank Seiden (1976), *Advertising Pure and Simple*, New York: Amacom, ISBN 0-8144-7510-8.

David L. Malickson and John W. Nason (1977/1982), *Advertising: How to Write the Kind that Works*, Revised Edition, New York: Charles Scribner's Sons, ISBN 0-684-14771-8.

John Caples (1974), *Tested Advertising Methods*, Fourth Edition, Englewood Cliffs, N.J.: Prentice-Hall, ISBN 0-13-906909-7.

Elbrun Rochford French (1958/1959), *The Copywriter's Guide*, New York: Harper and Brothers.

W Keith Hafer and Gordon E. White (1982), *Advertising Writing*, Second Edition, St. Paul, Minnesota: West Publishing Company, ISBN 0-314-63246-8.

Philip Ward Burton (1984), *Advertising Copywriting*, Fifth Edition, New York: Wiley, ISBN 0-471-84152-8.

Aesop Glim (1945/1961), *How Advertising is Written --and Why*, New York: Dover Publications Inc.

Hal Stebbins (1957), *Copy Capsules*, New York: McGraw-Hill Book Company, Inc.

Clyde Bedell (1940), *How to Write Advertising that Sells*, New York: McGraw-Hill Book Company, Inc.

Richard Bayan (1984), *Words that Sell*, Chicago: Contemporary Books, Inc., ISBN 0-8092-4799-2.

Hanley Norins (1980), *The Compleat Copywriter*, Melbourne, Florida: Robert E. Krieger Publishing Company, Inc., ISBN 0-89874-117-3.

Books about Copywriting

Robert Bly (1985), *The Copywriter's Handbook*, New York: Dodd, Mead and Company, ISBN 0-396-08547-4.

Dick Wasserman (1985), *How to Get Your First Copywriting Job*, New York: Center for the Advancement of Advertising, ISBN 0-525-48281-4.

S. Watson Dunn (1956), *Advertising Copy and Communication*, New York: McGraw-Hill Book Company, Inc.

Dennis Higgins (Ed.) (1965), *The Art of Writing Advertising*, Chicago: National Textbook, ISBN 0-8442-3100-2.

Walter Weir (1960), *On the Writing of Advertising*, New York: McGraw Hill Book Company, Inc.

Specialized copywriting techniques

Peter B. Orlik (1986), *Broadcast Copywriting*, Third Edition, New York, Allyn and Bacon, Inc., ISBN 0-205-08750-7.

Judy Young Ocko (1971), *Retail Advertising Copy: the How, the What, the Why*, Revised Edition, New York: National Retail Merchants Association, ISBN 0-87102-069-6.

Herschell Gordon Lewis (1984), *Direct Mail Copy that Sells*, Englewood Cliffs, New Jersey: Prentice-Hall, Inc., ISBN 0-13-214750-5.

Excellent books about writing

William Sloane (1979), *The Craft of Writing*, New York: W. W. Norton and Company, ISBN 0-393-30050-1.

John Fairfax and John Moat (1981), *The Way to Write*, New York: St. Martin's Press.

Karen Elizabeth Gordon (1983), *The Well-Tempered Sentence*, New York: Ticknor and Fields, ISBN 0-89919-170-3.

17

Visual Messages in Advertising

Visual elements in advertising can be the most powerful communicators. Many different parts of a print advertisement or a broadcast commercial could be considered part of the **visual communication strategy** for an advertising campaign. Photographs, illustrations, logos, layouts, and the use of white space are all **visual** or **graphic elements** of print advertisements. Videotaped segments, animation, special effects, headers and trailers are visual elements of broadcast commercials.

Visual images in print or broadcast are used to establish a product identity, to provide a suitable competitive distance, and to grab the attention of the target market. These are the same goals as those for verbal communication. **Nonverbal communication devices** are different.

Think about a corporate logo or trademark, like the "Golden Arches" of McDonald's. When the logo was first introduced with an advertising campaign, a connection had to be made between the "Arches" and the corporate name. Consumers had to learn the relationship. Once the relationship was established, the **sign** or "Golden Arches" became a **symbol**. In plain English, a symbol is an object that stands for something else. Here the visual element, "the Golden Arches," stands for or represents the company (McDonald's) in the mind of the consumer. Some people would say the sign acquired **symbolic meaning**. Notice that the sign has no meaning associated with it until it is coupled with some other object or concept. This association is accomplished in advertising through repitition of commercial messages. Through repitition brand names, which could be considered verbal signs, are often associated with other characteristics, concepts or qualities in the mind of the consumer. But, there are important limitations. Corporate symbols and signs can be associated with negative factors if the consumer experiences dissatisfaction with a company's products or service.

The visual communication strategy for an advertising campaign must send the same message as the verbal campaign. Visuals must communicate the primary benefits of the product. They must be different enough so consumers can recognize different corporate sponsorship of the ads. Grabbing attention and stimulating recall are important objectives for advertising visuals, because consumers will remember effective visuals. A primary consideration for any advertiser is the relative importance of pictures over words. Let's examine that decision.

What to Show in Visuals

Two questions must be answered before visuals are discussed. *Should visuals be used at all?* In certain circumstances, advertisements or commercials may be more effective without visuals. Competitors using highly visual print advertising campaigns may force a "type only" approach in order to establish a competitive distance. Temporary product shortages, or quick deadlines may force an interim approach which is more heavily oriented to type than visualizations. A product may have attributes that are not easily pictured.

The second question is, *"What is the relative importance of verbal to visual message?"* When you look at a print advertisement, does the picture or the message in type occupy the most space? In television, is the mood created by the commercial, or the verbal message more important? A new hairstyle may have to be dramatically photographed and presented. A new feature of a life insurance policy may not. Competitive approaches, and the message strategy must determine how important visuals are to an advertising campaign.

Once the decision has been made to use visuals, then you have to decide what to show, and how to show it. In different ways, several famous advertisers have said, what you say is more important than how you say it. The statement is true as long as you say it effectively.

Like advertising strategy, advertising visuals should establish the product identity, maintain a suitable competitive distance, and signal the target market. If the desired product identity highlights a unique physical feature, like a new automotive design, the physical feature should be dramatically pictured. If the product identity is tied to a product benefit, such as selling a "family car," then the visuals should support the selling concept. Many forceful demonstrations have been created to sell the primary benefits of products from glues to automobiles.

Look at the competition. If you want to be different, your visual strategy must use a different visual approach. If you want to mimic a competitor, then similar styles must be selected.

Actors, actresses and models must represent your target market. Credibility must be established for the visuals as well as the message with target audiences.

Visual strategy requires simple common sense. If you're selling indoor tennis, a visual must say indoor tennis. If you want to tell someone they'll have a great time at your bar, then you show them having fun. You don't show them paying their bar tab. If kids love your product, show kids loving your product. Advertising visuals must consistently convey the creative strategy for a campaign.

Visual Choices and How They're Made

Designers, art directors and layout artists work with advertisers and marketers to connect the visual strategy to overall advertising and marketing strategy. To do this several choices have to be made. In print, the designer must decide what types of visuals to use. **Photographs** may be used to add realism. They might also be used to create surrealistic fantasies. An **illustration**, or **line art drawing**, may show product features more clearly than a photograph of a product. These illustrations might also add a "fine arts" look to a campaign. In television, the art director must decide whether to use the **product, people, animation,** or **situations** to express the message. Commercials may be created using a **studio set**, or produced **on-location**.

There are many conventional principles of **layout and design**. All have been effectivley violated in print advertising campaigns. A great designer knows the principles and when violation of the principles will be a more effective creative approach. Here are a few of the principles.

Unity means that an advertisement or illustration tells a singular story. There is a focal point for the visual or layout, and other elements complement the focal point. Eye movement revolves around the focal point. **Symmetry** and **balance** are used to communicate **formality** or **informality**. Symmetrical layouts and illustrations are thought to be more formal than assymetrical layouts and illustrations. **White space** and **graphical elements**, including type, are balanced with each other to make a layout more readable. Layouts often communicate openness when white space is used effectively.

Color is used to capture attention. It may also be used to express a mood or feeling about a product. Many people associate moods with colors, so the selection of color can provide an association of mood with the product.

In television commercials, **cuts** and **fades** can be used to create action and elegance. **Sequencing** of visuals can tell a story, or describe a product's features more simply. Again, color can draw attention or create a mood for the product.

Visuals, whether print or broadcast, are very important elements in an advertising campaign. They can be the largest part of the production budget; but they must communicate the campaign strategy. The best designers and art directors in advertising know how to make visual elements of advertising sell the product and company.

To find out more about principles of advertising design and layout, see Roy P. Nelson's *The Design of Advertising*, Jerome Jewler's *Creative Strategy in Advertising*, and *Systematic Approach to Advertising Creativity* by Stephen Baker.

Study Questions

❏ What is the difference between a sign and a symbol?

❏ How does a logotype acquire symbolic meaning?

❏ When are visuals important to an advertising campaign? When are they not important?

❏ What is the primary goal of advertising visuals or advertising layouts?

❏ How does an advertiser decide what to show in an advertising visual?

❏ What types of visualization are important for television commercials?

Making Effective Storyboards

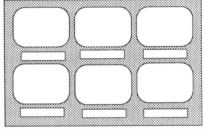

Storyboards are graphic summaries of television commercials. Since they are designed to provide idea sketches for visual and verbal elements, their content must be carefully chosen.

Here are a few hints for selecting and presenting visuals in storyboard form.

1) *Select the six most important visuals for presentation.* The visual images must convey the theme of the advertising campaign; but at least one visual must present a clear picture of the client's product. 2) *Design a consistent 8 1/2" x 11" presentation format for storyboards,* and keep them uniform. 3) *Use the same illustration method for each illustration in the storyboard.* Select the method of illustration carefully. For Macintosh presentations, images can be scanned and placed in the storyboard using Pagemaker, or another page-layout program. 4) *The Copy should be clean, accurate and relate to the pictures described by the storyboard.* 5) *When possible, use large presentation size storyboards for client presentations; use small sheets when presenting storyboard material one-to-one.* 6) *For corrections, use self-adhesive labels, cut to size* (Many come in large squares or sheets). 7) *Make sure the copy fits in your storyboard format sheet.* Association of the verbal and visual elements in television commercials is extremely important during approval and production phases. 8) *Use color renderings to create impact.* Close-up photographs or illustrations also create more product drama, if the copy is relevant and strong. 9) *Present storyboards as if they are actually happening.* Excitement is catching; but remember, storyboards are static. By themselves, they aren't inherently exciting. 10) *Double-check the copy to make sure it has television impact.*

Designing Ads When You're Not an Artist

For many of us there isn't time to learn the skills of the advertising designer. Some of us wouldn't have enough talent if we did have enough time. Here's a simple way to improve your print advertising layouts if you don't have a lot of money. For people who hire graphic artists, it's a way to communicate the effect you'd like to create.

Step 1. In a single statement say what you'd like to communicate to your audience. Do you want to tell them about the product, or the benefits of buying it?

Step 2. Do you want your advertisements to emphasize pictures or advertising copy? Based on your need to describe product features, or competitive advertising, either approach could be profitable.

Step 3. Decide how big your advertisements are going to be. Will you use single column, double column or full-page ads?

Step 4. Look at advertisements as layouts. Think of the illustrations as black boxes, and the copy as straight lines. See which layouts will tell your story best.

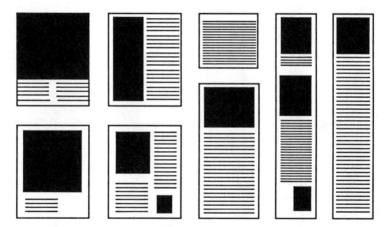

Step 5. Choose a layout from a graphic awards annual. Go to the *Graphis Annual*, or another book of print advertising awards. Look at the designs for ads which are the same size as yours. Select a layout which will communicate your story well. Remember, the larger the illustration or photograph, the better it's quality must be. You can also get good hints for typestyles in the award books. Communicate this information to a designer, then let the designer earn his or her money. Don't try to imitate headlines and copy, because the ads you see were not built on your strategic situation.

18

Production Decisions

Advertising campaign effectiveness and efficiency are two important byproducts of skillful **advertising production**. Production is the process of making print advertisements or commercials, printing **advertising collateral** materials, shooting and scripting audiovisual presentations, and manufacturing exhibits and displays. Advertising departments and agencies haven't traditionally produced all of the materials of advertising. Instead, art directors, production managers or traffic coordinators, oversee the work of various **production houses** or **independent producers** and **suppliers**.

Many processes of production, like producing color separations, designing exhibits, and shooting film or still photographs require the skills of specialized professionals. In the advertising agency business, some of the reliance on outside professionals may be ending. In recent years, several advertising agencies have set up their own broadcast production departments to produce commercials. The impetus for the change comes from two sources. Advertisers constantly complain about the rapidly increasing costs for commercial production. Advertising agencies, like other businesses, see the production department as another profit center for the agency. Success or failure will ultimately depend upon the ability of producers to make effective advertising at the best price.

There seem to be two extremes in advertising production. Every year a new campaign is created for a product, people in charge want to see something innovative and more creative than the past year. A natural consequence is the search for more sophisticated and complex extensions of production techniques. Pushed in this direction, simple advertising messages may be overshadowed by special effects and dramatic visuals. As production techniques gain sophistication, they require more specialized professionals. Production costs naturally go up. This is only one possible extreme.

At the opposite extreme, is the local advertiser who refuses to pay any money for production. Instead, this advertiser relies solely on the services of local media for production. If these production services are bad, then an entire advertising budget can be wasted. The most common problem with local media production is not that production services lack technical quality. Many different production personnel work on advertising for a client, so the individual print advertisements, or radio commercials, lack **continuity**. Each is an individual advertisement, rather than an integrated part of an overall campaign.

In advertising, production costs are usually determined before production personnel get involved with advertising. An art director who specifies on-location shooting in an exotic location sets a high cost for production. Using an actor-endorser for a product adds cost to an advertising campaign. The most important principle to remember is that *the purpose of advertising is to deliver messages to target audiences. If production costs are so high that they significantly diminish media exposure, then the costs are probably too high for maximum productivity.*

A Few General Production Principles

Clear objectives are important for efficient production. This doesn't mean clear objectives will result in cheap production. It means the production will be matched to the selected product identity, competitive distance, and target market. For some advertising contexts, it's important to have television production in far away places. Sometimes the complicated special effects are important to communicate the nature of the product, and the company behind it. These decisions are justified by well reasoned objectives.

One of the most important ways to minimize production costs is to *plan the production for an entire campaign.* When the visuals are planned ahead of time, a photographer can be hired to shoot all visuals at one time. Commercial producers can shoot television spots with fewer set-ups. Producing the visuals at one time also makes it easier to have products available. When large products, or large numbers of products are involved, this simplifies the job of coordinating the production.

Production costs can also be reduced by *reusing entire ads or visuals during a campaign.* Consumers don't tire of advertising as fast as advertisers. Minor alterations in visuals can produce several derivatives of an advertisement which look different to readers, and may be equally effective.

Aim for the simple message. In advertising, consumer processing time is very short. Simple messages are clear. They can be remembered easily. Two television examples illustrate this simplicity. A national gun control coalition wanted to compare the number of handgun deaths in the U.S. with other countries. They dramatically showed flags getting shot by hand guns. A simple technique telling a simple story. A spark plug manufacturer showed hands pulling rope starters on small engines with a background of classical music. The spot required a small production budget, but again was very effective in communicating the product's primary benefit.

There is one principle related more to effectiveness, than cost. *Pay for the best primary campaign visuals you can get.* These visuals are not always the highest priced, but sometimes they're not cheap. Let's illustrate the problem with a print advertising example. College towns are overrun by amateur photographers who want to be professionals. They often search out advertising agencies and advertisers in order to get professional assignments. What many of these photographers lack is the ability to get consistently good advertising photographs. They often have a few good prints in their portfolios, but when faced with shooting a machine-tooled gear, they can't seem to solve all the technical problems. Many professional photographers have similar problems. Some photographers can't shoot people realistically. This may be a problem in recruiting models, or it may be a problem in directing the models. Whatever the reason, ineffective campaign visuals can be the result. Selecting the producer for film, or a print photographer, can be one of the most important campaign decisions. Advertisers should look for people who have consistently produced the type of visual necessary for their campaign.

Print Production Hints

There are several places to reduce print production costs which may not diminish the effectiveness of advertising materials. The first guideline is to simply *know what you're paying for*. A beginner's knowledge of print production steps will help cut costs.

Advertisements and brochures begin with the first ideas and visuals, called **thumbnails**. These are the first scribblings made by doodling copywriters, artists, managers and account people. Thumbnails are used to test different ideas among co-workers. Once interest in a design is stimulated, an artist will make a **rough layout**. Rough layouts have rough illustrations and lines or squiggles to indicate type. Headlines and logos are usually included. Once rough layouts are approved, the artist or designer prepares a **finished layout** which has type and a facsimile of the illustration. This illustration may be an illustrator's rendering of finished artwork, a photocopy of the photographic print, or an actual photograph. After approval, the finished layout must be converted into a form ready for printing. The final form is called a **mechanical**. It includes the actual type and the final photograph. If the printer needs to process the photograph further, such as transforming a black and white photograph into a **halftone**, or a color print into **color separations**, then the photograph will usually be mounted away from the layout.

Making a halftone is a process which converts a black and white photographic image into a series of black dots. Newspapers use the halftone process for newspaper photos. Grays are less dense black dots than darker areas in the photograph. Making color separations is a process where a full-color photograph is converted for printing into **four process colors**, cyan, magenta, yellow and black. In this conversion, a printing plate is prepared for each color. By using varying combinations and percentages of the four colors, all colors can be represented. Since all colors in a photograph are represented by combinations of the four colors, each printing plate has an actual image of the ad on it. Advertisers are shown **color keys** of color printing jobs before they are printed in order to evaluate the color separations.

Another method of getting color into an advertisement is by using **spot color**. Spot color requires making printing overlays which indicate where color should be placed. Since the entire ad is not made up of these colors, the overlays will only produce an image which has the designated color. Spot color can be used in one, two, three, four and more color advertisements. To get the effect of color photographs, you must use the four-color separation process.

Proof prints for black and white printing jobs, and for spot color jobs are usually called **bluelines** or **silverprints**, or some similar name. Proof prints should be ordered for most jobs, in case the printer makes a mistake. This is particularly true when photographs are included. Photographs may be inserted backwards or upside-down.

To reduce print production costs, *alterations in copy or photographs should not occur after production begins*. Except in an emergency, copy and illustrations should be approved and examined before production.

Using spot color rather than color separations will reduce production costs because color separations are expensive. But, if color photograph quality is needed, then separations are required.

Putting words and advertising copy into type is called **typesetting**. There are three ways to reduce typesetting costs. *Proofread advertising copy carefully*, so mistakes are not produced by poorly typed copy. *Standardize headline, subhead and body copy type for advertisements*. Standardizing reduces typesetter errors, and aids campaign continuity. *Shop around for good typesetting services*. Typesetting costs vary considerably depending on the specific type supplier and on the amount of copy to be typeset.

Smart media purchasing and planning can make advertising more efficient. For example, in newspaper advertising, a two-thirds page ad can produce similar effects of a full-page ad at reduced space charges. Some production costs may be smaller because of the reduced copy. Small ads with large type may be as effective as somewhat larger ads.

Off-prints of print ads, black and white or color copies of actual advertisements, can be used in other advertising. Retail stores can put copies of newspaper ads near the cash register to make people aware of sales. A national advertiser may include four-color advertisements in a direct mail campaign so retailers know they are going to support purchase through national advertising.

About Broadcast Production

Once the strategy has been developed, scripts for radio and television commercials are written. With television spots, the scripts are combined with rough visuals in a **storyboard**. Some people produce a simulation of a commercial called an **animatic** where the script is read against a background of still photographs or illustrations. From an approved storyboard or radio script, production begins.

In radio, an announcer is hired. **Voice talent** may be used for several different characters in a script. **Jingles** may be written and produced by a broadcast production house, or independent producer. Studio production produces the audio script for the commercial. During post-production processes, music and voices may be **mixed.**

Radio scripts are usually simple to produce, unless complicated sound effects or celebrity talent is used. To reduce costs, an advertiser can *produce as many spots as possible during the studio session.* He or she should also *avoid extravaganza type spots*, unless they are being used to support the overall campaign strategy.

Television production is similar to radio production. The equipment is more sophisticated and cumbersome to move. That's why on-location shooting costs more than studio shooting. Exotic locations usually require more money because support systems for television production are not in place. Electrical generators and specialized vehicles may be needed.

From the approved storyboard, television producers film the primary visuals during production stages. Post-production processes are used to add special effects, and to complete the mix of verbal and visual message. As you would expect, celebrity talent and trained animals cost more. Purchasing the rights to popular music sound tracks may also be an expensive addition to television commercials. Like other production processes, *simplicity pays dividends*, dividends in production costs. There are dividends in recall, with one exception. An expensive and dramatic commercial may be strong enough to cut through the clutter and produce improved awareness for an advertiser.

Nothing is more important to the success of an advertising campaign than effective and efficient production. Poor production can kill an effective message. Expensive production can reduce media exposure. In the next chapter, we are going to see how one tool, the Macintosh computer, has changed advertising production.

Study Questions

❏ How does campaign planning affect the production processes for a campaign?

❏ How can continuity of an advertising message be strengthened through effective production?

❏ What is the relationship of production costs to media exposure?

❏ What are the steps of print production? Broadcast production?

❏ How do corrections or changes in copy affect production costs at different stages of production?

❏ What is the difference between process color and spot color?

Print Production Costs and Why They Go Up!

You can do everything yourself; but the savings in money may totally destroy the effectiveness of your advertisements.

Designers examine the total package of advertisements and prepare thumbnails, sample layouts and finished layouts for the final ads. All design costs are related to the time spent by the designer, so anything you can do to speed up the design process will make design services more economical. Good designers can tell you how to get the most impact in print for the money you spend. You must tell them the range of your promotion budget so they don't spend time designing unneeded materials. Typography costs vary according to the uniqueness of the typestyle and the method of production. Phototypesetting is the highest quality and most expensive. The difference in cost for short jobs is small. Changing copy always results in higher type costs.

Photographs can be purchased from stock photography houses, a photographer can be hired by hour or day, a non-professional may be used. The quality and price of professional photographers varies greatly. The best photographers can make exciting visuals from your ideas; the worst can fail miserably. Examine a photographer's work with products like yours. If you set up photograph sessions for each ad, it's more expensive than shooting all ads at once.

Illustrators vary like photographers, but illustrative style is usually easier to see in an illustrator's portfolio. If the illustration is a prominent illustration, used frequently, it pays to hire a top-notch illustrator. A good supply of freelance artists can produce simple illustrations inexpensively.

Color printing requires color overlays or color separations for the printing job. Insist on seeing color keys before a job is printed for process color jobs.

Keyliners get your artwork camera-ready for printing. If you don't have a good working knowledge of the printing process, many errors can result from do-it-yourself artwork. Most print shops will have paste-up artists who can help prepare a job from your roughs. Bypassing a designer can also reduce the continuity and effectiveness of your ads.

For brochures, don't forget bluelines. If you have trouble selecting colors for multi-color jobs, ask for color keys. You will be charged for them; but they will give you a preview of color combinations. Look for color accuracy in color separations. Many companies have specified colors for logos, product identification, and even equipment colors.

Learn to proofread carefully. The costs for changes and mistakes skyrockets as your job gets closer and closer to the printing press. Printers can help you correct mistakes, if you tell them what you need.

19

Making Ads on the Macintosh

Many people would think it insane to have an entire chapter devoted to making ads on the **Apple Macintosh computer**. Others would be gleeful. But, there are three important reasons for looking at how the Macintosh has changed the process of advertising. No other piece of computer **hardware** has had such an impact upon the quality of advertising production. Many myths have been created about what computers can and can't do for advertising. The Macintosh is one of the easiest ways for a person to experience print advertising production.

If you believe the marketers, and a few over-excited educators, the Macintosh computer will let anyone create outstanding print advertisements, newsletters and brochures. The Macintosh doesn't give you the ability to write exciting copy. It doesn't give you ideas for visuals. It can't tell you how to layout an advertisement. If you don't have an eye for the visual content of advertising, or the ability to write well, the Macintosh will only give you a good looking copy of bad advertising.

Because of the computer's outstanding graphics capabilities and output devices, Macintosh **software** can produce finished, **camera-ready mechanicals** for some print advertisements. Professional quality reports and outstanding presentation materials in black and white and color can also be effortlessly produced. Used in this manner, the computer can be a **tool** for the advertiser.

In the hands of an artist or graphic designer, the Macintosh is a **medium**. Just like oils or watercolor, the screen and its characteristics can be used to create unusual illustrations and dramatic animations. The beauty of the computer as a medium is its ability to perform transformations on pieces of artwork instantly. Different color combinations, graphic effects and manipulations can be examined within minutes. Complex illustrations still take hours of work at the computer; but the flexibility in design makes the computer a medium of choice for many designers and graphic artists.

Praising the characteristics of the Macintosh doesn't mean other types of computers are unimportant for advertising. Graphics capabilities and simplicity make the Macintosh important for advertising production. From the beginning of its evolution, two attributes have distinguished the Macintosh from other computers, its **mouse** and its **interface**. Let's examine those features first.

The Macintosh Mouse

The mouse is an **input device,** just like a keyboard. It's called a mouse because the cord connecting it to the computer looks like a tail. The mouse is not unique to Macintosh. But, Macintosh has always used a mouse as an important part of the computer system. There are several operations that can be performed with the mouse.

To **point** with your mouse, you move the mouse across the desk. A pointer moves on the screen. On the screen are icons, or symbols, which represent programs or folders where programs are stored. Figure 10 shows the Macintosh screen with its file folders, and an open folder. Inside the

Figure 10. Macintosh Folders and the PageMaker Icon [4]

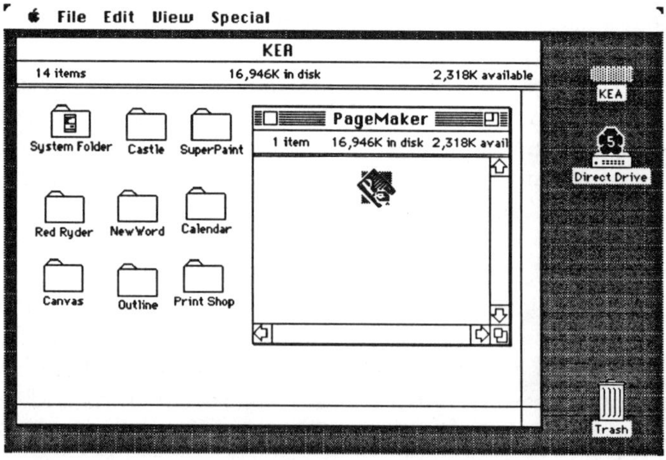

```
 ┌ ★ File  Edit  View  Special                          ┐
        ┌──────────────── KEA ────────────────┐        ▓▓▓▓▓
        │ 14 items      16,946K in disk    2,318K available│  KEA
        │                                     │
        │  ┌───┐   ┌──┐   ┌──┐ ┌═══ PageMaker ═══┐│    ▓▓▓
        │  │ E │   └──┘   └──┘ │1 item 16,946K in disk 2,318K avail│  Direct Drive
        │ System Folder Castle SuperPaint│               │
        │                    │                │
        │  ┌──┐   ┌──┐   ┌──┐│                │
        │  └──┘   └──┘   └──┘│                │
        │ Red Ryder NewWord Calendar         │
        │                    │                │
        │  ┌──┐   ┌──┐   ┌──┐│                │
        │  └──┘   └──┘   └──┘│                │
        │ Canvas  Outline Print Shop         │     ▓▓▓
        │                                     │    Trash
        └─────────────────────────────────────┘
```

open folder is the program icon for PageMaker. There are also menus across the top of the screen which can be pulled down. See Figure 11.

To **click,** you press the mouse button once and release. When the pointer is on an icon, clicking will **select** the icon; the selected icon turns black. The PageMaker icon in Figure 11 has been selected. Selecting means the icon is ready for your next operation. A **double-click** will *open a folder,* or *start a program.* Double-clicking is pressing and releasing the mouse button twice. **Dragging** is an operation where you point to an icon or folder, press and hold the button down. You can then pull the icon across the screen to another place. A **drag** is used to move and copy files. If you

---

[4]Apple screens, Figure 10-12, copyright by, and used by permission of, Apple Computer, Inc.

Figure 11. Macintosh Pull-Down Menus

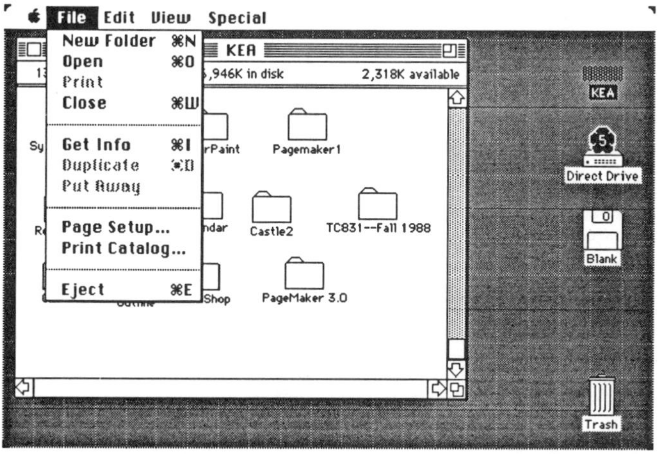

point to a menu, click and hold, the menu will pull-down. From the pull-down menu, you can release at any line. This **release** in a pull-down menu is called **choosing**. Figure 12 shows how to choose an item on a pull-down menu. Choosing lets you pick the operation you would like to perform in any software program.

These are the basic mouse operations. After a little practice they become second nature. Apple attempted to make the Macintosh a

Figure 12. Choosing an Operation on the Pull-Down Menu

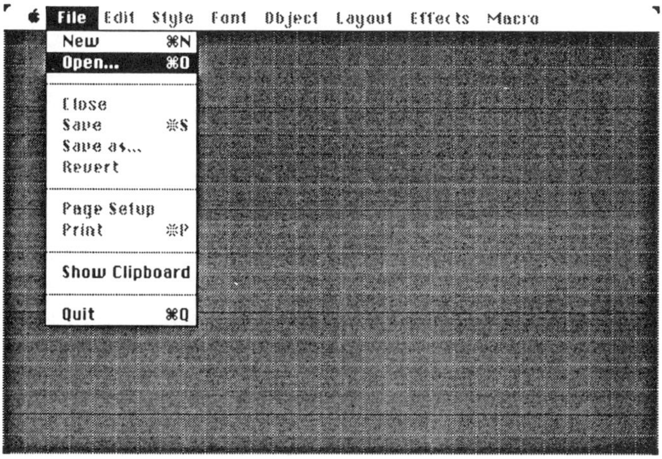

simple computer for the user. That's why the Macintosh **interface** is so important.

The Macintosh Interface

By standardizing and controlling how software programs operate, Apple has achieved consistency in the interface. The **interface** is the system of pull-down menus, double-clicking, selecting and choosing which is used to run software programs. Instead of typing commands, like other computers, the Macintosh is a graphically-oriented interface. In recent years, Apple has used litigation and the threat of litigation to protect its screen characteristics.

Figure 13 shows three different Macintosh screens, from three different pieces of software. The tops of the screens look very similar. They all have pull-down menus. Operation of any of the program functions is very intuitive. Most people who use a Macintosh feel comfortable double-clicking open a piece of software, then pulling down the menus to see how the program operates. The Macintosh interface standardizes cut and paste, copy and duplication operations.

The mouse and the interface are responsible for the easy to use features of the Macintosh. Without great software for advertising, the Macintosh would be just another computer. Let's look at the hardware and software that makes the Macintosh a powerful computer for advertising.

The Macintosh and Advertising

In advertising, the Macintosh is both a tool for the production of ads and a medium for the advertising illustrator. We'll examine both roles more closely. During its early stages of growth, Apple attempted to lure the business market with high quality laser printer output. The ability to make pages look professionally typeset, and the ability to include sophisticated graphics, launched the field of **desktop publishing** (DTP). More recently, Apple has broadened its product line to include more sophisticated computers with color capabilities. Both hardware and software innovations are important for advertising production.

A plethora of Apple compatible hardware products has been produced to meet increasing consumer and business interest. **Laser printers**, which are similar to photocopy machines produce pages which resemble typeset pages. These machines have image resolutions of 300 to 600 dots per inch (dpi). Because of the demand for even higher quality images, several manufacturers provide software interfaces so Macintosh pages can be output to **laser imagesetters** with resolutions between 1250 and 3000 dpi. These sophisticated machines can produce output on paper or film negatives, which makes them especially appealing for the production of print advertisements.

Because many companies were interested in newsletter production, numerous manufacturers have developed **scanners** which can be used to

Figure 13. Macintosh Screens from Deneba Canvas, Aldus FreeHand, and Microsoft Excel [5]

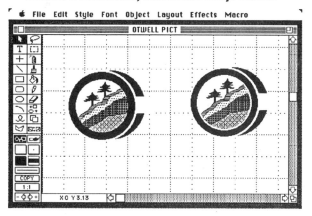

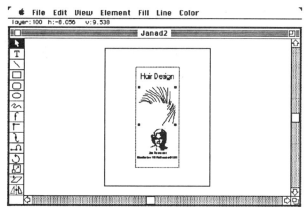

File Edit Formula Format Data Options Macro Window

G44

ADV 205 Lecture Data

	A	B	C	D	E
1	1	Advertising Contrasts and Collisions	9582	2443	8754
2	2	Advertising and its Environments	9508	2489	8755
3	3	Advertising and the Economic System	9510	2492	8756
4	4	Social Conflicts over Advertising	9529	2493	8757
5	5	Advertising and the Portrayal of Women	9515	2529	8758
6	6	Advertising Regulation and Responses	9530	2540	8759
7	7	Advertising Agencies	9517	68	8760
8	8	Advertisers and Media	9514	298	8761
9	9	Video Update: Contraceptives and Subliminals	9507	400	8762
10	10	The Advertising Industry Responds	9588	516	8763
11	11	Marketing I: Environmental Forces	9511	570	8764
12	12	Marketing II: Strategy and Objectives	9518	571	8765
13	13	Marketing III: Appropriation and Marketing Mix	9519	581	8766
14	14	Advertising Campaigns	9520	593	8767
15	15	Advertising Consumer Research	9527	926	8768
16	16	Creative Strategy in Advertising	9521	2116	8769
17	17	Great Advertising Ideas	9553	2584	8770
18	18	Making an Advertisement	9586	2597	8771
19	19	Graphics in Print Advertising	9533	2608	8772

[5]Screens used by permission, and courtesy of Deneba Systems, Inc., Aldus Corporation, and Microsoft Corporation.

input photographs into a computer **file**. It's easiest to think of a computer file as a sheet of paper with your information on it. This can be stored in a folder on the Macintosh. Actually, the file is information in digital form stored on a 3 1/2 inch flexible disk, or a **fixed disk**, known as a **hard disk**. Scanners vary in the resolution of their output, the number of grays they can translate from a photograph, and their ability to scan color images. Each scanner is accompanied by software which builds the computer file from the scanned image. Most software produces a computer file which can be used by paint, draw, illustration, image manipulation and desktop publishing programs.

As the desire for graphics and photographic images has increased, so have the storage requirements for graphic computer files. Complex graphics require tremendous amounts of storage space. In addition to increasing the size of **mass storage**, or hard disks, new forms of storage have appeared. Most people believe **optical** or **compact disks** will revolutionize the computer industry, like they have the music industry. Two forms of compact disk technology have appeared. One is a disk which stores information only. This is called the **CD-ROM drive**, or Compact Disk with Read Only Memory disk drive. The other form of optical disk allows the user to store files once, but doesn't allow erasing and rewriting. This is called the **WORM drive**, or Write Once—Read Many compact disk drive. The ultimate compact disk technology would be erasable compact disks; but WORM drives do allow archiving of clip art and other materials used by advertisers. CD-ROM disks have now been commercially prepared with advertising clip art, type fonts and scanned photos.

New advances in video displays and music interfaces will have an influence on future production of broadcast advertising. But, systematic use of these output devices for advertising has not yet occurred.

The most useful categories of Macintosh software for advertising are: paint and draw programs, illustration programs, image manipulation programs, page-layout programs, advertising templates for page-layout programs, and advertising design and layout programs.

Paint and draw programs are similar, except for the way they allow illustrations to be manipulated. **Paint programs** produce pictures and illustrations in a form called **bit-mapped graphics**. Each dot on the screen, or **pixel**, is manipulated independently to produce a picture. In order to produce laser quality images from a paint program, it must have a capability for producing 300 dpi images. In **object-oriented draw programs**, entire objects are manipulated and drawn. Individual advertisements can be produced in either paint or draw programs; but control of text for advertising copy can be a limiting factor. In some draw programs, copy blocks cannot have mixed type styles, such as italics and bold words in the same copy block. The most flexible programs are those which combine paint and draw functions, such as Canvas and SuperPaint. These programs let the user construct an advertisement using paint or draw characteristics. SuperPaint has paint and draw layers; Canvas uses paint and draw objects. Both programs permit transport of advertising materials to page-layout programs, using different **file formats**. Understanding which file formats produce the highest quality output is important.

Paint and draw programs are limited by the mouse interface. Extremely precise illustrations cannot be easily drawn with a mouse. This deficiency has been addressed by the illustration software packages. Illustration software programs are the most sophisticated drawing programs for the Macintosh. They permit the creation of illustrations through a dot-to-dot outlining method called vectoring. This dot-to-dot method enables the user to produce smooth **bezier curves** which reproduce well on high resolution imagesetters. Extremely precise drawings are possible because the output is produced using a sophisticated language called **PostScript®**, or a derivative called **Encapsulated PostScript (EPS)**. Illustration packages usually offer more sophisticated output features than simpler drawing programs. They provide mechanisms for producing illustrations using spot color, and some provide techniques for producing color separations. Because of the precise registration needed, files with advanced color instructions must be sent to high resolution imagesetters. The two best illustration packages are Aldus FreeHand™, and Adobe Illustrator™. FreeHand is the easiest program to use; but Adobe Illustrator has become a standard tool for many graphic artists.

Two programs, Letraset® ImageStudio™ and Silicon Beach Digital Darkroom™ are image manipulation programs. Both programs permit greater control of scanned images. It's wrong to restrict the description of ImageStudio to an image manipulation program. Outstanding artistic effects can be created with its special effects tools, such as the water drop, and finger smoothed edges. These features make ImageStudio an outstanding paint program. Altering shades of gray is also easily accomplished in ImageStudio. ImageStudio also provides excellent file manipulation and conversion features. An outstanding attribute of Digital Darkroom is its ability to automatically convert bit-mapped artwork to line art. The conversion process is rather rough. A comparable feature is included in Adobe

Figure 14. Digital Darkroom Conversion of
Bit-Mapped Image to an Outline Image [6]

---

[6]Burger clip-art, from WetPaint™ Classic Clip-Art. Used by permission and courtesy of DublClick Software.

Illustrator. Figure 14 shows a bit-mapped image of a hamburger which has been outlined by Digital Darkroom. No retouching was used.

Page-layout programs are probably the most useful tools for advertising production. Advertising layouts can be developed in a page-layout program. Then, artwork and copy can be imported and moved around the page. Most page-layout programs allow more precise control of type and graphics than paint and draw programs. The three leading page-layout programs are Aldus PageMaker, Quark Xpress™, and Ready-Set-Go™ by Letraset. Making an ad in a page-layout program will be demonstrated in the next section.

Many different types of illustration, from clip art to scanned photographs and original illustrations, can be used to construct advertisements in page-layout programs. Copy can be written in a word-processing program and placed in an ad. To **place** graphics or copy in a page-layout program is a specific operation. The place command is usually located on the pull-down file menu on the Macintosh.

Many retailers, newspapers, advertising agencies and consultants use **page-layout templates** to create advertisements. These templates range from simple border outlines of correct advertising sizes to dummy layouts of ads where new copy and graphics can be added. For those people who have to meet regular advertising schedules, templates can greatly reduce production time. If the original templates are designed effectively, they also insure a consistent presentation of advertising messages. In order to use a template, the artist or designer copies the computer file with the template, renames the file, and puts in new artwork and copy. The file is then stored under a new name. For anyone designing and writing advertisements for local media, templates are an efficient solution for producing quick advertising. If they're not used to produce actual photo-ready artwork, they can also be used to describe strategy to a graphic artist or to a media representative.

The most specialized software programs for print advertising are those specifically designed for display advertising. Software developers who create programs for single business applications, like advertising, are aiming at **vertical markets**. Because the size of the target market is much smaller than the general software market, and because of the unusual needs of individuals in the vertical markets for training and support, this specialized software is expensive. Essential training and support functions are an important part of vertical software. Off-the-shelf software would require similar support functions if it was selected by advertising intensive organizations, like newspaper display ad departments. A screen from DisplayAdBuilder is shown in Figure 15. Programs like DisplayAdBuilder, permit more flexible use of type, and provide tools for the manipulation of artwork. AdWorks™, from Concept Publishing Systems is another vertical system that permits more flexible use of type than most page-layout programs. The choice between specialized software for advertising and page-layout programs should be based on efficiency in production, and the

Figure 15. DisplayAdBuilder Shows Enhanced Ad Making Features of Vertical Market Advertising Software [7]

ability to output high quality advertisements. These criteria will be discussed briefly in the next section.

Two Methods of Admaking

Before we make an advertisement, let's talk about the ideal case. Many designers and graphic artists would like to be able to construct a complete advertisement on a computer, from initial scribblings to camera-ready art-work. The best scenario would include the ability to make color separations on the computer for 4-color print advertisements, and the ability to retouch photographs if they need it. There's one important limitation. Any artwork or photograph must be put into the computer before it can be used in an advertisement. One way is to create the artwork on the computer using an illustration package, like Adobe Illustrator or Aldus Freehand. Both programs provide spot color and color separation capabilities. It's too early to tell if the color separation quality, and the economics of production, will be able to compete with traditional color separation methods.

The other method of getting illustrations into the computer is by using a scanner. Once an image is scanned, it can be retouched and altered using many different types of software programs. Compared to existing methods for using photographs in advertisements, either making black and white halftones or color separations, scanning photographs is more risky. Critics of the scanning process cite several limitations. Normal halftone processes are relatively inexpensive; scanning is expensive because images must be output on a high resolution image-setter. Scanned photographic images

---

[7]DisplayAdBuilder screen used by permission and courtesy of Digital Technology, Inc.

take a tremendous amount of computer storage space. The quality of scanned pictures has not been consistently good. With regular halftone processes, the printer takes the responsibility for the quality of halftone
images. Printed results from scanned images are more variable because of
differences in the way dot patterns are used.

There is no doubt that some scanned images can be nearly as good as
halftones; but most aren't. For this reason, display ad software often uses a
place holding box for illustrations. An exception to the quality rule is the
use of clip art, or line art created from illustration software, in advertisements. Excellent clip art is available for many different types of products.
Some advertising agency designers and artists use scanned images to show
what the final advertisement will look like. Some high resolution color
printers can produce impressive color images. For presentations and planning, ads produced on a Macintosh in black and white or color can be very
effective. Let's look at two ways to produce newspaper and magazine
advertisements on the Macintosh. The first method uses PageMaker, a
page-layout program. The second method uses Aldus FreeHand and several
other software packages.

The first example demonstrates a simple method for producing ads with
black and white **line art**, in a page-layout program. This technique involves little risk. Like all newspaper advertisements, areas where there is too
much black need to be avoided. But the production process is straightforward. The second example, with beauty salon ads, was developed to
illustrate two important points. Macintosh software has tremendous
potential for dramatic illustrations, and efficient admaking. However, some
production processes can become more complicated through the use of
computers. An advertiser must weigh the benefits of high tech production
methods against personnel and time efficiencies. Let's look at the golf
course ads first.

Advertisements, like the one shown in Figure 16 for Pine Lake Golf
Course, can easily be designed and written in a page-layout program. Here
are the production steps for the Pine Lake ad.   First, the logo was created
in SuperPaint, Figure 17 (page 142). It could also have been created in
Canvas, or another drawing type program. Once drawn, the logo had to be
saved in a PICT file format. PICT files are object-oriented, rather than bit-
mapped. Bit-mapped files from paint programs don't produce the desired
type quality on a laser printer.

After the logo was created, it was time to produce the camera-ready
advertisement. If an advertisement has lots of copy, the copy can be written
in a word-processing program. Since the Pine Lake ad had so little copy, all
of the remaining work was done in PageMaker.

A box was drawn to represent the one-column ad size, Figure 18 (page
142). If you don't want this box later, you can easily change the color of the
borderline to white, making it invisible. Next, the headline was produced
and moved to the top of the ad, Figure 19 (page 142). Reverse type was
used to make it stand out from the rest of the ad, and to achieve consistency
in the promotional campaign. The price promotion copy was added next at

Figure 16. Newspaper Ad for Pine Lake Golf Course

the focal center of the ad. Then, the PICT logo file was placed in the ad.
When bringing a logo to a page-layout program, you'll often have to resize
the logo. Putting the arrow tool on one of the handles allows resizing; but
you usually have to press the shift key to make it hold its proportion,
Figure 20 (page 143). If you don't take such precautions, your circle can
turn into an ellipse.

Finally, the disclaimer copy and identifying information was put into
the bottom section of the ad. Instead of designing a traditional coupon, the
advertisement was designed like a ticket for an athletic event. This matched the other promotional materials in the advertising campaign. The
camera-ready advertisement was sent to the newspaper as it appears in the
original advertisement. Page-layout programs, like PageMaker also let you
vary the sizes and formats of advertisements easily.

Figure 17. Creating the Pine Lake logo in SuperPaint [8]

Figure 18. The Ad Size Outlined in PageMaker [9]

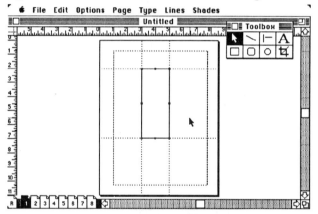

Figure 19. Adding Headlines and Copy in PageMaker

Figure 20. Resizing the Logo in PageMaker.

If single column ads for the golf course were regularly used in promotions, then a template with the ad outline, a black headline area, a logo, and the bordered disclaimer area should be made. Then, each time an ad is needed, only the headline, body copy, and disclaimer would have to be added. The golf course ad was easy because it was all black and white. In the hair salon example to follow, several different techniques were employed. Let's examine the strategy first in order to understand the components of the advertisement.

The hair salon advertising campaign (Figure 21, page 144) was designed to present an exclusive message for a specific stylist who already had considerable name recognition in the market area. Instead of promoting permanent wave or hair color prices, these advertisements attempted to emphasize the design aspects of hair styling, "Designs in Hair". In order to do this, upscale and unusual hairstyles were selected as features in the ads. But unlike competitive advertising which used photographs of models for their ads, the campaign used tracings of unusual hairstyles. These tracings would let the ads stand out in the newspaper. A simple open layout would also provide contrast between this ad and adjoining newspaper advertisements. Since this campaign was developed to demonstrate the admaking capabilities of the Macintosh, we'll describe the individual elements of the ad first. Then, we'll look at the methods of production.

All of the ads in the campaign used three pieces of copy: the headline "Designs in Hair," the name of the stylist, Jan Rasmussen, and the salon address line. Draw, page-layout and illustration software would all be able to produce type for headlines and copy; but an illustration program was

[8]Screen used by permission and courtesy of Silicon Beach Software, Inc.
[9]Screens in Figures 18-20, 22 and 25, used by permission and courtesy of Aldus Corporation.

Figure 21.
Three Hair Salon
Ads Produced on
the Macintosh

These advertisements
were produced in Aldus
FreeHand and Adobe
Illustrator 88. Hair
drawings were traced
from pictures scanned
from magazines. The
stylist's photograph was
scanned from an original
photograph, and mod-
ified in ImageStudio.
When placed in this
page-layout program,
each ad required 900K of
disk space. See the text
for a step-by-step
description.

Designs in Hair

Jan Rasmussen

Altogether Salon•2277 West Columbia•962-0902

Designs in Hair

Jan Rasmussen

Altogether Salon•2277 West Columbia•962-0902

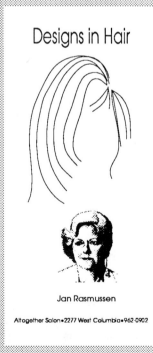

Designs in Hair

Jan Rasmussen

Altogether Salon•2277 West Columbia•962-0902

chosen because it provided more type flexibility. In addition, illustration software would permit finer lines to be drawn for the hair tracings.

In order to produce accurate outlines of hairstyles, photographs of hairstyles were scanned. These scanned images were then **imported** into the illustration software to be used as a template for the drawings. Importing is a process similar to the place command in page-layout software. After the drawings were completed, the imported template was removed.

The stylist's photograph was also scanned to be used as a place-holder in the advertisement. Unfortunately, because the only photograph available had a dark background, a software program was used to outline and retouch the image. After it was retouched, it was imported to the advertising layout. While some people might argue that the quality of this place-holding image is irrelevant to advertising production, it does provide a better guide for the printer.

If the advertisement was going to be placed in a newspaper or magazine, then it would have been sent to a high resolution imagesetter. Photographic prints of the pages, or film negatives would provide the best quality image. Let's outline the specific steps and software used to design this hair salon advertising.

Figure 22. Ad Outline and Copy in Aldus FreeHand

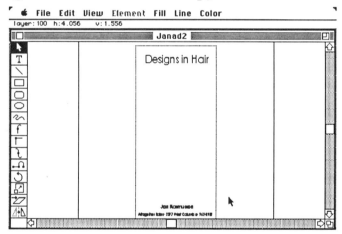

Figure 22 shows the outline of the advertisement on the screen of Aldus FreeHand. Even though a border is visible, the ads are borderless. The headline, stylist's name and salon address have been added to the advertisement. Aldus Freehand has a tremendous amout of flexibility in type design and modification. Using the arrow tool, type can be squeezed and stretched for special effects.

ThunderScan was used, Figure 23, to scan the stylist's photograph. Magnifying the scan with ThunderScan increases the resolution of the photographic image. The inset photograph shows why retouching and outlining was necessary; the background was extremely dark.

Figure 23. Stylist Photo Scanned with ThunderScan [10]

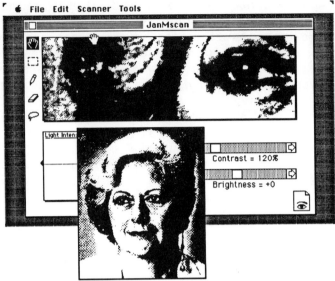

Retouching and outlining an image in ImageStudio, Figure 24, is like using a regular paint or draw program on the Macintosh. Using several different tools, a graphic image can be enhanced, shaded, outlined or modified to create special effects. For this advertising series, the photograph was outlined, and some of the dark shadows were removed. After finishing the picture was saved in an Encapsulated PostScript file.

Figure 24. Retouching the Sylist Photo in ImageStudio [9]

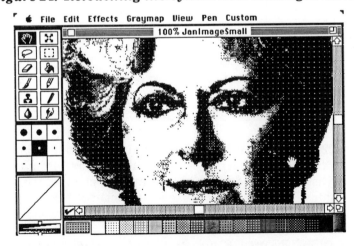

---

[10]Screens in Figure 23 and 24 used by permission and courtesy of Thunderware, Inc., and Letraset USA.

In order to produce accurate, stylized images of hairstyles, photographs of hairstyles were scanned with ThunderScan. These MacPaint files of hairstyles were then imported to the FreeHand advertising layout. Using the scanned photo as a template, line art representations of hairstyles were made. In Figure 25, a white rectangle was pasted behind the drawing so it would be more visible. In Adobe Illustrator, the template would have been gray, rather than black and white.

Figure 25. Using a Scanned Image as a Template in FreeHand

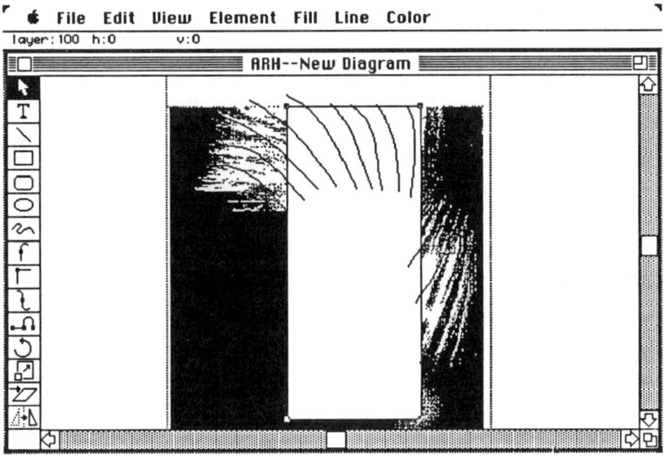

Using scanned images to create unusual illustrations is one technique graphic artists use to build illustrations on the Macintosh. Not everyone has the vision and imagination to create powerful selling illustrations on the computer; but most don't have that power in other media either. Illustration and design skills transcend media. That's why illustrators and designers will always be needed in advertising.

How Revolutionary is the Computer Revolution

For advertising, the Macintosh has added much presentation power to the work environment. Excellent representations of final print advertisements can be constructed using popular page-layout and illustration software. Final production of print advertising has been improved by the development of Macintosh products; but some production processes still require too much manipulation and risk. The best example is the production of halftone images.

New scanners have higher capabilities for resolution, and depth in recording gray-scale information. Yet, the software manipulation required to get good, not great, halftones is considerable. File sizes are monsterous; printing time is lengthy.

In the hair salon example, all of the advertisements could have been produced by tracing the hairstyles on paper, and using traditional halftone methods of production. The stylist's photo could have been sent to a printer, with dimensions and halftone screen specifications. It would have been sent back ready to paste into a layout. However, the hair salon ads weren't a feeble attempt to destroy the benefits of computer graphics on the Macintosh. Many production processes are simplified by computers.

Programs like Letraset ImageStudio, Aldus FreeHand and Adobe Illustrator have stimulated new interest among advertising creative people. Using these tools, many new and different types of advertising illustration are possible. Logo design is much easier using the computer because changes can be made and viewed instantly.

For presentation materials, newsletters and some print advertising, the present scanning technology is adequate. The selection of the appropriate file format is critical for the task desired. For simple place-holding graphics, MacPaint and PICT formats may be acceptable. For complete reproduction of gray-scales, TIFF or EPS files must be used. See Figure 26 for a summary of Macintosh file formats for graphics.

In summary, the revolution is here. The results are exciting. But, the final production quality has a relatively short way to go before it will be universally accepted by advertising professionals.

Study Questions

❑ Why were the Macintosh mouse and interface important to the acceptance of the Macintosh by advertising professionals?

❑ Why was the laser printer and high resolution imagesetter necessary for advertising?

❑ What is the difference between a bit-mapped and object-oriented image?

❑ What are the general steps for laying out an advertisement in a page-layout program?

❑ What is a computer file? Which file format types provide the best reproduction of gray-scale images for advertising?

❑ What are the basic operations (like dragging) on the Macintosh?

❑ What are the economic and time factors to be considered before using the Macintosh for advertising production?

Figure 26. Macintosh File Formats for Graphics

MacPaint™
File size*, 7K.

MacPaint files are bit-mapped
file images which can be manipulated by paint programs, and
they can be placed in page-layout programs.
Images are all black and white. Files are small
and easy to work with; but used primarily as
place holders for graphics.

PICT
File size, 119K.

PICT files are object-oriented file
images. Like MacPaint images,
they don't have gray tones, so they are
more useful for rough layouts. By converting a
MacPaint image to a PICT image, you can move
entire objects, like the woman's head, around
an advertising layout.

TIFF
File size, 406K.

Tagged Image File Format is a
more sophisticated bit-mapped
format. Scanner manufacturers like
the format because it can produce gray tones
well. There are several different TIFF formats, and
different levels of image resolution are possible.
Lack of standardization can cause some problems.

EPS
File Size, 830K.

Encapsulated PostScript files
contain PostScript language code
to produce high-resolution images.
For halftones, EPS files can be enlarged or
reduced without losing image information. Careful
planning must be used to match the resolution of
images to the screens used in the printing process.

*File size is the size of the file needed to store the scanned image at the right.

Macintosh Software and Who Needs It!

The software listed below is particularly relevant to advertising. Like all computer software, the usefulness is determined by the goals and abilities of the user.

Combination paint and draw programs are useful for advertisers who want to create in-store signs, logos and simple advertisements. SuperPaint by Silicon Beach Software, Inc., and Canvas, by Deneba Software, are two easy to use programs which can be used for simple illustrations. For graphic artists, Aldus FreeHand and Adobe Illustrator are essential. Both programs add capabilities for spot and process color; the ability to send files to a high-resolution imagesetter makes them very valuable for the production of advertisements and complex graphics. Illustrators, artists, and people who produce newsletters would want to add the enhanced paint and retouching capabilities of Letraset ImageStudio. Newsletter editors and public relations professionals may want to add scanning capabilities to their computer production systems. Scanners range in price from the inexpensive ThunderScan to flatbed scanners which cost several thousand dollars. All scanners have scanning software associated with them. Professionals searching for a scanner should examine the output from several different machines by testing a typical newsletter or production visual, before purchasing.

By far the most universally important software for advertising is page-layout software, like Aldus PageMaker, Quark Xpress, or Letraset Ready-Set-Go. In order to test these packages, the advertiser should design a simple advertising task and attempt to reconstruct the task using the software. Since these companies are continually competing for market share, their features are quite comparable. Personal preferences for the interface and features of each program will be important in the final choice.

There are several situations where the more expensive vertical market advertising software is an appropriate choice. AdWorks, from Concept Publishing Systems of Beaver Dam, Wisconsin, and Display AdBuilder, from Digital Technology of Orem, Utah, make sense when the output of advertising is the primary function of a department. By selecting an integrated system like these, advertising production will be more systematic and efficient. Because advertising intensive operations need extra training and support, the support services offered by producers of vert-ical software are an important part of the product purchase. The integration of clip art materials is an adjunct to retail advertising systems.

The products mentioned above are available from several different sources; but some specialized products are very helpful. The Electronic Clip Art Digest, a directory of clip art, is produced by SSG LaserWorks, 6376 Quail Run, Kalamazoo, MI 49009. No illustrator or artist would want to miss the Xris Xros file conversion utility produced by Taylored Graphics, P.O. Box 1900, Freedom, CA 95019. For users of line and clip art illustrations, two scrapbook utilities for the Macintosh are very important. Smartscrap™ is a more extensive scrapbook utility; ScrapMaker™ is an inexpensive scrapbook maker. Both are available from Solutions International, P.O. Box 989 Montpelier, VT 05602.

20

Media Strategies, Concepts and Objectives

Advertising media planning decisions are critically important to the success of advertising campaigns. In order to understand media concepts, some people like to use an analogy to biological mediums or environments to talk about various media characteristics. The analogy is useful for describing some characteristics of media, like speed of transmission and the effect of the environment on the messages transmitted; but the analogy has some important weaknesses.

When discussions of advertising media become too focused on media characteristics, they often lessen the importance of audience characteristics. Conflicting methods of audience measurement and computer modeling also tend to dominate discussions of media and divert attention from the importance of strategic media arguments. Let's re-examine the relationship between media decisions and other marketing and advertising decisions.

Structured Strategies and Media Decisions

Early marketing decisions about the product identity to be communicated, the appropriate competitive distance and the selected target market are crucial for the media director and media planner. For example, a complex product identity may require using print advertising, rather than television. Heavy competitor advertising in one medium may force a choice of alternative media or larger advertising expenditures in the same medium. Widely dispersed target market members may also restrict media choices. Budget constraints always set boundaries on the media selection process.

From the definition of the **target market**, the first media decision is to define the **target audience**. *The target audience is the group of people who are the intended receivers of advertising messages.* Several observa-tions should be made about the relationship of the target market to the target audience. Many writers use the terms as synonyms.

Definitions of the target market which are made during early market planning can be simple or complex. If an **undifferentiated marketing strategy** is used, then a very broad target market will be defined. Marketing plans which use a **differentiated strategy**, where **primary and secondary target markets** are defined, will have multiple definitions of the target market. Target audiences will be defined in the same way as the target market. Multiple target markets are related to multiple target audiences. It's also possible for a marketer to define target markets geographically, or by distribution channel such as wholesalers or retailers. When multiple segments or audiences are chosen, the advertiser must establish the relative importance of each segment. This is called **weighting**. Weighting determines what proportion of the expenditures will be spent on each segment. (Further description of the weighting concept can be found on page 183.) In all cases, the target audience will be smaller than the target market because some target market members are not accessible through advertising media. But practically, the terms can be interchanged if we assume marketing programs can only be directed at the **accessible audience**.

Once the target audience is defined, the media strategist must set **media objectives**. Media objectives, like other forms of objectives, are designed to provide criteria for performance evaluation in an advertising campaign. Several different elements are often included in media objectives, such as: a) specification of the media-related **creative requirements** for advertising messages, like high reproduction quality of print images, or 60-second broadcast messages; b) message delivery goals in terms of **reach**, *the number of people (or households) exposed at least one time to the advertising message*, and **frequency**, *the number of times an average member of the target audience is exposed to an advertising message within a specified time period*; c) proposed **timing patterns** for message delivery which consider seasonal purchase patterns, repurchase cycles, and competitive advertising. The most common timing patterns are **continuous** media scheduling where advertising is placed regularly. **Flighting** patterns schedule media in waves which usually coincide with periods of increased audience interest in the product. **Pulsing** schedules combine the attributes of continuous and flighting patterns. Pulsed advertising schedules use added media emphasis during promotional times while maintaining a continuous advertising program.

If target audiences are separated geographically, then geographical weighting patterns and goals should be included in the media objectives. All media objectives must be based on prior marketing decisions about product identity, competitive distance and target markets.

Setting media objectives requires strategic decisions about creative format, the breadth and depth of message delivery, and the timing of advertising messages. A formal **media strategy** must include a plan for achieving the objectives.

The next series of strategic decisions for the media director or advertiser is the choice of media, to be used in the campaign. While the description above makes it seem like a sequential series of decisions, the decisions are actually made at the same time objectives are set. For major campaigns, the **media choices** are: national and spot television, cable television, national and spot radio, magazine, newspaper, Sunday supplement, outdoor, transit, yellow page, point-of-purchase and direct mail. These choices must be justified by prior marketing decisions and evidence of consumer behavior which supports selection of the medium. Most advertising campaigns include a primary and one or two support media; the largest campaigns include most major types of media. Local campaigns often use a single medium. When more than one medium is used in the campaign, relative importances of the media must be estimated. Expenditures should be made in proportion to the estimated importance of each medium.

The strategic decisions above are followed by **tactical decisions** which are implemented by a media planner. These tactical decisions are: a) **selection of media vehicles**, which means specific magazines, television programs or stations where advertising will be used; and b) **scheduling of advertising messages** in the vehicles. Before we examine the vehicle selection process, let's take a closer look at media audiences.

Audiences

To an advertiser no concept is more important or mysterious than the concept of an **audience**. A media audience is a collection of people whose common bond is their pattern of media usage. While many different types of audiences have been described, some audiences are much more valuable to advertisers than others. The preferred measures of audience value seem to be **media efficiency formulas.** These formulas are used to calculate how many audience members are delivered for a specified advertising expenditure. Print media comparisons are based on **cost-per-thousand** formulas. Broadcast media comparisons use **cost-per-rating point**. These concepts will be discussed later, and summarized on pages 179-183. **Audience composition** factors may have dramatic effects upon the efficiency calculations, so the media planner must be aware of the composition of vehicle audiences.

Media planners don't always include the total audience in media calculations. Instead, they may use weighting to produce more accurate estimates of response to advertising. Here's how.

The **total audience**, *circulation and pass-along readers for print* and *viewers or listeners for broadcast*, is reduced to **target audience** members. As you can see, the accuracy of audience composition estimates is critical for this calculation. National advertisers often use Simmon's (*SMRB*) data for these estimates. When Simmon's data are not available, the media planner must trust his or her own primary research data, or data from individual media vehicles.

For local campaigns, where audience composition data are not readily available, there are two options. Each media vehicle can be assumed to have an audience whose composition mirrors the general population. Proportions of audience members within certain demographic ranges can be estimated from individual market data in the *Survey of Buying Power*, or from U.S. Census data. These estimates may provide a more realistic estimate of the target audience size for a medium, but comparisons between

media don't make sense. This calculation assumes all media have audiences with the same proportion of adults, children and teenagers. They don't.
The second option is to pressure local media into providing audience
composition data.

After the total audience size is adjusted for the number of target
audience members, the **advertising audience** may be estimated. *Advertising audience is a term used to describe the percent of readers, viewers
or listeners who are exposed to an advertising message.* Since exposure
generally means that an audience member has an opportunity to read, see
or hear the message, some media planners use other characteristics to
adjust for different levels of message processing. Using primary research,
or syndicated data, a media planner may adjust target audience estimates
based on the average recall of advertisements, or average response to advertisements from past campaigns. This precision is only possible when careful post-evaluation of media schedules has been performed, or when **test
market** research has been performed to determine media and advertising
use by consumers.

When all of these adjustment calculations are added to efficiency
formulas for media vehicles, several observations should be made: a) as the
number of adjustments increase, the efficiency and cost estimates go up;
b) if the adjustment assumptions are applied to all media vehicles, it is just
as valid to omit the adjustments entirely, since all vehicles would be adjusted by the same proportionate amount; c) when the adjustments are based
on assumptions, rather than research, they are only crude guesses.

Other methods of adjusting the total audience are possible. For
instance, if we were interested in a differentiated marketing strategy, we
might adjust a total media audience in proportion to various levels of product interest. Purchasers of the product class, competitive purchasers, or
frequent users could be separated for these estimates. These estimates
would have to be made on the basis of research studies or primary sales
data.

One new research technique has appeared in recent years. It's called
single-source measurement. The technique measures advertising
exposure variables and couples them to scanning information from product purchases. The purpose is to provide information about the impact
of advertising copy and media schedules on the target audience from
the initial advertising message to product choice in the marketplace.
BehaviorScan™ from Information Resources, and a new system called
ScanAmerica™ being developed by the SAMI/Burke and Arbitron Ratings
units of Control Data Corporation, are the most prominent research
systems. This type of research generates **single-source data.** Because
single-source data links media behavior to product purchase and brand
selection, some experts expect battles over who gets access to the data.
They predict that advertisers would be more likely to do their own media
planning and placement if reliable information about audiences and purchase decisions was readily available. Obtaining single-source data is still

very expensive and unrealistic for many advertisers. The scanning-based technique does promise to offer more insight into advertising processes.

So far, we've only examined audiences from the perspective of an advertiser. *Media vehicles are actually marketing their audiences.* In order to sell advertising, a medium has to demonstrate it has a large audience, or a profitable audience for advertisers. Since advertisers always want descriptions of the audience for media planning, many media pay to have **audience research** performed. Reports from audience research become support for advertising rates. In direct response advertising, highly responsive audiences can be marketed for more money. To build audiences for any mass medium, we usually have to promote the medium through advertising, maintain estimates of audience characteristics, and demonstrate the size and potency of the audience for potential advertisers.

Making Media Comparisons

Media planners and advertising strategists make media comparisons every day. When media choices are made for a campaign, several factors must be compared. **Creative factors** determine the impact and potency of messages delivered by a medium. **Audience factors** are related to a medium's ability to deliver messages to selected audiences in a timely manner. **Management factors** are related to production and cost efficiency. Figure 27 outlines the differences between major media on these three factors. Let's examine some dimensions of each factor.

Message impact could be called the "Wow! factor." A medium like television, with its visual drama can astound viewers; huge outdoor boards can create spectacular visuals that are bigger than life. **Message permanence** is the length of time the message can be processed by the consumer. Broadcast commercial messages are fleeting and transient; magazine messages may be available for one or two months. **Message immediacy** is the timeliness of messages as they are perceived by consumers. Radio and television are news-oriented media. Newspapers also convey an immediacy for retail sales messages. **Copy complexity** is the ability of a medium to deliver a complete sales message. Print advertising and direct mail deliver the most complete messages. Messages on outdoor boards, and in television commercials may be much less complete, especially in :15 second commercials.

Advertising media vary in their ability to deliver highly targeted audiences. **Audience selectivity** is an indicator of how easily audiences can be targeted by the medium. Direct mail is the most selective; yellow page may be the least selective. Special interest magazines and business magazines are certainly more selective than consumer magazines. Radio, because of its station formats, is more selective than network television. **Geographic flexibility** is ability to make different media buys in selected markets. Spot television is more flexible than network television. Network radio has less geographic flexibility than local radio. Direct mail advertising, because of its access to zip codes, probably has the highest degree of

Figure 27.
Summary of Media Characteristics

	CREATIVE FACTORS				AUDIENCE FACTORS			MANAGEMENT FACTORS		
	Message Impact	Message Permanence	Message Immediacy	Copy Complexity	Audience Selectivity	Geographic Flexibility	Timing Flexibility	Production Flexibility	Production Cost	Unit Cost
Television	H	L	M	L	M	H	V	L	H	H
Network	H	L	M	L	L	L	L	L	H	H
Spot	H	L	M	L	M	H	M	V	M	M
Cable	H	L	M	M	M	H	M	M	M	L
Network	H	L	M	M	V	H	M	M	M	M
Local	H	L	H	M	V	H	M	H	L	L
Radio	M	L	H	M	H	H	H	H	L	L
Network	M	L	M	M	L	L	M	M	M	M
Local	L	L	H	M	H	H	H	H	L	L
Newspaper	M	M	H	H	L	M	H	M	M	L
National	M	M	M	H	L	L	H	M	M	M
Local	M	M	H	H	M	H	H	H	L	M
Supplements	M	M	M	H	L	L	M	M	M	M
Magazines	M	H	L	H	H	H	V	M	M	M
Consumer	M	H	M	H	M	M	V	M	M	H
Business	M	H	M	H	H	M	M	M	M	M
Farm	M	H	M	H	H	M	M	M	M	M
Outdoor	H	L	L	L	L	M	L	L	H	H
Transit	L	L	L	L	L	M	L	L	H	H
Yellow Page	L	M	L	L	L	L	L	L	L	M
Direct Mail	H	M	M	H	H	H	M	H	H	H
P-O-P	V	L	L	L	L	M	L	V	H	H

H = High on the characteristic
M = Moderate
L = Low
V = Wide variations

geographic flexibility. **Timing flexibility** is an indication of the amount of lead time needed to place advertising in a medium. Radio commercials can be produced in a few minutes and put on the air minutes later. Outdoor boards are much more restrictive. Posters must be printed, and installation requires advanced planning. Point-of-purchase displays also require pre-production planning.

To be effective, advertising messages must be produced efficiently. Advertising media vary in the amount of production assistance given to advertisers. They also vary in production and commercial costs. **Production flexibility** refers to the amount of time needed to produce different commercial messages. Overall cost for producing a single commercial or print advertisement is called the **production cost** for an advertising medium. Television has the highest production cost. Local newspaper ads may be most inexpensive to produce. The **unit cost** is the price of a standard advertising unit, a commercial or print advertisement. These costs vary greatly. A single television commercial may sell for $200,000 on prime time; a local cable television spot may sell for $135. National magazine ads may sell for $5,000; newspaper ads might sell for $65. Media choices may be shaped more by the budget available than creative, audience and management factors. But, the advertising media selected for an advertising campaign must efficiently deliver messages to a profitable part of the target audience. In order to produce more quantitative comparisons of media vehicles and media plans, several formulas for comparisons have been developed. They'll be outlined in the next section.

Quantitative Media Comparisons

Numerical formulas have been developed to compare media vehicles, and to compare and evaluate entire media plans. In this section, some of the most popular measures will be reviewed. Before we start, two concepts need to be examined. A comparison of five radio stations is called an **intramedia comparison** because the comparison is made within the same media class, radio. Since the audience, creative and management factors within the media class are similar, numerical comparisons are appropriate. Numerical comparisons across media classes, or **intermedia comparisons**, are not valid because characteristics of the media are so different. Watching a highly involving commercial on television, is not the same as speeding by a billboard at 65 mph. Consumer processing differences for magazine advertisements also makes it difficult to compare them with radio or television commercials.

Even though intermedia comparisons are not valid, some numerical indicators of total media impact have been developed. To understand these indicators, we need to look at the **rating** concept for media vehicles. Television ratings are the most prominent form of ratings; but in recent years, the rating concept has been broadened to include other forms of media.

Ratings are always measured in reference to a population. Often the population is defined as U.S. households or persons in households. The result is a **household rating** or a **person rating**. *A rating is the percent of a population exposed to a media vehicle within a specific time period.* Before using ratings, the population should be carefully defined. While ratings are an important measure for intramedia comparisons; they can also be summed to compare media plans.

The sum of rating points for media vehicles results in a total called **gross rating points,** or **GRP's.** Gross rating points are a rough measure of total audience delivery by a media schedule or plan. *When ratings are calculated for the target audience, instead of the general population, the measure is called* **target audience rating points or TRP's.** Ratings, GRP's and TRP's are all expressed as percents, so 200 gross rating points means 200 percent of the audience was exposed to the message during a specified time period. Because people use media differently, 200 gross rating points doesn't mean every person actually saw the advertising. It means the equivalent of 200 percent of the audience saw the message. Some advertisers like the numbers to represent people, rather than the percent of a defined population. In those cases, they calculate gross impressions.

Gross impressions *is the sum of audience members delivered by each media vehicle in a media schedule or plan.* This measure, like gross rating points, is a distorted measure of the total audience because some people see a commercial message in two or more media. There can be considerable duplication in these gross measures. Advertisers would like to know how many different people in the population are exposed to their advertising messages. This measure is called reach.

Reach *is the percent of homes or persons exposed at least once to an advertising campaign during a specified time frame.* Net reach and unduplicated audience also refer to the same concept. When reach is calculated for a campaign, the duplicated audience must be subtracted from the gross rating points, in order to count individual audience members only once. It's apparent that larger number of media vehicles in a plan will lead to more complicated patterns of exposure in the audience. *The average number of exposures for those audience members reached by advertising is called the* **frequency, or average frequency.** Frequency is an important concept because many advertising campaigns force consumers to learn associations between brand names and product attributes. For these tasks, consumers must be exposed to advertising messages more than once. Media planners realize there is a trade-off between reach and frequency. Whether to concentrate on reach or frequency strategies is a question partially determined by the life cycle of the product. Audiences must be made aware of new products, so high reach schedules are used. Complex products and complex messages require frequency strategies. In major advertising campaigns, the reach/frequency question becomes slightly more complicated.

To describe media plans and schedules which use several vehicles with a number representing reach and a number representing frequency is too simplistic. Instead, media planners refer to an **exposure distribution**. An exposure distribution is a table which lists the number of exposures for an audience member followed by the percent of the audience exposed to each number of exposures. For example, with two magazines, a target audience could be exposed 0, 1 or 2 times. With large media schedules frequency distributions may list 10 or more exposures. Two media plans can be compared to see what percent of the audience has been exposed at certain frequency levels. *Effective reach is the percent of homes or persons exposed at a specified frequency level.* This level is set by the media planner to accomplish a desired communication goal with advertising messages. Choosing between media vehicles is still one of the most difficult tasks for the media planner.

Comparisons of Media Vehicles

One of the most obvious comparisons that can be made between media vehicles is a comparison between ratings. Ratings provide an estimate of the percent of households or persons using a media vehicle. Ratings for broadcast vehicles can be deceptive because the viewing and listening audience varies by time of day, or daypart, and seasonally. To compensate for this problem, several broadcast concepts have been introduced.

Households using television, or HUT, is used to describe the percent of households where television sets are on during a specified period. PUT's or persons using television, expresses the percentage in terms of people rather than households. During late night viewing hours, fewer households have sets turned on, so the total viewing audience is much less.

Share of audience, or share, is the percent of households using television which are tuned to a specific program. HUT, rating and share can be expressed in several formulas. Pages 179-183 provide a summary of quantitative formulas for media evaluation. The formula for a rating is: Rating = HUT X Share. Several other comparisons have been described in previous sections.

Cost-per-thousand, or CPM, is the cost for an advertising unit divided by the audience delivered by the media vehicle, multiplied by 1,000. CPM can be used to compare total audiences or target audiences; but the calculations for each media vehicle must be based on the same population. *Cost-per-rating point, or CPP, is the cost for an advertising unit divided by the GRP's.* Cost-per-rating point is often used to determine how much advertising effect can be purchased with a fixed media budget.

Comparisons of media vehicle audiences can be done on many different variables by **indexing** the variables of interest. With indexing, each vehicle is compared to a standard, called a **base**. For example, suppose we know 54 percent of the women in the U.S. have four years of college. From a survey, 62 percent of female readers of Magazine A have four years of college; 48 percent of Magazine B readers have four years of college. To index these numbers, we divide the variable of interest—readers with four years of college--by the base, then multiply by 100. In this case, Magazine A's index is 115 (62/54 X 100); Magazine B's index is 89 (48/54 X 100). Indexes are usually rounded to the nearest whole number. Indexes are easy to understand because they show what percent of the base is represented by each media vehicle.

Quantitative comparisons of media vehicles offer an objective way of comparing audience and cost data. But as we said earlier, some of the qualitative variables in Figure 27 can make media scheduling more of an art than science. The final section of this chapter will examine the role of the computer in media planning and scheduling.

Computers and Media Decisions

Computers are excellent tools for repetitious calculations. To determine reach and frequency, and exposure distributions, and to compare media schedules, several different **media models** have emerged. **Linear programming models** attempt to find the best media solution given cost and audience parameters. Media **simulation models** attempt to estimate real world exposure patterns using vehicles that have been chosen by the planner. **Mathematical models**, like the **beta binomial model**, use formulas to estimate reach and frequency from media schedules. Computers can solve complex mathematical formulas very rapidly; but the validity of the media models named above depends on the assumptions made about consumer processing of advertising.

Some media departments have approached the media vehicle choice question from a different direction. They have used decision-support software, like **LightYear**™ from Thoughtware, Inc., to establish qualitative and quantitative decision rules for media choice. Using a simple type of artificial intelligence, the program orders media choices for the planner using both qualitative and quantitative information.

Regardless of their numerical sophistication, computers must have existing decision criteria in order to evaluate media vehicles, plans and schedules. Computers can't create assumptions, but they can sometimes project outcomes when the assumptions change. Computers have revolutionized the media buying process, and they continue to provide interesting insights into complex media scheduling.

Study Questions

❑ How are media objectives related to other forms of advertising objectives?

❑ What strategic media decisions must an advertiser make? How are media decisions related to overall marketing decisions?

❑ What are some of the most important qualitative differences between media classes?

❑ What is the major limitation in using gross impressions or gross rating points to evaluate media schedules?

❑ How is effective reach different from reach?

❑ Describe the major timing patterns for media schedules.

❑ What is the advertising audience, and why is it important? How can weighting be used to adjust audience estimates?

❑ Distinguish between rating, HUT, PUT and share.

Support Software for Media Planners

Large-scale media departments usually are tied into mainframe computers at major service bureaus, like Interactive Market Systems, or SMRB. Individual media planners must use additional computer support in order to analyze subsets of national data, to make decisions about media vehicles, and to present media data to the rest of the marketing team. You'll notice that the software listed here is mostly IBM-compatible software; some Macintosh alternatives are listed, as well.

By far the most important piece of support software for the media planner is a spreadsheet program. For IBM machines, Lotus 1-2-3™ represents the largest installed base; Microsoft Excel for the Macintosh is a powerful program. With spreadsheets, the planner can examine market characteristics, calculate efficiencies based on audience statistics and media costs, and plot and graph important relationships.

As indicated earlier, some advertising planners are using decision-support systems to evaluate choices between media vehicles. In addition to LightYear, mentioned earlier, several other programs are available, including: Expert Choice from Decision Support Software, Prism from Tempus Development Corporation, and What's Best! from General Optimization, Inc. Most of the advertising applications for these programs have been developed by individual users, and the primary determinant of effectiveness is the set of decision-rules and assumptions added by the advertiser. Certainly, expert systems and artificial intelligence will play more important roles in future advertising planning.

Two Macintosh programs, FlowMaster™ and GeoQuery™, provide graphical presentations of media information. FlowMaster charts advertising budgets and media expenditures; GeoQuery provides market data mapping.

Presentation software, a strength of Macintosh, is also important for the media planner. Programs like More™, Cricket Presents™ and PowerPoint™ can make media presentations more effective because of their overhead and slide transparency output capabilities.

21

Broadcast Media

Broadcast advertising media include: network and spot television, network and spot radio, cable television and theater advertising. To purchase **network time,** radio or television, an advertiser contracts with the network for commercial placement. Commercials are sent to the networks and are scheduled on all network affiliates. **Spot television** and **spot radio** media buys are purchases of time from individual stations. Spot radio could also be called local radio if media buys are made in a limited geographic area, such as a single market. **Cable television** purchases can be made from cable networks or from individual stations, but regional marketing companies called **cable interconnects** offer larger audiences by selling time on a group of cable systems. The time sold by interconnects is usually local time scheduled during cable network programming.

Media planners justify using network television in media plans because of its *broad coverage* and *high impact visuals.* Products look good on television. Because of its high visibility, television *communicates prestige* to the audience. Spot television adds *geographical flexibility* to a media schedule, while providing the advantages of network television for a more limited audience. For retailers and local advertisers television gives *immediacy* to the message, a necessary characteristic for generating store traffic.

Cable television commercials preserve many creative advantages of television, and supply more *upscale audiences.* While cable audiences are much smaller than network television audiences, cable subscribers generally have higher income and educational levels than network viewers. Cable purchases on networks like MTV, CNN, and ESPN, can be used to provide additional television support for a campaign at a *lower unit cost.* Because of the lower unit cost, *longer commercials can be used.* The development of 2 to 5 minute **infomercials** for cable television offers innovative creative options for advertisers. The smaller size of the audience for cable programs is the medium's most limiting factor. If media scheduling on cable reaches the right audience, cable media buys can be very *cost efficient and effective.*

The major limitations for network and spot television are *high production costs* and *high unit costs.* Network and spot television offers broad coverage of mass audiences, but *lacks the specificity* of cable or print media audiences. Media purchases on cable are usually less justifiable economically because of the **fragmented audiences**. An abundance of cable channels lessens the chance that viewers will regularly watch a small number of programs or networks on a cable system.

Both **network and spot radio** advertising are justified by their *immediacy, low unit costs* and *low production costs*. These characteristics make it easy to add radio to print or television intensive media schedules. *Some audiences, like teens, can be reached more effectively* through radio advertising. Because of a variety of station formats, *radio is a more selective medium* than television. Radio is also a mobile medium. People take it to the lake and listen while they drive. Like cable television, the large number of stations and formats contributes to radio's major weakness, **audience fragmentation**.

Decisions to use broadcast media can be justified by the individual strengths and weaknesses of each medium. But, a decision to use broadcast media in a media schedule must also consider consumer attention factors and creative limitations of broadcast messages.

Broadcast Messages

Advertising experts describe broadcast messages as transient, or fleeting, which is a reference to differences in **permanence** between messages in the broadcast and print media. With the exception of cable television infomercials, which may run 2 to 5 minutes, broadcast commercials run 15, 30, 60 and sometimes 120 seconds. There is little time to sell a set of product features in a commercial. Consumers can't re-process the information, as they might be able to with a print advertisement. Another contrast between print and broadcast messages is the nature of message processing by consumers.

When commercials appear in television programs, consumers usually can't skip over them. Nor can consumers look for and seek out broadcast commercials they'd like to see. For magazine or newspaper readers, advertisements can be skipped, skimmed or re-read. Videotape technology has clouded this distinction a little.

Consumers now use videocassette recorders to record their favorite television programs. When they replay the programs, there is a tendency to fast-forward during commercials. Media researchers call this **time-shift zapping**. Zapping makes it easy for a consumer to avoid commercials. The effects of zapping on advertising audiences will be examined later.

More selective exposure to commercial material occurs on computer databases where shopping information is stored. Comp-u-store Online™ and the Electronic Mall™ are shopping sections of CompuServe®. Using personal computers, consumers can access vast amounts of information about products and pricing. Database access is actually an electronic form of print advertising media, rather than a separate broadcast medium. Most soothsayers believe electronic information retrieval for product information will be important in the future. For years, two-way interactive cable television has been touted as the the next wave of technological innovation. The advertising potential hasn't been realized, yet.

Broadcast messages, with a few exceptions, still have creative limitations. *Messages must be simple* because of the speed of transmission, and because consumers can't re-process the information. Complex messages must be simplified for use in radio or television formats. In a typical 15 or 30 second spot, there may be time for the product name and company name or one product attribute. When 60 second commercials are used, *one selling idea must predominate.* Radio commercials for retail stores often use a **donut** format where changing sale information can be inserted in the middle of a jingle or mini-drama.

Consumers use radio, and sometimes television, as background noise while they are performing other tasks. This practice results in *less attentiveness to commercial messages,* so even though television or radio receivers are on in a household, the messages may not be processed as thoroughly as print messages.

Describing the creative limitations of broadcast commercials can be deceptive and depressing unless these weaknesses are balanced against the major advantage. Broadcast commercials can have potent **impact**. Visual dramas can be created for television. Unusual theatrics can be used on radio. These dramatic messages can then capitalize on the audience strengths of each broadcast medium.

Broadcast Audiences and Their Measurement

Since the price of advertising is determined by the size and quality of an audience, **audience measurement** is critical for media and for advertisers. Dramatic changes in audience measurement have occurred in recent years, and these changes have fueled many debates among advertising experts.

On September 1, 1987, media history was made when two network television rating services, **A. C. Nielsen** and **AGB--Audits of Great Britain**, began measuring audiences with a device called the **People Meter**. When television is monitored in a home with a People Meter, family members are assigned an identification number. As people in the household watch television programs, they check-in and out with the People Meter. The meter monitors channel selection and VCR use. Demographic information about the family is collected before program monitoring begins. Like earlier **audimeters**, viewing data is transmitted directly to the parent company's data banks.

People Meters replaced the earlier system of audimeters, which monitored channel selection. Audimeter results were coupled with **diaries**, where family members recorded the programs they had watched. The new People Meters were designed to overcome human errors of program entry, since writing in a diary requires considerably more effort from test families. Critics of the People Meter maintain that family members don't always check-in and out as they should. They also say the check-in system doesn't work for children. As you might expect, the major critics of the People Meter audience measurement system are representatives of the major networks.

After three months of People Meter operation, network television audiences were estimated to be 5 to 10 percent lower than they had been during the same months a year earlier. When audiences fell short of promised viewing levels, the networks had to provide **makegoods**, which are commercials added to fulfill contractual requirements for audience delivery. The reduction in viewers reported by People Meters was so large that spot television time had to be used to correct scheduling discrepancies. Video-cassette recorders and subscriptions to cable television have also reduced network television viewing. The major networks believe there are biases in the People Meter measurement system. The reliability and validity of the measurement system is now being examined by independent researchers.

Broadcast audience measurement has been in a state of flux. Since People Meters were introduced in 1987, AGB has decided to cease operations in the U.S. Competition among media research firms is heavy. While Nielsen holds a virtual monopoly on network television audience measurement, Arbitron Ratings plans to provide national audience estimates by 1990. Both Arbitron and Nielsen monitor local television viewing in some markets. Arbitron Ratings, Nielsen and Information Resources are also competing to provide single-source data which relate viewing habits to product purchases.

In radio ratings, **Arbitron** has been a leader in providing audience estimates for local radio listening for many years; but, it has recently been challenged by **Birch Research**. **Radio's All Dimension Audience Research (RADAR)** measures network radio audiences. Companies like Nielsen have already begun talking about ultimate audience measurement devices which measure more information from viewers, including emotional response to programming and commercials.

Viewing audiences for television, and listening audiences for radio, vary by time of day and by season. That's why it's important to know how many households are using television, or HUT levels. It's also important to know who watches during different dayparts in order to provide more precise targeting for commercial messages. **Dayparts** are specified time periods for viewing or listening during the day. Television distinguishes between morning, afternoon, early fringe, prime time, and late fringe or late night, dayparts. Radio divides dayparts into morning drive, mid-day, afternoon drive, and evening.

Targeting must also be done based on the type of program. Television ratings tell how much interest there is in a program, but without demographic and share of audience information, effective media planning is very difficult. Radio planners must evaluate ratings by station format, since station format is more important than specific radio programs for listeners. Station loyalty doesn't exist for network television; but cable television networks like ESPN do attract regular audiences.

Cable television growth is only one of the factors contributing to diminished audience size for network television. Videocassette recorders, because of time-shift zapping, can reduce network advertising audiences. Another form of zapping, **electronic zapping**, occurs when viewers switch channels during commercial breaks. Satellite dishes (TVRO's), with large numbers of channels, provide many viewing opportunities for an audience. This can also reduce network viewing time.

In order to effectively buy broadcast media, the media planner must know the size of the audience by household or individuals, the share of the audience compared to alternative media, and the cost of commercial time. Many media planners also develop goals for efficiency, such as cost-per-rating point, as purchasing criteria for broadcast media.

Purchasing Broadcast Media Time

Network television purchasing begins in July when advertisers and advertising agencies make **upfront buys** of commercial time for the new fall television seasons. The prices charged are based on the networks' ability to deliver a specified audience rating. If the ratings are lower than specified, the network will provide **makegoods**.

There are three popular ways to purchase network television time: a) a **scatter plan** purchase, where you purchase a package of commercials on several different programs; b) **full or partial program sponsorship**, where an advertiser agrees to purchase all or some of the commercial time for a specific program; and c) a **one-time special** purchase, usually for entertainment or sporting events.

Scatter plan purchasing *reduces the risk of losing advertising effectiveness because of a programming flop.* By distributing commercials across several programs you are also *increasing the unduplicated reach* for your commercials.

Full program sponsorship has almost disappeared from network television since it is so *expensive.* Program sponsorship may be accompanied by extra mentions of your company or product, called **billboards**, when a program is promoted. Program cast members may also be available for promotional events. Because of audience loyalty, program sponsorship for a media plan emphasizes *frequency, rather than reach.* Audiences for programs also get larger as programs keep airing. Media planners refer to the increase in viewership as the **cumulative audience**, or **cume**. Cume is another word for unduplicated reach over a specified time period. One of the biggest disadvantages to sponsorship is the *high risk for new shows,* because purchases are made before the new season begins.

One-time specials are often *good media vehicles for new product introductions.* They're also *good for seasonal advertisers* because seasonal advertisers use more flighting objectives than continuous advertisers. Many one-time specials or events can be marketed heavily with sales promotions, contests and publicity. Unfortunately, advertising purchases *for entertainment specials are very expensive* . Audience size increases may not keep pace with higher commercial costs.

Spot television buys requires more complicated pre-purchase evaluation and preparation than network buys. The reason for the complication is obvious. Spot television commercial time is purchased from individual stations, rather than the major networks. So a media planner must negotiate with individual stations for the media buy. Audience selection forces a planner to decide which markets, which stations within the markets, which brands to advertise, and which dayparts for commercial time must be purchased. Finally, a tentative flighting schedule must be established. This schedule indicates when the advertiser would like the commercials to begin and end. All of this activity takes place before the media planner communicates with the individual station.

Once contact is made with the stations, the advertiser is supplied with a list of **avails**. Avails are the available slots for commercials. From the list of avails, the media planner must reconcile differences between the avails and his or her flighting schedule. Then, prices must be negotiated. Broadcast media rates are quite negotiable. After commercials are produced, they have to be sent to each of the stations where spot time was purchased, an immense coordination task for the media and production departments. Spot markets are often used as test markets for new promotional strategies.

Cable television network time is purchased similar to network television time; spot or local cable time is individually purchased, like spot television. Cable interconnects act as intermediaries between the advertiser and several regional cable systems.

There are similarities between network and local radio purchases, too. Network radio purchases are made for network radio programs, like Rick Dees Weekly Top 40 and NBC Talknet. Local or spot radio purchases are made like spot television with, one important difference. Because the radio markets are so fragmented, commercial time must be purchased on many more radio stations than spot television stations, in order to reach a sizeable audience.

Radio and television commercials must meet the marketing needs of the advertiser. As we've said earlier, broadcast messages are transient. So, the advertiser must decide how long commercials must be. Radio commercials are usually 30 or 60 seconds. But, television advertisers have begun using **stand-alone 15 second spots**. Most media specialists believe the decision to allow stand-alone 15's will result in network advertising by more companies. Stand-alone 15's have lower unit costs, so an advertiser could advertise for less total expense. In 15 second spots advertisers will only be able to reinforce brand or company names.

Both 30 and 60 second radio and television commercials are common; longer commercials are sometimes used for special effects, or to provide additional information. Some long infomercials on cable were designed to provide cooking tips using specific products; many of these commercials provided recipes and hints. Since these longer commercials generally have been used only on cable stations, their effectiveness has not been studied extensively by researchers.

Broadcast media play an important role in advertising. Like all media, television and radio deliver messages to an audience. The effectiveness of the media depends upon the quality of the audience. Quality of the audience determines how much an advertiser is willing to spend for commercial time.

Study Questions

❏ Distinguish between network and spot television and radio.

❏ What are the strengths and weaknesses of broadcast advertising messages?

❏ How are network television and radio audiences measured? How have People Meters changed audience measurement?

❏ What decisions must an advertiser make when purchasing spot television time?

❏ What effect will stand-alone 15 second spots have on network television advertising?

❏ How is network television time purchased?

❏ Why would networks be against People Meter measurements, and advertisers be for it?

Satellite Dishes and Media Audiences

At one time, satellite dish (TVRO) sales were booming. Then, when the cable television networks, and HBO, began scrambling their signal, dish sales dropped. Several controversies arose. Advertisers complained that scrambling reduced the viewing audience considerably, and should be postponed. Cable system revenues were affected, because dishes were positioned against cable. "Pirating," a term applied to those who illegally tap into cable systems, was also applied to dish owners who received unauthorized signals.

Since dishes are able to receive many signals, the viewing alternatives are different. Also, different timing for satellite transmission of programs means audience composition for shows can be different from network, or cable network viewing. As a practical solution, most advertisers disregard dish audiences. The audiences are too hard to measure, and not large enough to provide large fluctuations in program ratings. Dish owners who purchase descramblers, which allow access to cable networks and HBO, can be counted with cable subscribers.

22

Newspapers, Magazines and Supplements

As the major print media, newspapers, magazines and supplements have unique attributes which interest media planners. They also share some common creative strengths and limitations. The ratio of national to local advertisers provides a clue to some advantages and disadvantages of each medium. Newspapers are supported by a large proportion of local advertisers; magazines have a large proportion of national advertisers. Supplements vary depending upon their scope. Some supplements are like regional weekly magazines. These tend to have a higher percentage of local advertisers, while national weekly supplements have characteristics and advertisers which are more like magazines than newspapers. As you might expect, national newspapers, like USA Today, have a combination of characteristics which differ from either newspapers or magazines.

Newspaper advertisers often justify the selection of newspapers in their media schedules because of the *intense coverage*. In many communities, 70 to 80 percent of the homes subscribe to the community newspaper. Since local news is of primary interest, newspapers become a *primary source for shopping information*. Community interest also endows the local newspaper with *prestige* in the local marketplace. Like other print media, *consumers determine their own rate of reading* for features and advertising. Sometimes this results in slower processing; sometimes faster. Newspapers have always had a reputation for *flexible advertising production*. Retail advertising departments provide advertising assistance to retailers, and can change advertising quickly. *Sales promotions and coupons seem to work very well* in newspapers.

Unlike magazines, newspapers do not have a long life. *Permanence is low* because most people throw newspapers out with the daily garbage. With today's lifestyles, many newspaper readers only have time to skim editorial features, so *reading time may be short*. Advertisements may be missed. Even with new advances in printing and color technology, the *quality of printing in most newspapers is inferior to magazines*. If the primary selling point for a product is elegant beauty, then magazine reproduction may provide a better representation of the product's image.

Magazine media buys are justified by the *enhanced selectivity* of magazine audiences. While there is considerable variability across magazines, from broad consumer weeklies to special interest and business magazines, there is *more opportunity for selecting specialized audiences* with magazine advertising. Some broad consumer magazines offer regional editions. Magazines also have *more permanence than newspapers or broadcast media.* In fact, pass-along readers are an important part of magazine audiences. Color and black and white *reproduction quality can result in outstanding advertising images.* Editorial content of magazines often provides a *supportive environment for advertising,* when related products are advertised. In recent years, many *magazines have attempted new creative approaches,* such as holograms on the cover, pop-up advertisements and new formats.

Even though regional editions are available for some magazines, *advertising copy cannot be tailored to local audiences.* Except for news-weeklies, *magazine advertising production is much less flexible than newspapers or the broadcast media. Longer lead times are necessary;* but knowing editorial content in advance can help an advertiser plan product advertisements for special magazine issues. *Copy changes cannot be made efficiently* because of the large coordinated printing task for major magazines.

Supplements are often selected over newspapers and magazines because they offer *better reproduction quality than newspapers,* a little *more permanence than newspapers, more immediacy than monthly magazines,* and *the broad coverage of newspapers.* Their selection is often an attempt to compromise on the advantages of both media types.

National newspapers have attempted to offer advertisers an *upscale, national audience,* with *excellent reproduction quality.* Daily publication provides *immediacy.* But, many national advertisers have continued to use multiple newspaper buys in major markets to get more coverage than that offered by national newspapers.

Characteristics of the print media make them quite different from broadcast media. These differences interface with different consumer attention and processing capabilities to make print advertising messages unique.

Print Advertising Messages

Most of the attention and consumer processing characteristics of print advertising messages are related to prestige of a publication and the length of persuasive messages. Magazine readers range from consumers shopping for ideas, such as those who read magazines like *Family Circle* and *Vogue,* to professionals who use magazines to keep up with their profession. Regardless of the profession, business advertising gets high marks for readership because the professional products advertised relate to success in professional careers. Both consumers and professionals can be persuaded effectively through magazine advertising.

High quality illustrations and minimal copy have become the standard for fashion advertising in both men's and women's magazines. Product dominance in illustrations combined with unusual photography creates interest in the product, and favorable associations with a brand name.

In contrast, business readers may read an advertisement which carefully argues the advantages of a certain product. Since special interest and business readers will read more copy, it's important to provide essential selling points in magazine copy. David Ogilvy was a champion of reason-why copy and national brand images. An interesting visual can be used very effectively in magazine advertising to support a brand image. But, headlines and body copy must entice and persuade the active reading audience.

Print Advertising Audiences

Several different variables have been used to describe print media audiences. As we discussed in the previous chapter, the concept of a rating has been extended to include print media; but **circulation** is by far the most common characteristic used to describe print audiences. *Circulation refers to the total number of magazine issues that get into the hands of readers.* There are several different types of circulation.

Paid circulation, found primarily in consumer publications, is the same as subscriptions. *Controlled circulation means the publication controls the audience by delivering only to selected individuals or households.* Some suburban newspapers have controlled circulations; but one of the most common types of publications with controlled circulations is the specialized business publication. Magazines, like *MacWeek* for Macintosh product developers and consultants, circulate the magazine to professionals so they can use the base to establish advertising rates for a very specific audience. Non-professionals may subscribe to the magazine, but the professional circulation makes the magazine desirable for advertisers. *Non-paid, non-controlled circulation magazines or newspapers are distributed free, usually through distribution points, rather than individual delivery.* Many local advertising weeklies use this type of circulation.

For advertisers, the type of circulation is important because messages are being sent to specific audience members. Advertising rates are determined by circulation, so the advertiser wants to make sure he or she gets maximum delivery of the message for every dollar spent. Free circulation magazines and newspapers may not be picked up. Free circulation media may report a community's population as its circulation, even though distribution never reaches the entire population. Several different auditing organizations regularly monitor magazine circulation. These are important to an advertiser because they allow estimates of advertising efficiency.

Magazines with a large proportion of paid subscriptions may become members of the **Audit Bureau of Circulation** (ABC). The organization reports distribution and circulation figures for magazines. Publications which don't meet the circulation requirements of ABC, and who have controlled circulations, may use the **Business Publications Audit of**

Circulations (BPA). Print media circulation data, specifications for printing sizes, and advertising prices are published annually by **Standard Rate and Data Service (SRDS)**. Media planners depend on SRDS for audience planning estimates.

Unlike broadcast media, print media often have **secondary** or **pass-along readers**. Most media research firms would say *a reader is anyone who looks into a particular issue of a magazine or newspaper within the last publication interval.* Given this definition, readers will outnumber the circulation estimate for any magazine or newspaper. *Primary readers are people who live in a household where there is a magazine or newspaper subscription. Secondary readers do not purchase their own copy of the magazine or newspaper.*

Some magazines or newspapers periodically do research to establish other statistical measures of their audiences. One measure is the **Average Issue Audience** (AIA). The Average Issue Audience is the number of readers expressed as a percent of a base. For example, a magazine with 60,000 hair salon owner readers has an AIA of 33.0%, since there are about 180,000 hair salon owners in the U.S. This measure is similar to a person rating for broadcast media vehicles.

Readers per Copy (RPC) is another indicator of print media audiences. Newspapers usually have about two readers per copy. Other publications vary. RPC goes up when the publication has a weekly frequency, and newsy editorial material. It also goes up when the publication is popular for use in public places, like medical and professional offices. RPC goes down when editorial material is complex, because then it takes longer for the primary reader to process the information. Short life publications, like *TV Guide* also have lower RPC values because the information is quickly outdated.

Like a television program or series, audiences accumulate over time. **Audience accumulation** is again the term used to describe an increasing unduplicated audience. Publications have different accumulation periods. Newspapers accumulate audiences during the day; monthly publications accumulate over a 30 day period. The greater the number of pass-along readers, the longer the accumulation period. Accumulation is an important concept for time-sensitive campaigns. If information must get to consumers rapidly, then vehicles with faster accumulation periods should be chosen for the media plan.

Several other qualitative differences between publications are important for an advertiser. Magazines and newspapers vary in the number of days a reader spends with an issue, the number of pages opened, the frequency of coupon redemption, reader interest in advertising, and reader opinion of the publication. All of these qualitative variables must be considered by the media planner in purchasing print media space.

Purchasing Print Media Space

Advertising rates are generally determined by the circulation of the publication. Media planners and advertisers use **media rate cards** to make media buys. Lower media costs can be obtained in several ways.

By planning newspaper or magazine schedules several months in advance, the advertiser can make **bulk media buys**. Bulk media purchase plans provide lower costs per inch because the advertiser has a contractual agreement to purchase space more frequently. Many newspaper bulk contracts specify a number of inches per week. This system favors the continuous advertiser. For some publications, the advertiser can purchase space across a group of related publications at reduced cost.

Depending upon a publication's advertising policies, special placement of advertising may be negotiated. Premium space, such as the front or back cover or center spread, will cost much more; but increased attention to the ad may be worth the added expenditure.

Cost-per-thousand (CPM) is probably the most common yardstick used to measure the effectiveness of a magazine or newspaper. CPM usually goes up with the selectivity of an audience. In comparing magazine audiences, it's important to calculate CPM using the same base. If target audience is used to calculate CPM for one magazine, then target audience data must be used for all other comparisons of CPM. This may be difficult because target audience information may not be available for local and regional publications. Without access to a uniform source, like Simmon's (SMRB) data, target audience data may not be reported in standardized categories.

Once the media buy has been made, the advertiser must send camera-ready artwork or negatives to the publication. Print advertisements should be collected after publication because several problems may occur. Collected advertisements are called **tearsheets**. They are needed in order to support claims of poor reproduction quality or faulty placement. If a publication fails to deliver the guaranteed audience, or if poor reproduction occurs, an advertiser may be entitled to a rebate or credit.

Study Questions

❑ What are the major differences in strength between newspapers and magazines as print media?

❑ How is consumer processing of print messages different from the way they process broadcast messages?

❑ Outline the differences in circulation types for magazines. Why is circulation type important for an advertiser?

❑ How is circulation and readership different?

❑ Define Average Issue Audience and Readers Per Copy. How are they important to a media planner?

❑ How can print media costs be lowered?

Space Sense for Newspaper Advertising

Effective newspaper advertisers save money by using good judgment in their media buys. The most obvious savings can be made by planning advertising early. Once advertisements have been outlined for several months in advance, bulk space buys can result in the most economical media rates. In order to determine the costs, the advertiser should compare the total media costs without the bulk buy to bulk buy rates for the same time period. For intermittant advertisers, the question to ask is "How much unneeded space am I purchasing with a bulk buy?" Also related to this question is, "How much extra advertising am I getting for the same price?"

Advertising layouts can sometimes be reduced in size without reducing their effectiveness. If you look at the pages of a newspaper, either a daily or advertising weekly, you'll see that an advertisement that is 2/3 of a page will have the same attention-getting power as a full-page ad. For example, from the rate sheet of a shopping weekly, the full-page rate for 96 inches was $414.72. Purchasing 60 inches of space, 5 columns by 12 inches, the cost was $279.60. Both ads will command nearly as much attention because they dominate the page in the newspaper. But, the smaller ad cost $135.12 less than the full-page ad. For every two ads at the lower cost, you save enough money to place an additional advertisement. Space sense like this, is related to dollars and cents in an advertising budget.

When you run small space ads, there are a couple of techniques that will provide more effectiveness. These techniques will aid visibility, rather than reduce costs. Tall narrow ads usually get better position placement than square ads. But, they should only be used when the format fits your advertising message. As ads get smaller, headlines should get shorter and larger. This will help get attention. Using larger graphics can also produce better results for small ads.

Good close-up photographs of people get good readership in ads. Product photographs and headlines also are important ways to signal the target market. Headlines must attract the attention of your most likely customers. Gimmick photography never works as well as good advertising strategy. Some advertisers say everyone looks at "babies"; but everyone who looks at "babies" isn't a customer for your products. If you make your ads relevant to your target market's needs, they will be much more effective.

Coupons increase readership, when they are applicable to your products. Consistent graphic design, similar borders and logo placement, may be the strongest principle of advertising effectiveness. Your customers need to learn to identify your store or product by looking at the format of your ads.

Outdoor and Yellow Pages

Outdoor and yellow pages advertising are two support media used by both national and local advertisers. In a few isolated cases with small retailers, outdoor or yellow pages may be the only medium used. National advertisers use outdoor and yellow pages advertising to support national campaigns. To support local dealers and distributors, national advertisers may offer cooperative advertising programs which include outdoor and yellow pages subsidies. While national advertisers use more outdoor than local advertisers, yellow pages is used more heavily by local advertisers. Both yellow pages and outdoor advertising add breadth to a media plan, which can't be offered by other media. As support media, the individual strengths of outdoor and yellow pages must be used to extend the effectiveness of major media buys.

Outdoor Advertising

As an advertising medium, the **outdoor industry** has experienced indecisive growth for two reasons. For a few years, consumer protest movements against the medium placed considerable pressure on the industry. Some restrictions and plans for the replacement of outdoor boards were included in the 1965 **Highway Beautification Act**. Insufficient governmental funding has added to industry indecision because regulation and replacement of outdoor boards has been stalled.

Outdoor advertising must be defined according to standard industry categorizations, otherwise any hand-made poster or business sign would be considered part of the industry. Outdoor advertising, as discussed here, will include three types of outdoor structures. These range from individually produced painted bulletins and spectaculars to mass produced posters which are affixed to outdoor structures. The structures described below are managed and produced by **outdoor advertising companies**.

Painted bulletins are individually-produced outdoor structures. Because they are painted singly, messages can be localized for audiences in different geographical areas. Extenders can be added to the top of boards for more dramatic effects. *second most expensive*

Spectaculars are the most complex outdoor structures. Many have dramatic lighting and mechanical or electronic elements to create attention. ↑ 3-D   *most expensive revolving   panels*

Because of their complexity and construction, spectaculars are the most expensive outdoor structures. In order to justify the large expense, spectaculars must be placed in major metropolitan areas where traffic is heavy.

Posters are outdoor boards which use printed sheets affixed to the outdoor structure. Several different sizes are available. Most advertisers now use 30-sheet posters; but 24-sheet posters are also used. Some markets have smaller sizes available. The advantage of posters is their ability to be mass produced.   *least expensive*.

As an advertising medium, outdoor advertising is *a high frequency medium.* Boards can't be put up and taken down easily. When many boards are purchased in a geographical area *high reach levels* can also be obtained. *Geographic flexibility is high* because almost every neighborhood has outdoor structures. *Outdoor messages have impact because they're huge.* Outdoor posters provide ideal *opportunities to reinforce product identities when consumers are away from home.*

Consumer *processing time for messages is limited* because they are traveling at highway speeds. *Selectivity is low* because the only constraint on the audience is geographical neighborhood. *CPM's for outdoor advertising are artificially low* because of the length of time posters are displayed, and audience duplication biases in outdoor audience measurement. *Absolute costs are also high* for using outdoor advertising. An advertiser must pay production costs, costs for changing displays and illumination costs.

Purchased from an outdoor advertising company, advertisers establish the size of audience they would like to reach, and the company offers structure locations which are available. Lead time is a critical variable for outdoor advertising, since prime locations may be contracted for long periods of time.   *lighting*

Outdoor Messages and Audience Measurement

Outdoor messages must be short. Graphics must be dramatic. And, the most important creative requirement is that artwork be readable. One rule-of-thumb says there is a seven word limit for outdoor messages.

Regardless of the creative limits, outdoor messages must quickly create interest and associations between brand names and product packaging. The creative task for outdoor may be one of the most difficult creative tasks in advertising. Audience measurement is nearly as difficult.

The effectiveness of outdoor advertising is influenced by driving speed and distractions while driving. Typical recall studies are ineffective because outdoor advertising is a support medium. It's impossible to tell whether product recognition or recall is due to an outdoor board or other advertising messages.

National audience data for outdoor is compiled by SMRB; local audience data is compiled by two organizations, **Audience Measurement by Market of Outdoor** (AMMO) and the **Traffic Audit Bureau** (TAB).

These organizations use a **map-recall method** to estimate reach and frequency for audiences. Drivers are asked to use a map to recall their travel behavior. This is correlated with the placement of outdoor advertising. Driving by an outdoor structure is considered exposure. Demographics are also compiled for the mobile audience.

The outdoor industry has changed its method of calculating market coverage for outdoor advertising. In the past, advertisers would purchase enough posters to be seen by a percentage of the market, usually 50 or 100. To make the audience data more consistent for advertisers, a gross rating point system was created. An ***outdoor gross rating point** is equal to one percent of the population passing by an outdoor board each day.* To calculate outdoor GRP's, you divide the number of people passing an outdoor structure (or set of structures) by the population, and multiply by 100. So, if 40,000 is the population of a city, 20,000 motorists would have to pass by the structure to achieve 50 gross rating points. *Remember that this is a duplicated audience so the numbers for reach are exaggerated.*

Yellow Pages Advertising

Since government deregulation of the telephone industry, considerable changes have taken place in yellow pages advertising. Independent directory producers have arisen to challenge the industry mainstay Ameritech. In recent years, directory publishers have attempted to encourage use of the yellow pages by inserting sales promotion coupons and other sales promotion devices. In some areas, where competition for yellow pages advertising dollars is intense, directory producers may offer additional premiums and promotions. These promotional expenditures are designed to provide support for yellow pages advertisers, and to promote consumer use of a specific directory.

For local and national advertisers, *directory selection may be an important choice in a market area.* This decision should be based on competitor selection of directories, estimated use of directories by present customers, advertiser support by the publisher, and cost considerations.

Customers go the directory to find retailers and businesses they need. As industry propaganda and research says, most trips through the yellow pages result in a purchase. In the yellow pages, small businesses can appear large by using the appropriate size advertisement and effective copy. A poor ad can reduce the effectiveness greatly. *To be effective, yellow pages ads should tell potential customers how to get to a business, when the business is open, and what products or services customers can expect to find.*

Yellow pages advertising isn't cheap. *Display ads are quite expensive.* Their cost should be weighed against the number of directory-assisted customers a business expects each year. In multiple directory markets, expenditures on yellow page advertising should be weighted by estimates of the consumers' use of each competing directory.

Telecomm   Career Expo

Feb 21 10-4   2nd Floor M.S.U. Union

Study Questions

❏ How do absolute costs of yellow pages and outdoor advertising compare with local radio and television absolute costs?

❏ Why are audience estimates for outdoor advertising biased?

❏ What is the primary advantage of outdoor posters to painted bulletins and spectaculars?

❏ How do the creative requirements of outdoor advertising restrict advertising messages?

❏ How are outdoor gross rating points different from gross rating points in other media?

❏ What is the map-recall method used for?

❏ How has deregulation affected a businessperson's use of yellow pages advertising?

❏ What consumer and product factors influence the effectiveness of yellow pages advertising?

Buying Yellow Pages Advertising

One of the most frequently asked questions by businesspersons is, "How much should I spend on yellow pages advertising?" As with newspaper advertising, it's easy to overspend. Yet, some businesses fail to spend enough on yellow pages advertising. Asking your present customers two questions will help determine how much to spend. Ask them, "When you decided to come to our (store or business), did you look at our yellow pages ad?" and, "Do you usually look up our telephone number in the yellow pages before you visit?

When customers use yellow pages in their decision-making, yellow pages advertising is extremely important. It's also important if customers refer to it often, because they are being exposed to competitor ads at the same time. You should also look at competitor ads in the yellow pages. Determine how many businesses like yours are using yellow pages ads. If they are your major competitors, then you should probably purchase a similar ad size. But, like newspapers, a 2/3 page ad will dominate a page; a quarter page ad will get noticed easily. Several factors require more spending in the yellow pages: brand name merchandise, small advertising budgets where other media are not often used, and a desire to increase visibility of your business in a market area.

You can also increase visibility with mutli-color ads. Blue or green and black are easier to read than red and black ads. Always list store hours, telephone numbers, and directions if they are needed.

Doing Media Calculations

Comparison Technique	What it means and how to calculate it.
Rating	A rating describes how many households or people are using a specific advertising medium. Ratings are expressed as percents of a population. You have to define the population. Typical populations are actual population in a geographic area, or target audience population in the advertising area. Since many local media don't have target audience statistics, it is.often better to express local media ratings in terms of actual population. Another way of defining it is the ratio of the vehicle audience to the population. Therefore, the formula for rating is:

$$\text{Rating} = \frac{\text{Vehicle Audience}}{\text{Population}}$$

If a weekly newspaper in a city of 40,000 has an audience of 32,000 people, then the newspaper rating is 32,000/40,000 = 80%. Eighty percent of the population were exposed to the medium.

Comparison Technique	What it means and how to calculate it.
Gross Rating Points	Gross rating points is one measure of the total impact for an advertising campaign. It is the sum of all ratings for advertisements and commercials in a campaign. When national media are used, GRP's are often calculated for the target audience. Because of the biases in outdoor GRP's, outdoor GRP's should be reported separately. Remember, GRP's include audience duplication, so they are not indicators of unduplicated audiences. GRP's are simply an indicator of total advertising weight for a campaign.

$$\text{GRP} = \text{Rating}_1 + \text{Rating}_2 .. \text{ etc.}$$

Notice, that because duplication is allowed, two advertisements in a single vehicle will double the rating points for that vehicle. Suppose we run 2 ads in a regional magazine with a rating of 15, 20 radio spots on a radio station with a rating of 11. The GRP calculation would be:

$$\text{GRP} = 2(15) + 20(11) = 250$$

Notice, the magazine rating is multiplied by 2, and the radio station rating by 11.

Gross Impressions	Gross impressions is similar to gross rating points, except that it is expressed in numbers of exposures to advertising. Impressions can also be expressed in numbers of impressions for a target audience. This measure is another crude indicator of total advertising weight.

$$\text{G. I.} = \text{Impressions}_1 + \text{Impressions}_2...\text{Etc.}$$

If we run 15 spots on a television program with a 10 rating, and a newspaper ad from a newspaper with a 30 rating, (all from a city of 40,000), then we will have 72,000 gross impressions. Here's how. Each spot on the television program will expose 10% of the population, or 4,000 people. The newspaper ad will expose 30% of the population, or 12,000 people. The total is calculated as $15(4,000) + 1(12,000) = 72,000$.

Reach **Unduplicated Reach**	Expressed as a percent, reach is the number of *unique* households or individuals exposed to one advertising message. For a single insertion in a single vehicle, reach is simply the percent of individuals or households exposed to the message. When two ads or spots are used in the same vehicle, or when multiple vehicles are used, the audience duplication must be removed to provide the unduplicated audience. In complex media schedules, advertisers usually look at effective reach (see below), rather than reach. Another way of expressing reach is by relating it to GRP's.

$$\text{Reach} = \text{GRP's - Duplication}$$

Calculating duplication is beyond the scope of this book. For more information about that calculation, consult *Strategic Media Planning*, by Kent M. Lancaster and Helen E. Katz. Many practitioners assume no duplication; but that solution will result in inflated estimates of reach.

Frequency **Average Frequency**	Frequency is the average number of times an audience member is exposed to a message. Frequency is an indication of repetition in media scheduling. Campaigns which have more complex brand associations to make usually seek frequency in their media objectives. Multiple vehicles can produce distorted estimates of frequency, so most media planners choose to look at exposure distributions instead.

It's important to examine the relationship between reach, frequency and gross rating points.

$$\text{GRP} = \text{Reach} \times \text{Frequency}$$

From this formula, it's possible to derive the other relationships:

$$\text{Reach} = \frac{\text{GRP}}{\text{Frequency}}$$

$$\text{Frequency} = \frac{\text{GRP}}{\text{Reach}}$$

Exposure Distribution	Exposure distributions are tables of two values, the frequency of exposure and the percent of the audience exposed at each frequency level. For two magazines, A and B, we might have the following exposure distribution.

Frequency	Percent Exposed	
0	53%	
1	41%	
2	6%	Sum=100%

As exposure distributions get more complex, the list of frequencies is usually shortened to a maximum number, 10 to 12. The Lancaster and Katz book describes exposure distributions more completely. Exposure distributions are essential for estimating effective reach.

Effective Reach	Effective reach is the percent of the audience which is exposed at a defined frequency level. Effective reach is a better indicator of message repetition when learning requires multiple exposures. By setting the desired frequency level, the planner can match exposure and learning goals for advertising.
HUT PUT	HUT or PUT levels tell what percent of households or persons are using television during different periods of the day, or during different seasons of the year. HUT and PUT levels are estimated by Nielsen, and they're important because they indicate the absolute size of the audience. These values are useful for audience estimates when the concepts of share and rating points are discussed. Following the definition of share, the numerical relationships between rating, share and HUT will be described.

Share	Share is the percent of total television viewers or radio listeners who are watching a specific program or listening to a specific station. Remember, the percent of viewers or listeners is equal to the program or station rating.

$$\text{Share} = \frac{\text{Rating}}{\text{HUT}}$$

This also means the following formulas are equivalent:

$$\text{Rating} = \text{Share} \times \text{HUT}$$

$$\text{HUT} = \frac{\text{Rating}}{\text{Share}}$$

Suppose there are 120 households, and 100 households which are using television. Fifty households are watching Program A, 40 are watching Program B, and 10 are watching Program C. HUT = 100/120 = 83.3%. Ratings are as follows: Program A, 50/120 = 41.7%; Program B, 40/120 =33.3%; Program C, 10/120 = 8.3%. Shares of audience for each program: Program A, 50/100 =50; Program B, 40/100 = 40; Program C, 10/100 = 10.

CPM **Cost-per-Thousand**	Cost-per-thousand is the most common efficiency formula used to evaluate advertising media audiences. It relates the cost of a unit of advertising to audience size. It can be expressed for the entire population, or for the target audience.

$$\text{CPM} = \frac{\text{Unit Cost}}{\text{Audience Size}} \times 1{,}000$$

CPP **Cost-per-Point**	Cost-per-rating point is a measure of the cost for an advertising schedule. It relates advertising expenditures to gross rating points.

$$\text{CPP} = \frac{\text{Advertising Costs}}{\text{GRP's}}$$

CPP is useful for comparing the efficiency of schedules and for comparing competitive media expenditures.

| Indexing | Indexing is a widely used technique for comparing media, and any other, variables to a standard. Inflation rates are often described according to some base year. Media planners must establish their own base, in order to effectively describe differences between media vehicles. The formula for an index is as follows: |

$$\text{Index} = \frac{\text{Variable of Interest}}{\text{Base Value for Variable}} \times 100$$

If we know that out best market produces 982 product per year, then we could develop an index of test markets based on projected sales for the next year. Suppose predicted sales for Market A were 1,242; Market B were 745; and Market C were 1,000. Indexes for each market would be as follows: Market A, 1,242/982 x 100 = 126; Market B, 745/982 x 100 = 76; Market C, 1,000/982 x 100 = 102. An index of 126 means the test market performed 26 percent better than the base market value.

| Weighting | Weighting is a procedure which allows an advertiser to adjust estimates of markets, media or advertising response to make the estimates more realistic. Weighting can be done on the basis of subjective estimates, or objective measurements. In both cases, the weighting procedures must be justified by some rationale. For example, suppose we wanted to estimate exposure to one tennis club advertisement in the newspaper. In a city of 40,000, newspaper penetration or coverage is 70%. So, only 28,000 (.7)(40,000) are potential readers. Since only 20% are tennis players, (.2)(28,000) or 5,600 are in the potential audience. The estimation process could proceed with other subjective percentages, such as percent of the population between specific target ranges, or on the basis of income levels. The purpose is to provide more careful estimates of response, so conservative estimates should be used at each step. |

By collecting media use data, target audience information, and other information about the target audience, advertisers can make more meaningful estimates about advertising effectiveness. Starch scores would allow weighting for vehicle differences.

When used judiciously, weighting can add precision to marketing and advertising plans.

24

Direct Mail

For the last few years, direct response advertising has been one of the fastest growing segments of the advertising industry. **Direct response advertising** *is any advertising message that attempts to get an immediate response from consumers, using any advertising medium.* While **direct mail advertising** immediately comes to mind, *direct mail is only one of the media employed to deliver direct response messages.* Not all direct mail advertising is direct response advertising. The major focus of this chapter will be direct mail advertising because it is an important part of the media mix for many advertising planners. Several other key terms must be examined first.

For a long time, magazines and newspapers have used response coupons as incentives for consumers to seek more product information, purchase sales promotion items or sample products. Cable television systems have stimulated new growth in direct **response television** where 800 telephone numbers are used to order products. Virtually every advertising medium can be used as a direct response vehicle, including outdoor boards.

The only criteria required for direct response advertising is an objective which has a *response goal for consumers.* Two other distinctions should be made. **Direct marketing** *is the exchange of goods and services which results from direct communication with the target audience.* **Mail order** *is a method of selling and distributing products which relies on mail or telephone orders of products.* Catalogs are frequently used. Mail order may be promoted and catalogs distributed through direct response advertising; but some mail order business may be the result of in-store transactions.

Direct Mail as a Medium

Direct mail is the *most selective and most accountable medium* for advertisers. Response to advertising can be measured quite easily, and the results can be judged against costs. Direct mail is *high in geographic and production flexibility.* Consumers from almost any segment of the population can be geographically segmented for more effective mailings. Any legitimate mailing package can become part of a **direct mail advertising package.** This may range from mock-up products to samples, or supportive product literature. When catalogs are part of the direct mail package, *messages have a long life with the consumer. Impact is high* when unusual packages are delivered.

Because of its selectivity, *CPM for direct mail may be unusually high. Production costs can be astronomical,* if the mailing package isn't designed efficiently. *Inaccurate mailing lists can reduce the effectiveness* of direct mail and cause considerable waste. But, despite this potential for waste, direct mail has more potential for success because of the highly targeted messages it carries.

Contrary to the popular belief that consumers hate direct mail advertising, several studies have shown that many consumers look forward to receiving direct mail catalogs and literature. In fact there are segments of the target audience who are heavy users of the medium. These groups purchase regularly through the mail, and many prefer mail order to traditional shopping methods. Busy professionals like the ease of ordering, and decreased shopping time. Catalog suppliers have also learned that fulfillment is the key to success. Speedy delivery and fast return processing results in a continuing customer base, which is necessary for profitable performance.

Mailing List Management

Direct mail advertising requires careful mailing list management in order to guarantee effectiveness. Advertising planners can choose from several types of lists, and several types of list maintenance. An advertiser may maintain his or her own list of customers. Regardless of other direct mail activities, a customer list is always an excellent way to evaluate advertising and build customer relations. In many situations, the advertiser may enlist the services of a **direct mail house** which brokers mailing lists for list suppliers. These direct mail organizations have staffs of planning advisers to help suggest the most effective mailing list for campaign objectives. Thousands of lists are available.

Three types of lists are useful for an advertiser. **A house list** is a list of present customers. These lists are valuable because the present customers already like and trust your business. If this list has past purchase information on it, the value of each customer can be determined from the list. **Response lists** are lists of consumers who respond to advertising. It's helpful if response lists can target consumers who have responded to similar offers. Occasionally, direct competitor lists are available; but sometimes there are restrictions on the type of mailing that can be sent to your competitor's customers. Response lists from several sources can be merged to find buyers who purchase from different mail-order sources. **Compiled lists** are lists developed from directories, membership lists and subscription lists. Consumers listed on compiled lists don't have a record of responding to advertising, so the response levels will be lower than the other two types of lists.

The most effective direct mail advertisers maintain records for list control which establish histories for customers. These controls monitor the recency of customer purchases, the frequency of customer purchases and the average expenditure made by the customer. Non-profit and religious organizations often use this type of system to solicit contributors.

Direct mail houses maintain large banks of mailing lists, and they often merge lists to find **multibuyers,** or people who purchase from several different mailing sources. Huge lists require large mainframe computers; but smaller lists can be managed on personal computers. There are two primary requirements for direct mail management programs, **bulk mail sorting routines** and **duplication elimination.**

Bulk mail sorting routines print mailing labels according to government bulk mail standards, so mailing costs are reduced. Duplication elimination is a feature that not many personal computer programs have. Duplicate mailing addresses can cause considerable waste in a mailing list. Most computer software uses **match codes,** or a system of coding and comparing information so duplicate records are eliminated. Without this feature mailing lists lose their efficiency.

Creative and Legal Parameters

Direct mail packages must contain complete product and response information if a response is expected. The package usually includes the mailing envelope, a cover letter, product literature, a response device and a reply envelope. All are important physical parts of the package.

Direct mail advertising copy must also be complete reason-why copy. Short sentences and a great writing style helps persuade an interested audience to purchase a product. Effortless ordering information increases the response rate. There are several excellent direct mail advertising guides, including: *Successful Direct Marketing Methods* by Bob Stone, *Direct Marketing* by Edward L. Nash, and *Profitable Direct Marketing* by Jim Kobs.

Direct mail advertisers must also be aware of the legal restrictions on the medium. Because of early misuse of the medium, government regulation is stringent. Competent legal review should be made of all direct mail advertising to insure that it meets governmental standards.

The **delayed delivery rule** says that a mailing piece must say how long before a product is delivered. If it doesn't, delivery must occur within 30 days. If delivery will be delayed, the consumer must be notified and given the option of cancelling his or her order.

Publishing companies lobbied for the **negative option rule** which allows companies to send books, if the consumer fails to tell the company not to send a featured book. Companies who use this direct mail technique must handle the resulting consumer problems efficiently.

Guides for the use of endorsements and testimonials were outlined in 1975. These guidelines require endorsers to be consumers, and they require companies to disclose all endorser information when asked.

When **unordered merchandise** is sent, the government considers it an unfair trade practice. Consumers may keep the product as a gift. They are under no obligation to pay.

There are also guidelines about "bait and switch" practices, use of the words "free" and "new," deceptive pricing, and dry testing or the practice of promoting products that don't exist.

In recent years, direct mail advertisers have experienced extraordinary growth because of the efficiency of the medium, governmental monitoring and an active and responsible trade association, the **Direct Marketing Association** (DMA). Information about direct marketing practices and regulations can be obtained from the Direct Marketing Association, Six E. 43rd Street, New York, NY 10017.

Study Questions

❏ What are the advantages and disadvantages of using direct mail as an advertising medium?

❏ Distinguish between mail order, direct marketing, direct response advertising and direct mail advertising.

❏ What kinds of direct mail lists are available for advertisers, and how do they compare in effectiveness? What are the key variables for mailing list effectiveness and efficiency?

❏ What does accountability mean in reference to direct mail advertising?

❏ How does direct mail advertising copy differ from other forms of advertising?

Direct Mail Response Rates

Most advertisers want to know what kind of response rates direct mail gets. In 1988, several financial institutions reported response rates as high as 15%. Their rule-of-thumb was less than 1% was a failure, 2-5% was good, 10% was outstanding. One bank boosted deposits by $15.5 million with a 7% response rate. Integrated promotions, where consumers were enticed to act quickly, work better than general mailings. Success must be measured against the overall sales goal. For example, a 1% response rate for signing up credit card customers was successful because of the long term increase in revenues from this small group. The total marketing package is important; technical details like return envelopes and high quality paper are important. Targeting the mailing list is essential for attaining the highest possible response rates.

Making a Local Media Plan

There are several sources of information about media planning for large national advertisers, including: *Advertising Media Planning*, by Jack Z. Sissors and Jim Surmanek; *Strategic Media Planning*, by Kent M. Lancaster and Helen E. Katz; and *Advertising Media*, by Anthony F. McGann and J. Thomas Russell. Using national market and audience data, national advertising plans can integrate large quantities of data in order to select the best media plan. The focus of this supplementary section will be on local media plans.

Local advertisers rarely have access to national data. They often have little audience data from radio and television stations. Manufacturers are often too enthusiastic about spending the local advertiser's budget. Like other advertisers, local advertisers have difficulty comparing media. The following system for building local media plans assumes the local advertiser has customers already. If you wanted to extend this system to a new business, then the customer media habits would have to be estimated from local media information. There are four steps: 1) measure the media habits of target customers; 2) examine the media rates and efficiency; 3) select media and scheduling periods; 4) evaluate the effectiveness of the media choices.

Measure Media Habits

In order to plan media more effectively, it's a good idea to know what media your best customers use. Here is a sample questionnaire for "Fitness One," a health club in a city with a population of 40,000 within it's city limits, and about 78,000 in the total metropolitan area.

Dear Fitness One Customer:

In order to offer more services to more people, we're trying to evaluate our advertising and promotion. Would you please take a couple of minutes to fill out this questionnaire. Your answers will help us become more efficient.

About how many times a week do you visit Fitness One? _____

Do you subscribe to the *News & Times* [local newspaper] (circle one) Yes   No

Whether you subscribe or not, would you circle the days of the week when you read most of the *News & Times*.   Sun Mon Tue Wed Thu Fri Sat

Do you read most of the *Shopping Advisor* [Advertising Weekly] each week? (Circle One) Yes   No

Metro Monitor [Regional Magazine] comes out once a month, do you get to read most issues of that magazine? Yes   No

During what period of the day do you watch the most television?
_____ Morning _____ Mid-day _____ Evening

Do you subscribe to cable television? (Circle One) Yes No

If you do subscribe to cable tv would you tell us when you are most likely to watch MTV, CNN, USA or ESPN?_____Morning_____Mid-day_____Evening

Now, we'd like to know which radio stations you listen to? Would you put an (x) in the box to indicate what times of day you listen to your favorite radio stations. You only need to mark those stations you listen to most.

				Morning	Mid-day	Evening
AM	WCCJ	95.7	"The Hot One"			
AM	WWB	106.5	"Heavy Rock"			
FM	WTCK	90.2	"New Age Rock"			
FM	WACF	114.2	"Campus PBS"			
FM	WMGC	116.4	"Religious Station"			

If we wanted to find out demographic information, questions could be added at the end of the ques-tionnaire. Skills Supplement 2: Writing Simple Question-naires, provides some sample demographic questions.

In this questionnaire, we began by asking how many times a person visited the fitness club per week. This let's you sort questionnaires by categories of customer. We could have examined those who use multiple services, rather than examining those who come to Fitness One twice a week or more. Some commun-ities will have more newspapers; they can be added to the list. Getting the time of day for listening to radio and watching television is important because it will help reach those customers. Radio habits are a little difficult to measure because some people remember the call letters, some the numbers on the radio dial, and others remember the station slogan.

The questionnaires should be given to at least 100 customers; 200 to 300 would provide more reliable results. As the number of radio stations and news-papers increases, more customers should be included in the survey, if possible.

Next, we tabulate the number of customers for each media category. The easiest way is to make a summary table with large boxes and simply put a mark on the summary table for each customer response. Then, add up the number of marks in each box. Divide by the number of people who completed question-naires. This turns the number of people in each category into a percentage. These percentages, either as decimals or multiplied by 100, are a substitute for Target Audience Rating Points, TRP's. Look at the table below for a summary of 200 customer responses.

News & Times .64 Sun ..39 Mon .41 Tue .30 Wed .53 Thu .36 Fri .45 Sat
Shopping Advisor   .67
Metro Monitor .01
TELEVISION .12 Morning .14 Mid-day .35 Evening
CABLE TELEVISION .01 Morning .01 Mid-day .07 Evening
RADIO STATIONS

	Morning	Mid-day	Evening
AM 95.7	.36	.15	.02
AM 106.5	.01	.00	.02
FM 90.2	.05	.03	.02
FM 114.2	.09	.05	.03
FM 116.4	.01	.01	.00

Calculate Media Efficiency and Rates

By looking at the media habits of our customers, we are betting that similar customers are out there reading or listening to the same media. This is not a bad assumption, but we might not want to rule out some media because of potential new audiences. By looking at our summary chart, we see that the *News & Times*, the *Shopping Advisor*, and AM 95.7 radio reach the most customers. To compare the two newspapers, let's examine the cost for a 20 inch ad. There are two possible ways to look at cost-per-thousand; one way is to look at newspaper circulation data. The other way is to base coverage on our customer summary. Before we make the calculation, we need to know how many people live in our city, and how many are between the ages of our customers. Since Fitness One caters to adults, children would be removed from the estimate of media costs. To find the population breakdowns, we look in the *Sales and Marketing Management Survey of Buying Power*. Most libraries have copies.

In the *Survey of Buying Power*, our city has a population of 54,200 people. By combining age groups, we find 39,674 adults in the city. Local newspapers report circulation based on the first number. The Sunday *News & Times* reports a Sunday circulation of 39,000. The *Shopping Advisor* reports weekly circulation of 38,806. If we figure ratings based on these numbers, the rating for the *News & Times* is 72; the rating for the *Shopping Advisor* is also 72. From our customer summary table, we have found a smaller rating for both papers, 64 for the *News & Times* and 67 for the *Shopping Advisor*. We can calculate CPM for both sets of information. The cost of a 20 inch ad is $368 for the *News & Times*, $101 for the *Shopping Advisor*. This means the CPM from circulation data will be $9.44 for the *News & Times* ($368/39000 x 1,000), and $2.60 for the *Shopping Advisor* ($101/48,806 x 1,000).

To calculate CPM from our summary information, we first have to find the approximate number of people to use in the CPM formula. We do this by multiplying our rating times the number of adults from the *Survey of Buying Power*. For the *News & Times* we get 25,391 (39,674 x .64); we get 26,582 (39,674 x .67) for the *Shopping Advisor*. CPM for each newspaper would then be $14.50 for the *News & Times* ($368/25,391 x 1,000), and $3.80 for the *Shopping Advisor* ($101/26,582 x 1,000). The absolute prices indicate nothing because of the number of assumptions we have made in order to estimate CPM. What is important is the difference between the two numbers. Here, the *Shopping Advisor* is much less expensive than the *News & Times*.. Other factors may enter into the media decision. Reproduction quality of the *News & Times* may be better, or the daily newspaper may have a better image than the shopping weekly.

Calculating CPM for radio and cable television can be done in a similar way. For radio, the station would have to supply its Arbitron rating, in order to calculate the number of people in the audience. AM 95.7 has a morning rating of 17. This means a far greater number of our customers listen to AM 95.7 than people in the general population. Without calculating CPM, this looks like a good support medium. One 60-second spot on AM 95.7 costs $36.00. CPM is $3.91 ($36.00/9,214 x 1,000). This CPM was calculated using the entire population since the rating was not broken down by ages. Cable television bases audience data on the number of wired households. In the city described, 70 percent of the households are wired. You can convert households to people, again by going to

Survey of Buying Power. Divide the population by the number of households to find how many people per household (54,200/21,900 = 2.5). Convert the cabled households to people by multiplying people per household times households (23,300 x 2.5 = 58,250). Notice that the number we got was higher than the population. This is because the the cable system crosses different boundaries than those measured by the *Survey of Buying Power.* Multiply the number of people in cable households by the rating we found in the customer summary. For evening viewing, it would be 58,250 x .07 = 4,078. CPM would be calculated as follows: ($18.00/4,078 x 1,000 = $4.41). Again, other factors would enter into the media choice, such as potential for new audiences and impact.

Make a Media Schedule

Promotional periods for a retail store should be selected six months to one year ahead of time. For our example, we'll select a four week period. In four weeks, we'll purchase two 20 inch newspaper ads in the *News & Times*, one 20 inch ad in the *Shopping Advisor*, and 10 60-second radio spots on AM 95.7. Total cost for the promotion will be: 2($368) + 1($101) + 10($36) = $1,197. If we use the ratings determined by our customer summary, then we can calculate Gross Rating Points for the promotion as: 2(64) + 1(67) + 10(17) = 365 GRP's. The rating determined by the radio station was substituted for the cusomer rating because it provided a more conservative estimate. We could calculate gross impressions by using the population estimates which were included in the CPM calculation. Gross impressions would then be: 2(25,391) + 1(26,582) + 10(9,214) = 169,504 gross impressions. Many people like to make a chart to show when the media is being scheduled. They graph media on the side, dates on the top, and use bars to indicate advertising.

September																												
	S	M	T	W	T	F	S	S	M	T	W	T	F	S	S	M	T	W	T	F	S	S	M	T	W	T	F	S
News & Times				▄								▄																
Shopping Advisor			▄▄▄▄																									
AM 97.5	▄▄▄					▄▄▄																						

Evaluate Media Response

There are several simple ways to evaluate a media schedule. If the ads have to be returned to get a promotion, they should be counted. All print ads should have a code number which indicates where they were placed. Asking customers where they heard about a special, a promotion, or your store is also a good, economical way to evaluate media placement. For retail stores, customers should respond within four days. Remember that media audiences accumulate over time, so continued advertising will result in more response, as long as there is continuity in the advertising program. Experimentation with media is a good idea, if the unit cost and total cost for experimenting is reasonable. Care should be taken to make sure the media coverage doesn't extend far beyond the geographic distribution of your customers. Some store owners ask how far away, and in what direction customers live, in order to cut wasted media coverage.

25

Sales Promotion

Sales promotions are incentives or rewards given to consumers, wholesalers or retailers to stimulate immediate sales. Not all sales promotions occur through advertising; in fact a large proportion of sales promotions occur as trade allowances for retailers. These promotions from manufacturers to wholesalers and retailers are part of a **push marketing strategy**, and they're called **internal sales promotions**.

Internal sales promotions include: trade allowances, free products, product buybacks, merchandising assistance, point-of-purchase materials, cooperative advertising support and promotional contests for dealers. These promotional devices are used to get the manufacturer's product into stores. More money is spent by manufacturers on dealer promotions than consumer promotions.

Incentives for consumers are called **external sales promotions**. As part of a **pull marketing strategy**, consumer sales promotions may include: coupons, price-offs, free samples, in- on- or near-packs, self-liquidating premiums, contests and sweepstakes, refund offers and bonus packs. Consumer promotions are designed to move product out of retail stores.

Sales promotion strategy is important to an advertiser for several reasons. Many manufacturers can't wait for the long term establishment of brand franchises from national advertising, so sales promotion is used to get the product moving through the distribution chain. New products may need sales promotion to induce trial by consumers. Sales promotion may alter advertising schedules. Prior to a sales promotion, advertising may be needed to merchandise the promotion. Advertising response may decline after a sales promotion because consumers have stocked up on the product. Because of the interrelationship between sales promotion and consumer demand, sales promotion strategy must be coordinated with the overall marketing plan. If it isn't coordinated, other marketing and advertising efforts may be wasted.

Product identities can be enhanced through sales promotion. Bundling a new product to an established brand name can build an important association in the consumer's mind. Product identities can also be reinforced by selecting relevant sales promotion devices.

Competitive advantages can be established and maintained through innovation in sales promotion. Using sales promotion when competitors don't, or competing directly through sales promotion can result in strength against competitors. Many computer software developers try to attract a competitor's customers by offering trade-ins for competitive products. Sensitivity to target market needs is important because consumers vary in their susceptibility to sales promotions.

When to Use Sales Promotions

Consumer sales promotions can be used to induce trial, to encourage re-purchase, to increase the frequency of product sales, to enhance sales during promotional events and to move overstocked products. Sales promotions can't replace advertising, because advertising has a long range goal of building brand franchises and brand loyalty among consumers. Consumer perceptions of the "deals" offered is an important factor in the success of sales promotions.

Sales promotions to wholesalers and retailers can often add new outlets to the distribution chain. It can reduce inventories, and build morale for the sales force. Promotions can create excitement; but they must also generate measurable differences in sales.

New products, improved formulations of old products and trendy products can be promoted effectively . Because many sales promotions are expensive, overuse of promotional devices can reduce long run profitability for a brand. Let's briefly examine a few sales promotion techniques to see their strengths and weaknesses.

Sales Promotion Techniques

Billions of dollars are spent each year distributing **coupons**. Some consumers clip, collect and use them. This technique is generally *used to stimulate trial* of a product, or *to promote brand-switching*. Older target market members seem to be more responsive to couponing. There are two major problems with the technique. As with advertising clutter, the consumer environment is saturated with coupons. It's not unusual for a consumer to get four or five coupon inserts in the Sunday newspaper, and a package of mailed coupons weekly.

The second problem is **coupon fraud**, or misredemption. Some retailers have been caught clipping and redeeming coupons from the manufacturer, without selling products. Monitoring the coupon redemption system is costly and time consuming.

Product sampling is another technique used to induce trial of new products or new formulations of old products. The technique is extremely expensive. Decisions have to be made about the amount of product in the sample. There must be enough so a consumer gets an idea of product effectiveness; but too much product will not stimulate immediate sales. Samples may be hand delivered or distributed through the mail; either method is costly.

To stimulate purchase from existing users, manufacturers offer **price-offs**. Price-offs allow consumers to purchase the product at a reduced price, so they are more likely to stock up on the product. For many package goods, there are regular purchase cycles, which depend on the frequency of product use. By offering price-offs, consumers can stock up at a lower price. This also removes the consumer from the market for competing products in the product class. If the technique is used too frequently, consumers begin to expect the lower price for the product. When this happens, products may be perceived as discount products.

Selling two or more products together is called an **in-, on- or near-pack**. As mentioned in an earlier section, this is a technique that can be used to associate a well known brand name with a new product. The association may result in more sales if consumers think the products go together. It's also another way to stimulate trial of a new product. Consumers usually feel there is more value in one of these bundled product packages. In some cases, retailers may not like bundled packages because the featured product competes with an existing store brand.

Bonus packs reward consumers for purchasing regular-sized packages. This is an attempt to get trial buyers to start using the product regularly. It also provides reinforcement for regular users of the product.

With **self-liquidating premiums,** *the manufacturer offers a popular product with the company identification to consumers at dramatically lower price.* The low price is sufficient to cover the manufacturer's expense. That's why it's called self-liquidating. Kool cigarettes offered a $699 catamaran; the possibilities are endless. Since the price of the product is recovered, self-liquidating premiums may have more perceived value in the eye of the consumer. The major requirements for success are determining which products consumers prefer, and which products support the product's identity. Of course, brand identification on the premium must be highly visible in order to extend the product's brand image.

Some companies offer **free mail-in premiums**. Like self-liquidating premiums, selection of the product is critical. But, since the premium isn't self-liquidating, the premium cost must be lower. Total costs of the promotion will be higher. It's difficult to match a free premium with the target market. Higher priced premiums may require proof of purchase from several different packages, or from multiple purchases. These difficult consumer tasks can reduce the redemption rate.

The return rate for **refund offers** is quite low. Since proof of purchase, a sales receipt and refund application are usually required, only 25 percent of those who purchase the product may complete the refund process. Refunds take considerable time, and this delay can eliminate any association of the sales promotion with product identity.

Contests and sweepstakes are another form of sales promotion. When they are publicized properly, contests and sweepstakes can create considerable attention. Many consumers don't purchase products in order to enter, nor do they return many coupons as a result of a sweepstakes. Professional entrants are also attracted to contests and sweepstakes.

Continuity promotions use stamps, sets of glasses, raisin figurines, or any other set of items to attract repeat customers. Popular promotional items quickly run out; unpopular promotions may die in the second or third week. A critical variable for the success of continuity promotions is the amount of effort a consumer must expend to complete the process. If purchase patterns are reasonable, then a greater number of consumers will purchase repeatedly.

Two variables are very important for consumer sales promotion success, appeal and effort. Premiums and promotional items must represent a good value for consumers, so advance testing with the target market is necessary. Effort is also connected to value. As the amount of effort required by consumers increases, the perceived value of the promotion decreases. Or, as the perceived value of the promotion increases, the advertiser can expect the consumer to expend more effort for the promotion. Participation is related to effort and perceived value. Finding the right balance is important.

Trade promotions are also essential for new product survival. Shelf space is limited and competition heavy, so **trade allowances** are almost always used. Trade allowances are short term price reductions in order to get dealers or retailers to purchase the product. Manufacturers believe the price reductions will let retailers offer products at lower prices to consumers. This may not happen.

Cooperative advertising support is used to assist retailers or distributors with advertising costs, and to move products out of the outlet. Cooperative advertising plans usually reimburse about 50 percent of the local advertising costs. This reimbursement may be made in products, rather than cash. Cooperative advertising does give the manufacturer more control of the promotion of the product; but management of cooperative advertising programs can be costly.

Point-of-purchase display materials are offered to retailers because they provide some manufacturer control over the amount of space allocated to a product in the retail store. Point-of-purchase materials are expensive to produce, and many go unused by retailers. Point-of-purchase advertising will be discussed more completely in a later section.

Sales Promotion Principles

Sales promotion expenditures are growing rapidly. Whether it's because of frustration with the effectiveness of advertising, or competitive pressure, advertisers continue to use almost every technique to stimulate product sales. Some manufacturers measure advertising accountability only by product sales. In the long run, this procedure can be detrimental, especially if consumers perceive a brand as having less value because it is always discounted. For some products, sales promotions simply change the cycles of purchase. Special rebates on automobiles may create immediate sales; but a longer period of depressed sales may follow because potential purchasers have been removed from the marketplace. Too many discounts can also depress profits and affect the survivability of a retail store. Promotional offers depend on heavy increases in demand by consumers.

Consumers also differ in their use of sales promotions. Researchers have found a group of consumers who are **"deal prone."** This is a segment of the market which uses sales promotions exclusively. It's because of this segment that sales promotions fail to build brand loyalty. If consumers only seek the lowest price for a product, then brand-switching will occur more frequently.

Integrating effective sales promotion with advertising and publicity programs is important to the advertiser. Some stimulation of consumer and trade participation is necessary for effective sales promotion. Advertising programs can't be abandoned. Coupled with timely product publicity, the marketer can increase the effectiveness of the entire promotional effort.

In the next sections, two promotional areas will be examined more closely. **Point-of-purchase advertising (P-O-P)** is a sales promotion device; but it's also an advertising medium. *Point-of-purchase is a medium because it can produce the final advertising impression before a sale.* Following the discussion of point-of-purchase, the growing area of event marketing and promotion will be examined.

Point-of-Purchase Advertising

Many advertisers underestimate the effectiveness of point-of-purchase advertising because it is so difficult to coordinate and manage. Point-of-purchase displays are multifunctional. They are usually sales promotions for the retailer. As the point of last impression, they're an advertising medium. But, they also are product structures which hold and store the product.

Point-of-purchase displays are very flexible, and include many different types of product promotion. **On-the-shelf displays** may feature coupons, recipes and special offers, or they may be "shelf-talkers," which are small feature cards for product attributes. **Mobiles** are often hung in supermarkets to highlight floor displays of products. Some displays, like **cut-case displays** are simply packing boxes that open in an unusual way. **Large bins**, or **catch-all displays** are used to hold large quantities of product. These bulk quantities are perceived as being lower-priced by consumers. Many different types of **display stands** are used for books, sunglasses, cigarettes and other packaged goods. **Counter displays** often are used to suggest "a few more items" to daily shoppers. Since all purchasing customers have to pass the sales counter, it's an ideal location for a manufacturer's product. Most stores receive added incentives from manufacturers for space near the cash register.

There are point-of-purchase benefits for advertisers, retailers and consumers. The advertiser finds a purchasing audience, reduced advertising costs, and brand name prominence in the retail outlet. Retailers can extend shopping time in a store by using interesting displays. They can also use P-O-P materials to organize shelves and countertops. Since shoppers are in a purchasing mood, the volume of sales can be increased by point-of-purchase advertising. Consumers can use point-of-purchase displays to find the best prices and to access product information. In a self-service environment, effective point-of-purchase displays can perform some of the functions of the sales force.

The **Point-of-Purchase Advertising Institute (POPAI)** is the trade association for the point-of-purchase industry. To stimulate the industry, POPAI has co-sponsored many research studies to measure the effectiveness of point-of-purchase advertising. POPAI designates consumer purchases as **specifically planned purchases,** where the brand has been selected before shopping begins, **generally planned purchases,** where the product class may have been selected, **substituted purchases,** where alternatives are chosen, and **unplanned purchases.** In store surveys, nearly two-thirds of all product decisions are made in the retail location. Because the stores studied were drugstores and supermarkets, the estimates of in-store decision-making refer to packaged goods. For more involved products, like recreational vehicles and automobiles, point-of-purchase can support the efforts of the sales force.

As an aid to P-O-P planning, POPAI publishes lists of products and their **incidence of purchase** per 100 shoppers. This measure can be used to determine which products should be featured in store promotions to draw customers into the store. Most research by POPAI has found that point-of-purchase and advertising work best together, rather than separately. More information about point-of-purchase advertising can be obtained from the Point-of-Purchase Advertising Institute, 66 North Van Buren Street, Englewood, New Jersey, 07631.

Event Marketing

One of the hottest areas for promotion is **event marketing.** Corporations which use event marketing sponsor a multitude of athletic, music and entertainment events each year. The number of events and sponsors has grown geometrically. Sponsors of golf tournaments, the Olympics and other televised sporting events are usually required to purchase commercial time during the event. In music events, companies like Pepsi create commercials with rock stars, then sponsor tours for the artist around the country.

Like other areas of sales promotion, event marketing requires special coordination between marketing planners and event coordinators. The event and talent for music events must have an identity and image which is consistent with the brand identity. Event marketing management has been listed as a growth career by several popular magazines. The tasks of event marketing are very difficult.

To be effective, the event marketer must select the appropriate event for the target market and brand identity. In order to be unique, it has to be different from competitive events. Then, the coordination efforts begin. Sites for the event, if not already fixed, must be chosen. Publicity and promotional packages must be prepared. Nuts and bolts details must be worked out, like facilities rental, equipment rental and logistical support. Backup systems and tight control are necessary because events occur on a specific timetable. During and after an event, secondary marketing materials, like T-shirts and specialty items, must be available. Event evaluation must begin at the time of the event, and continue several weeks later. Local coordination with retailers and distributors is extremely important for regional sales success.

The results can be dramatic, whether the event is a success or failure. This means there is a high risk associated with event promotions. Since major events are newsworthy, a company's sponsorship can receive considerable publicity before and after the event. Not all events are major events. Many stores and companies sponsor local sporting events or teams in order to build a reputation of corporate citizenship. An evaluation of the outcomes for event sponsorship must be measured against the goals for the event. Event marketing is a sophisticated, and detail-oriented promotional skill, so it should be approached carefully in order to build stronger brand identities.

Study Questions

❑ How do push or pull marketings strategies affect the type of promotions offered by manufacturers? What is the difference between internal and external sales promotion?

❑ Which sales promotion techniques are designed to stimulate trial? Which reward continued use?

❑ Why are effort and perceived value critical variables for sales promotion?

❑ What is the effect of sales promotion on the product demand curve? How does a sales promotion affect product demand in the long and short run?

❑ Describe the role of P-O-P as an advertising medium. As a sales promotion device.

❑ How does POPAI describe consumer in-store purchases?

❑ What are the major requirements for event marketing success?

26
Product Publicity
and Public Relations

Every marketer and advertiser should have a formal public relations plan to complement marketing and advertising programs. **Product publicity programs** generate information to be used by the news media about a company's products. This usually includes news releases, product photographs, information sheets and feature articles. Unlike advertising, where space and time is purchased, publications and broadcast stations don't charge for product news coverage. Editorial coverage of a product and its features by newspaper columnists, magazine feature writers and broadcast journalists can enhance interest in a product, and create demand in the marketplace. But, coverage is determined by the newsworthiness of the publicity. Publicity must also support the validity of advertising claims made about a product and its features.

Corporate **public relations** programs are usually managed by a corporate communications director, or the head of a public relations department. These departments are responsible for communications between the corporation and its **publics**. Public, to a public relations professional, is a term similar to target audience for an advertiser. The difference between the two terms is the goal of communication, and the scope of the audience. Target audiences are potential purchasers of a product, so the ultimate goal is product sales and loyalty. Publics don't have to be product purchasers. Instead, *publics are groups of individuals who have an interest in the product, negative or positive.* Here's an example.

Suppose our company manufactures baby cribs. The target audience for our product will be mothers with small children. Target audiences are always one of the key publics for the product publicist. But, there are many more. Distributors and retailers of baby cribs must be part of the communication process, because they need to know the attributes of the product. Since past baby crib design by other companies has been faulty, consumer protection groups and legislators must be considered publics, and focal groups for our publicity efforts. In order to maintain good employee relations, internal employee groups must be treated as a separate public. Corporate stockholders must also be kept aware of the company's products, and the profitability of the corporation.

Local retailers often fail to understand the power of public relations programs. In addition to publicity about products, public relations professionals must keep the corporate name and product identity in front of the publics. Consumer satisfaction is important to continued product and company loyalty; it's also important for maximum growth. A small local advertiser can double or triple the effectiveness of his or her advertising through effective public relations. Sponsorship of community events, feature stories about store personnel and close contact with customers can build a credible store reputation. Unusual sales events or promotions can quickly become news items for radio and television news programs. Poor public relations, and consumer dissatisfaction, can completely destroy a company's marketing and advertising efforts.

Media Channels

To the public relations professional, media are outlets for information rather than suppliers of space and time. In order to disseminate information effectively, **media channels** must be provided with well-prepared material which meets their editorial requirements. Stories must be written in a proper journalistic style; broadcast material must be written for spoken delivery, rather than for a reading audience.

Competent publicists spend considerable time communicating with the editorial staffs of newspapers, magazines, radio and television stations. The media channels list for a product publicist will include: the major trade magazines in the product area, major consumer publications where the product is regularly featured, radio and television stations where product news features are regularly used in programming. A list of public relations directories which list media channels for publicity has been included at the end of this chapter.

Because public relations, and publicity distribution is such an inexact process, it is impossible to accurately determine audience coverage statistics for publicity programs. Some companies use inches of published coverage as a criteria for publicity success. Sponsors of major events sometimes use seconds of on-air logo visibility as a measure of their public relations effectiveness. Large corporations conduct public opinion polls before and after information campaigns in order to evaluate communication effectiveness.

In the last few years, public relations has become a more scientifically-oriented profession. **Management-by-objectives** has diffused into public relations training programs; quantitative methods have become a popular addition to many curricula. But, the practitioner's art still requires mastery of primary tools of the trade. Some of those tools will be examined in the next section.

Public Relations Tools

Product news releases are one to two page news announcements about the product. News releases must be written in good journalistic style; most follow the specifications in the *Associated Press Stylebook*. Like news stories and advertisements, facts in a news release should be presented in what some writers call an **inverse-pyramid style**. Facts should be discussed in descending levels of importance because editors shorten features from bottom to top.

Product news releases are usually disseminated with photographs of the product. Each photograph has its own caption attached to it. The best publicists usually try to get unusual photographs of the product because they are more newsworthy and interesting. All product photographs should build and reinforce the desired product identity, and they should be relevant to the target audience.

New product announcements are usually made at **news conferences**. By developing good relations with editors and writers, the publicist can comfortably ask the media to view and try new products. To prepare, the public relations professional will create **media packets** which describe the product and why it's different. The media packet usually contains relevant product literature, plus short and long news releases, one or two features about the product, and glossy black and white photographs. Color photographs may be offered, or included, in the media pack, depending on the sophistication of the media package.

During news conferences, and separately, the public relations director becomes a critical link between the press and spokespersons for the company. Sometimes the publicist speaks for the company; at other times corporate executives must be produced for interviews. The coordination task gets much more difficult when a company's product is under fire from outside groups.

Product publicity is one of the most neglected elements in the marketing mix. Students rarely study it as an adjunct to advertising and sales promotion. Advertisers usually don't understand the symbiotic relationship between effective publicity and advertising success.

Study Questions

❑ In what ways are publics similar and different from target audiences?

❑ How do messages in a public relations media channel differ from messages in advertising media?

❑ What are news releases? When should they be used?

❑ Why must news releases be prepared using an inverse-pyramid writing style?

❑ How do publicists evaluate publicity campaigns?

❑ How do publicists and media planners differ in their use of media?

Media Channels for Publicity

Effectiveness for the publicist is determined by the extensiveness and relevance of his or her media channels. A large number of public relations activities require face-to-face contact; but the distribution of news releases is largely a dissemination task. This is a list of the most popular sourcebooks.

All TV Publicity Outlets - Nationwide
National Radio Publicity Outlets
  Public Relations Plus, Inc., Box 1197, New Milford, CT 06776
Bacon's International Publicity Checker
Bacon's Publicity Checker
  Bacon's Publishing Company, Inc., 332 S. Michigan Avenue, Suite 900, Chicago, IL 60604
Broadcasting-Cablecasting Yearbook
  Broadcasting Publications, Inc., 1735 DeSales St., N.W., Washington, D.C. 20036
Editor & Publisher International Year Book: Encyclopedia of the Newspaper Industry
Editor & Publisher Market Guide
  Editor & Publisher, Co. Inc., 11 W. 19th Street, new York, NY 10011
Gale Directory of Publications
  Gale Research, Inc., Book Tower, Detroit, MI 48226
Gebbie Press All-in-One Media Directory
  Gebbie Press, Box 1000, New Paltz, NY 12561
Hollis Press and Public Relations Annual
  Hollis Directories Ltd., Contact House, Lower Hampton Rd., Sunbury-on-Thames, Middlesex TW16 SHG, England
Hudson's Washington News Media Contacts Directory
  Howard Penn Hudson, Editor, 44 W. Market St., Box 311, Rhinebeck, NY 12572
Internal Publications Directory
  National Research Bureau, Inc., 310 S. Michigan Ave., Suite 1150, Chicago, IL 60604
Media Guide
  Federation for Community Planning, 1001 Huron Rd., Cleveland, OH 44115
Media News Keys
  Television Index, Inc., 40-29 27th Street, Long Island City, NY 11101
Standard Periodical Directory
  Oxbridge Communications, Inc., 150 Fifth Avenue, New York, NY 10011
Standard Rate and Data Service
  Spot Radio Small Markets Edition
  Consumer Magazine and Agri-Media Rates
  Community Publications Rates and Data
  Spot Radio Rates and Data
  Spot Television Rates and Data
  Newspaper Rates and Data
  Network Rates and Data
  Business Publication Rates and Data
  Standard Rate and Data Service, Inc., 3004 Glenview Road, Wilmette, IL 60091
Television and Cable Factbook
  Warren Publishing, Inc., 2115 Ward Ct., N.W., Washington, DC 20037
U. S. Publicity Directory, Radio & TV
  John Wiley & Sons, Inc., 605 Third Avenue, New York, NY 10016

News Release Writing Hints

NEWS RELEASE

For Immediate Release
For more information, contact: Ken Burty, (517) 449-7865.

New Software Program Captures Viruses ❸

(SAN FRANCISCO) A new software program destroys computer viruses by imitating the computer's op❹g system software, and re-programming itself.

Annihilator™, a new computer protection program from SGC Software, represents a new way to attack computer viruses, according to company president, Phil Mathews.

"This new program imitates the opera❺stem software, so viruses become attached to it. After the viruses a❺ached, Annihilator destroys the linkages," Mathews said.

Experts agree that comp❻viruses have become the plague of the computer industry in the 1❻ Annihilator represents a new type of computer programming, called Self-Modifying Code Generators (SMCG). Because of the way these new programs alter their own computer code, they can re-program themselves and attack any new viruses that appear.

More information about Annihilator can b❼ned from: SGC Software, Inc., 115 Water Way, San Francisco, CA 9877❼

Here are a few short hints for writing effective news releases. 1) Most companies which have formal public relations programs use a corporate news release masthead. 2) The release date, or "For Immediate Release," should be near the top so editors know the recency. The contact person named should be knowledgable and available. Check the accuracy of the telephone number. 3) Writing a newsworthy headline helps establish the style and credibility of the release. It may not be used exactly as you write it; but sometimes it will be. 4) The body of the release is written in standard journalistic style. Datelines may or may not be included. The lead sentence should again establish the news value of the product announcement. Notice that the body of the release is double-spaced. This allows easier editing. 5) Quotes about the product from principals in the organization help establish expertise and credibility for the company, and its leaders. Newspapers also like to use quotes in their features. 6) In the later paragraphs of the release, background information, more technical information, and summaries of related information may be included. 7) Company name and address should be stated completely as the last line of the release. Other information may also be necessary. Trademarks should be noted and properly cited on all publicity, so when they are used by other organizations the citations will be accurate.

27

Campaign Evaluation

Once an advertising campaign has finished it's hard to get interested in **campaign evaluation**. If a campaign was successful, there never seems to be a need to evaluate. If a campaign was a failure, no one wants to go near it, because they might have to accept responsibility for the failure. These are exaggerations; but they do demonstrate some of the problems with evaluation research. After paying an astronomical media bill, a retail advertiser may be reluctant to spend more money on evaluation. Regardless of any hesitation, *every advertising campaign should be evaluated. If an advertising campaign is not going to be evaluated, then setting campaign objectives is a waste of time and energy.*

This doesn't mean expensive evaluation research needs to be done for every campaign. It means there should be an **evaluation plan** which *outlines the review procedures to be performed during, and upon completion, of the campaign.* The complexity of the evaluation plan will be determined by the size of the campaign budget, and the proportion of the budget designated for evaluation. This proportion typically ranges from .01 to 2 percent. Small promotion budgets may need as much as 2 percent, in order to support any research procedure. Large television-intensive campaigns may need a much smaller proportion in relation to their huge media expenditures. *Media complexity, or the number of media included in the media plan, and multiple sales promotion programs, can increase the evaluation budget considerably.* The evaluation plan becomes more complicated when multiple objectives are being evaluated. Ideally, all objectives in a campaign should be subject to review; practically, there usually aren't enough resources to evaluate all aspects of a campaign through formal research methods.

Formal research methods aren't always needed for evaluation. The smallest retailer can walk around the store and talk to customers after an advertising campaign. Customers can provide clues about what they read in advertisements, and what media they use. New customers signal a change in the target audience attracted by advertising. Product sales provide a good indicator of sales promotion effectiveness. Simple or complex, evaluation techniques can tell whether the campaign objectives have been met. There are also some secondary reasons to evaluate campaigns.

Campaign evaluations can provide clues to strategy development. For example, suppose we say that we'd like to establish a more sophisticated identity for our product in order to attract an older target market. After the campaign, our research may show that the advertising didn't create sophistication in the minds of consumers. But, we still may have attracted an older audience for some reason. The evaluation tells us if we accomplished our objective; but more importantly, it can tell whether that objective yielded more profitable results.

Media evaluations can provide evidence that the contractual agreements with media were met by publications or broadcast programs. If a review of weekly television ratings finds discrepancies between the actual and promised rating, then makegoods or rebates should be requested. Reviews of print advertising should also check the reproduction quality and placement of advertisements, in case adjustments need to be made.

Financial reviews may uncover efficient or inefficient advertising practices which can be improved or repeated in future campaigns. Some agencies closely examine **return on investment (ROI)** for advertising as a measure of success. Critics question ROI as a measure of effectiveness because there are so many intervening variables between advertising and sales. New requests for accountability have prompted many agencies to monitor the sales effect of advertising more closely. Certainly, advertisers and agencies need to know the total cost of advertising programs, and an accounting of promotional expenditures.

The Evaluation Process

Before we examine specific types of evaluation research, some general observations about research methods should be made. Like strategic advertising research, *evaluation research must follow the rules of science.* Objectivity and accuracy are important. Attempts to manipulate the results are highly unethical. If the goal is to improve advertising in the future, then it doesn't make sense to violate the rules for objectivity.

Each research method and technique has guidelines which determine how appropriate the method is for a specific evaluation. When used appropriately, each method can provide valuable information about the success or failure of strategic decisions. Different methods produce different kinds of conclusions. For example, suppose we have a very small advertising budget, and no funds for evaluation. In an organization with experienced professionals, we might use a **Delphi method** of evaluation. A researcher using the Delphi method asks several expert judges to evaluate some practice or event, in this case advertising. Even though the judges evaluations are subjective and based on their experience, the method achieves a degree of objectivity by not allowing judges to communicate with one another before presenting their evaluations. A quantitative evaluation of this same advertising campaign might reach an entirely different conclusion. In this example, the Delphi set of evaluations is based on experience, the quantitative evaluation is made on the basis of statistical analysis. Each method has individual strengths and flaws. There is definitely a quantitative bias in marketing and advertising. So quantitative studies are supported more strongly by corporate managers, and usually preferred over qualitative studies.

Another general evaluation principle is related to the timing of evaluation. Suppose we want to change our target market through advertising, or we want to change consumer perceptions of our brand, or store. *If our goal is change, then we must measure characteristics of the target market, brand or store, before we begin the campaign.* The amount of change can't be calculated without knowing the **baseline**, or beginning point. Scientists would say we need a **pre-test** and a **posttest**, a before and after measurement.

Not all evaluative measurements require a pre-test and posttest. When media contracts specify the audience rating to be delivered, that's an absolute value. So, in these cases, we only need to know actual delivery rate. Therefore, a posttest is all that is required.

Sometimes we want to know how fast advertising is changing attitudes, or purchase patterns. Public relations advertising is often interested in the rate of change for public opinion. Evaluation of the rate of change requires regular monitoring. These continual measurements are the basis for **tracking studies**.

Regardless of the method employed for campaign evaluation, the evaluation plan must match the evaluation technique with the objectives to be evaluated. In order to organize these techniques more effectively, we'll return to the hierarchical *structured strategies*.

Evaluating *Structured Strategies*

Strategic decisions for promotional campaigns were summarized in Figure 8 (page 106). This section will summarize the techniques that can be used to evaluate *structured strategies*. But first, let's review the relationship between strategy and objectives. ***Strategies are plans which tell how we intend to accomplish defined goals; objectives are measurable indicators which correspond to our strategic plans and goals.*** Every level of strategy will have plans, and goals or objectives. Evaluation for each level of strategy will answer different questions about promotional strategy. Let's work through the structured strategy example to demonstrate how evaluation can answer important management questions.

Marketing Strategy. Three inderdependent decisions were required for marketing strategy: selecting a desired product identity, determining an appropriate competitive distance, and defining the most profitable target market. These decisions outline the plans for reaching specified marketing goals. Marketing goals could be described in terms of the percent increase in sales, market share or markets.

It's quite easy to evaluate the marketing goals. Before and after measurement of sales, market share or market distribution outlets, and sales would supply adequate evidence of success or failure. Some myopic corporate executives might be content with these indicators, but marketing and advertising managers shouldn't be. Knowing the change in sales doesn't tell you whether your strategy was effective or not. Sales may increase or decrease as a result of other market variables. Poor strategy implementation, rather than poor strategy, may be responsible for decreases in sales.

Evaluation of the strategic implementation requires knowing whether the changes in product identity, competitive distance and target market were achieved or not. The objectives would be specific statements about changes in each of the three major decisions. For example, "We want to change the product identity from a discounted lesser brand to a moderately priced major brand." Changes in the communicated product identity can be detected through **before and after consumer surveys**. More elaborate measurement techniques, like **multidimensional scaling**, can determine distances between competitive products and product attributes. Once again, if a manager is looking for the change in product identity or competitive distance, then measurements must be taken before and after a campaign. The before measurement may be part of the pre-campaign strategic research. Other pre-campaign research procedures, like **preference mapping** and **conjoint analysis** can be used to determine what product attributes are important to consumers. By regularly **monitoring sales and purchaser profiles**, changes in the profitability of target markets can be estimated.

Evaluation of the three marketing decisions can provide evidence that the strategy was or was not implemented properly. If increases in sales, share or market distribution correspond to the predicted changes in strategy, then the manager has fairly strong support for his or her strategic decisions. Faulty implementation should also be evident from this evaluation research. This discussion of marketing strategy was provided as an example of the relationship between strategy and objectives. Campaign evaluations would usually evaluate advertising, rather than marketing decisions. But, the strong tie between marketing and advertising decisions in *structured strategies* means there will be overlap in some of the evaluation techniques.

Sales Promotion Strategy. Sales promotion is a short term incentive to purchase the product. Therefore, the goal for sales promotion strategy is to increase sales. Evaluating change in sales requires **before and after measurement** of product sales, to consumers for consumer promotions and to distributors for wholesale promotions. The time period for measurement, the evaluation markets, and method of recording sales need to be established before the promotion is implemented. This is the simplest form of sales promotion evaluation. Several research firms, including A. C. Nielsen, SAMI/Burke (Selling Areas-Marketing, Inc.) and scanner research firms, offer product auditing services to measure product movement.

Most sales promotion managers like to use redemption rates and participation levels as indicators of success; but these are not always appropriate measures. To test the product identity communicated by sales promotions, an advertiser would have to examine differences between consumers who had seen sales promotions, and those who had not seen them. Consumer surveys could also detect differences in consumer perceptions of sales promotions from all competitive products. Monitoring participants and redeemers of coupons periodically could determine the target market attracted to sales promotion techniques. While sales is still the best indicator of sales promotion effectiveness, these other evaluation techniques provide some evidence that advertising and sales promotion strategy are coordinated.

Post-promotion evaluation may be much more important for event promotion than sales promotion, because the sales effects from an event are much more difficult to isolate. In-crowd interviewers, and interviews from participant lists gathered at events, are important event evaluation techniques.

Advertising Copy and Visual Strategy. Much of the testing for communication effectiveness of copy and visuals will have been performed during pre-campaign strategic research. But, impact in the market environment is important. Several research suppliers provide services which test the communication effects of print and broadcast advertising during a campaign. Before we look at these national suppliers, procedures for evaluating general advertising objectives should be discussed.

Many advertisers specify objectives which list "increasing awareness of a new product" or "increasing comprehension of a product's major sales points." Awareness is a function of both creative and media factors. Ad size and design is important; but media placement is probably more important to the overall goal. Comprehension is also a function of both factors. Clear presentation of sales points requires effective copy and design. But, repetition in a media plan is needed for the consumer's learning curve. General objectives, like the two mentioned above, should probably be evaluated through a pre- and posttest survey of consumers in the target market. This is particularly true for smaller advertisers and local campaigns where national posttest services are unavailable. For large advertisers, the creative and media functions of general advertising objectives may be evaluated separately.

Several research firms offer advertising posttest services. Print advertisements in major consumer magazines are evaluated by Gallup & Robinson to determine readership, the communication of major sales points and consumer attitudes toward the ad. Gallup & Robinson's indicators of effectiveness are *proved name registration, idea communication* and *favorable buying attitude.* For posttest research, Gallup & Robinson also prepares reports of competitor performance. Another research firm, Starch INRA Hooper, offers the Starch Readership Report which measures advertising readership in consumer and trade magazines and newspapers. The indicators of effectiveness for Starch are *noted, associated,* and *read most.* The major difference between the two methods of posttest research is how consumers are tested. Gallup & Robinson measures consumer **recall** of ads and sales points; Starch examines communication effectiveness based on consumer **recognition** of ads. The Starch Impression Study provides more in-depth consumer attitudes toward advertisements they have read.

Several other companies provide posttest evaluations of print advertisements. SAMI/Burke provides a day-after recall test for magazines. Day-after recall is used by several television research firms. Readex, Inc., monitors business and farm publications to determine readership of editorial material and advertising.

Several methods of testing broadcast commercials also exist. SAMI/ Burke conducts day-after recall testing of broadcast commercials; but in recent years additional measures of persuasiveness have been added to their techniques. Gallup & Robinson also provides posttest services for broadcast commercials. One SAMI-Burke subsidiary, **AdTel**, uses a split cable system to experimentally test commercials. Split-cable experimental tests would be more appropriate for pre-testing than posttesting because of the higher expense. This list of research suppliers is not complete. There are several other national research firms which conduct similar types of measurement. Many independent research firms also conduct **proprietary studies**, or confidential studies for their clients.

All of the methods described above are expensive, so an advertising campaign must have a large budget in order to justify the evaluation techniques. Local and regional advertisers can evaluate their ads using less elaborate techniques. Members of the target market can view and talk about broadcast commercials in focus groups. In-store customers can also be asked about store advertisements. The major goal is to see whether the copy and visuals communicate the desired product or store identity, and competitive distance. Customer questionnaires can determine whether changes in targeting were effective.

Advertising Media Strategy. Evaluating media objectives is easier for large package goods advertisers than it is for local advertisers. Since media objectives are usually defined in terms of reach and frequency, an advertising schedule which is primarily network television can be evaluated by comparing promised audience sizes by networks with weekly ratings in *The Pocketpiece Report*, part of the Nielsen Television Index prepared by Nielsen Media Research. When audiences fail to reach the expected viewing levels, makegoods may be requested from network representatives.

There are several other broadcast media considerations that should be evaluated in addition to audience levels. Did the spots actually appear on the promised program? If they didn't, the media representative will usually contact the advertiser or advertising agency and negotiate a new position for the commercials. When commercial time is purchased on a specific program for four weeks, the spots will be rotated during the show. Rotations are fine, but the advertiser must make sure the rotations were fair.

Invoices from the station will usually indicate the rotations. Consistently poor rotations should be reported to media representatives so they can be corrected in future broadcast buys.

Tearsheets, actual advertising pages, should be collected from all print media. Since weekly or monthly audience information is not reported for most magazines, it is almost impossible to check audience delivery. Yearly publication audits should be examined to make sure circulation data used for media planning was accurate. Newspaper ads should be checked to see that color from a back or adjoining page did not destroy readability of the ad. Most newspapers guarantee that no coupon will appear on the back of an advertisement, since this might destroy readership of the ad. Also, newspaper tearsheets are important to make sure the reproduction quality was adequate. Sometimes faulty press runs will cause very muddy, or distorted visuals. Out-of-register color advertisements look blurry, some small type may be unreadable.

Media evaluations are routinely made to check the quality and place-ment of advertising. Network television audience comparisons can be worth a considerable amount of money to the advertiser.

Public Relations Strategy. *Product publicity is difficult to evaluate because the publicist sends out large amounts of release material, with no guarantee that it will be used by newspapers, magazines or broadcast stations.* Clipping services are available to monitor publications, and some companies will monitor visual coverage of events on television. Electronic database retrieval of articles about a company or product can be done to see what was used from news releases. Unfortunately, irregular updating schedules for electronic databases makes it impossible to determine how fast publicity disseminates. Once articles are collected, the publication date does provide a reference for how fast information was disseminated. By performing an analysis known as **content analysis**, the publicist can determine if the best information for the product identity, competitive distance and target market was communicated. In content analysis, the researcher develops categories of content and counts or measures the occurrences of the categories in news features.

Study Questions

❏ Describe the relationship between strategies, objectives and evaluations.

❏ How does evaluation research different from strategic research?

❏ How does the evaluation of general advertising objectives differ from the evaluation of specific copy or media objectives?

❏ Describe the differences between the Delphi method, tracking studies and consumer surveys as campaign evaluation tools.

❏ How is sales promotion evaluation different from advertising evaluation?

❏ How do Starch readership scores differ from Gallup & Robinson readership measurements?

❏ Why is the Nielsen Pocketpiece important to network advertisers?

❏ Why is product publicity evaluation so difficult?

Hidden Evaluation Costs

Campaign evaluation is important for many campaigns, but there are often hidden costs associated with it. The costs may be financial or psychological. Remember, an objective evaluation will discover whether the campaign objectives were met or not. If they weren't met, then the responsibility for not meeting the objectives may be associated with the most visible person connected to the campaign. People who know about advertising and marketing realize the large number of unpredictable variables associated with it. These unexpected variables can cause many problems. If advertising is viewed as an ongoing process, then every failure should provide more information for the next campaign. As long as the failures aren't continuous, then more effective marketing programs should result.

There are hidden financial costs to evaluation, as well. For every consumer survey, questionnaires need to be printed, data analysis must be performed, and evaluation reports written. For many industrial, trade and professional products, an evaluation of advertising must survey unusual samples of people, such as medical doctors, beauty salon owners, or purchasing agents for large corporations. These people are difficult to reach through telephone and mail surveys. Therefore, experienced interviewers and field workers must be hired. Completing questionnaires will take longer than expected, and all time-related work will be delayed. Delays and extended interviewing cost money.

Delphi evaluation methods require coordination of experts and participants in the evaluation. A coordinator may be needed for the logistics; the researcher will have to summarize the evaluation reports.

Laboratory experiments, where advertisements are evaluated or public relations devices tested, require getting large samples of people. These people may have to be compensated for their lost wages, as well as for participation in a research study. The test materials, sample ads or experimental videotapes, may cost more to produce because of the strict requirements for similar materials in the test environment.

Long term panel studies often lose participants. This mortality, as it is called, can affect the evaluation study. Recruitment procedures are usually continuous, since this insures the necessary number of participants for long term measurements.

Complicated measurement techniques require training. Complicated coding procedures require similar training. All training costs money and time.

28

Four Specialized
Types of Advertising

The advertising process is quite simple. Find the right audience and tell
them what they need to know in order to select your product. The process
becomes complicated because it's hard to tell what audience is best, and
what information the audience needs in order to make an informed choice.
There are four types of advertising which use the same marketing and
advertising processes described in other sections of this book; but, whose
objectives and audiences require special consideration. These specialized
types of advertising are: business, retail, public relations and international.

Business Advertising

Business advertising, or **business-to-business advertising** as it was
previously called, is different from consumer advertising because the target
markets are business purchasers of products. The promotion mix for business advertisers usually has higher expenditures for personal selling,
publicity and sales promotion than the promotion mix for consumer advertisers. Individual purchases of business products are usually much larger
than consumer purchases. Some companies may purchase millions of
component parts from other suppliers. Because of the size of purchases,
and the economics of manufacturing, the nature of decision-making is quite
different for business purchasers. Therefore, the goals for business advertising must also reflect these differences.

Purchasing agents are important targets for considerable amounts of
business advertising. In many corporations, there are well-defined and
documented procedures for becoming a supplier of component parts or
materials. Most purchase decisions require presentations from salespersons, or in some cases a sales team, before decisions are made. Bids are
usually required. Within a corporation, many large purchases, like computers, are joint decisions between several different groups of individuals.
Joint decision-making may require even more sales effort from the
business advertiser. *Business advertising plays an important role in
preparing targeted business purchasers for sales representatives.* This role
is often reflected in business advertising objectives.

Business advertising objectives will reflect some of the same goals, such
as increasing awareness or recall of sales points. But careful research must

determine what information is necessary for business audiences, before sales representatives arrive. For some smaller purchases, where no salesperson contact is anticipated, business advertisers may favor direct advertising or telemarketing. This direct response advertising requires purchaser response objectives. So, sales may be the ultimate goal of some direct business advertising. Media considerations are also different.

Business publications usually have more pages of advertising than consumer publications. *There is considerable clutter in business magazines; but readership of business advertising is high.* Business purchasers are highly involved in the corporate roles; therefore, they seek information about products which is role-relevant. *Absolute cost of business advertising is quite low* compared to consumer advertising. Reduced audience size means the *cost-per-thousand is usually higher* than consumer advertising. The principle generally holds that the more specialized or targeted an audience, the higher the cost-per-thousand. In recent years, some business advertisers have used network television advertising during sporting events to reach business audiences. Network television is not a typical business medium for most specialized business products.

In addition to differences in media, there are also some important creative considerations for business advertising. Because readers of business print ads are highly involved, most *require more copy* than consumer advertising. Most business advertising makes a *rational presentation about product attributes and benefits*. Because of this tendency toward rational presentations, *visual and design elements must create interest and readership in business advertisements*.

Retail Advertising

Retail advertising is consumer advertising for retail stores. When retail advertising occurs in a limited geographical area, it is also a type of local advertising. Local advertising also refers to lower-priced advertising, where a medium doesn't include an agency commission in the price of advertising. There is overlap between the two concepts. In recent years, shopping malls and multi-market retailers have changed the meaning of retail advertising. For the smallest stores, retail advertising may be a single yellow pages ad, or a few newspaper ads. But, the largest retailers now use network and spot television, and all other major media. One part of retail advertising that hasn't changed is its primary objective. Retail advertising *must create store traffic because of the close relationship between store traffic and sales*. The promotion mix for retailers places heavier emphasis on sales promotions for consumers and sales personnel than most other types of advertising.

A retailer's product mix has an overwhelming influence on advertising planning. Because of the seasonality of products, promotions must be planned well in advance. Promotions must also be coordinated with the cooperative advertising programs offered by manufacturers. Cooperative advertising is an important way for retailers to extend their promotional budget.

The close tie between product movement and retail advertising has also influenced the relationship between retailers and advertising agencies. Many advertising agencies can't produce and change advertising quickly enough to meet the needs of retailers. Quite often an overstocked item must be featured in a special sale to reduce the inventory. Agencies can't always respond quickly because of time-consuming approval and production processes. The number of different products also requires specialized knowledge by advertising agency specialists. Since some media don't add commissions to local advertising, agency fees would discourage a retailer from hiring an agency. Local media usually offer production help for free, or at a minimal charge. Ad agencies are often hired when a retailer's media or creative requirements become too complex for the in-house advertising department.

Whether retail advertising is prepared in the retail advertising department, or in an advertising agency, **continuity** is one of the most important variables for success. *Retail advertising must communicate product information and it must communicate the store's image.* Many writers have categorized retail stores into three types: promotional, non-promotional and semi-promotional. **Promotional** stores always have sales and are often viewed by consumers as discount stores. **Non-promotional** stores have more sophisticated store images. They usually sell brand name products, and rarely feature price promotions. **Semi-promotional** stores have strong store images, yet they still are known to have good sales and promotions by consumers.

The type of store is related to the product types discussed earlier. To review, **convenience** items are those items which are purchased as necessities, without much involvement on the part of consumers. Brand names are not important for these products, and substitution of brands is commonplace. **Shopping** goods are products where rational choices are made on the basis of product attributes, rather than brand name. Price is an important attribute for shopping goods. **Specialty** goods are products where consumers insist on brand names, and won't substitute. Convenience and shopping goods are important for promotional stores; specialty products are important to non-promotional stores.

Evaluation of retail advertising varies by the complexity of the advertising program. But, all retailers must measure store traffic and sales as a function of retail advertising and sales promotion.

Public Relations Advertising

Public relations advertising might also be called non-product advertising. The category has been broadened to include institutional or corporate advertising, public service advertising and political advertising. Public relations advertising usually seeks to change individual attitudes through advertising in the short term. Through continued advertising, the public relations advertiser hopes to influence later behavior. For corporate advertisers this may mean the consumer is influenced to invest in corporate stock, or is favorably disposed toward a company's products. Politicians hope to get a favorable vote. Public service advertisers usually hope to get contributions or support for their public service efforts.

Like audiences for publicity, the audiences for public relations advertising are more broadly defined than specialized audiences of business advertising. Corporate public relations advertising requires careful coordination between the public relations and marketing departments in order to provide consistent images of the corporation, and company products. Many corporations see public relations advertising as an important way to get controversial messages to the public and legislators. Some use **controversy** or **advocacy advertising** as the vehicle for this dialogue.

Public service, and non-profit, advertising is an important part of the total public relations program. Therefore, the advertiser must assess the relative advantage of advertising versus traditional publicity programs. Political advertisers depend on careful message construction and media selection to reach their constituencies.

There are many unresolved issues surrounding public relations advertising. For example, to what extent does advocacy advertising become lobbying, rather than advertising. Is advocacy advertising a justifiable, tax-deductible expense for doing business? Where is the demarcation line for religious advertisers who build profitable empires from broadcast advertising? Do they still meet the requirements for tax-exempt corporations? How do you police the claims and statements made in political advertising? Political advertising doesn't fall under the jurisdiction of the Federal Trade Commission. Should another agency handle complaints?

International Advertising

New economic power in Japan, Korea, Taiwan and the People's Republic of China, market changes in Europe, and growth of Third World countries, have stimulated new interest in international advertising. Global communities are much more interdependent than they were in earlier years, therefore changes in marketing policies and practices in one country have far-reaching effects on companies around the world.

Several new problems emerge when marketing programs span cultures, rather than local markets. While language may seem to be an obvious barrier to advertising and marketing, cultural differences are far more important, because cultural differences are often not as apparent as differences in language. Multi-lingual communicators can bridge and solve communication problems. But, critical marketing decisions must be made by marketing professionals who are part of the culture being targeted by advertising and marketing programs. In this way, cultural norms and expectations will be integrated into advertising messages.

Economic considerations are also important in international advertising. Advertising grew as a result of mass production. As companies became able to produce more products than those required by consumers, advertising was needed to sell products and reach new markets. Some international economies still do not have the production capabilities to meet consumer demand. Until production capabilities increase, advertising may be irrelevant to product sales.

Some of the most difficult barriers to effective international advertising are restrictive regulations against advertising, less sophisticated media choices and insufficient understanding of cultural differences between consumers. The payoff for solving the international advertising puzzle is a wealth of untapped markets. The cost of reaching these untapped markets is also high.

Study Questions

❑ How do business advertising audiences differ from consumer advertising audiences? Why is most business advertising rational, rather than emotional, in creative approach?

❑ How are the promotion mixes of business and retail advertising similar? How do they differ from the promotion mix of a national consumer advertiser?

❑ How do retail advertising objectives differ from consumer and business advertising objectives?

❑ How does type of store affect retail advertising approach? What about promotion mix?

❑ Why do many retail stores use media for production of ads, rather than advertising agencies?

❑ How do public relations advertising objectives differ from other advertising objectives?

❑ What are the issues associated with advocacy advertising?

❑ What are the most difficult problems for international advertisers?

29

Advertising Presentations

Advertising presentations are inevitable. Whether you're a copywriter, illustrator, account executive or manager, you'll have to sell your ideas to someone else. Every selling situation is unique; yet there are a few guidelines that can make these presentations much more effective. Let's look at some preliminaries first.

Before you start preparing and gathering materials, you have to **determine what outcome will make your presentation successful**. Getting a new account is usually an all-or-none outcome for account executives. So is winning a competition for students. Many presentations are partial selling situations. For example, a marketing manager may present the annual marketing plan for the president of the company. While he or she would like most of it accepted, it's likely that changes will be made after the presentation has finished.

Selling ideas is like selling a product. *Ideas are products*. They have attributes, selling points and must be distinguished from competing ideas in some way. Product, or idea packaging is extremely important because it communicates a message about the presenter. Great packaging of ideas tells the audience the presenter is detail-oriented and knowledgeable. Poor packaging tells the audience the presenter is sloppy and possibly misinformed.

As the presenter, *you are the medium for your message*. Just as advertising media have editorial environments which help advertisements sell, presenter style can create a a more relaxed selling environment. Presenters can also destroy the effectiveness of a presentation by saying or doing distracting things. In practice sessions, all presenters should ask a critic to tell them if body gestures or expressions become distracting or annoying.

The audience is your target market. This means *your message must be presented in terms your audience understands*. When you're presenting to the company president, you know there's a corporate language which provides guidelines for the occasion. Corporations often develop themes or ideas which are the focus for new company initiatives. These themes often have to be acknowledged in presentations.

There are a couple of dangers in thinking of the audience as a target market. In trying to tailor a presenta-tion to the likes and dislikes of the audience, the presenter may lose sight of his or her presentation goal.

Presentations must have strong content, as well as effective style. In advertising presentations, *the client must be sold before you get a chance to sell to the consumer.*

The Presentation Dialogue

In most cases, presenters hope a client presentation is the first step in an ongoing dialogue. To ensure this dialogue, **every presenter must be conversationally literate about the arguments in your presentation.** *If you organize the material for your presentation as arguments, then the reasons for your decisions will be more obvious, and easier to recall.* Let's look at a short argument, which might be the scenario for a graphic designer.

We want to argue that the client needs a new logo design. This is the claim of the argument. What evidence supports this argument? We have a consumer survey which shows consumers confuse the client logo with logos from other companies. We have a set of competitive logos which are more updated and contemporary than our client's. We can also demonstrate through enlargements that the client's logo has limitations for outdoor advertising, so it will probably need to be redesigned as his or her marketing program uses outdoor advertising.

Of course most arguments aren't this simple. For advertising presentations, you can construct arguments about all of the strategic decisions. As discussed earlier in this book, *these arguments make up the **strategic framework.*** They should be the focus for the presentation dialogue, and subsequent questions and answers. There are several important communication requirements for the presentation dialogue.

1) You must communicate excitement. Your client has invested a lot of energy and effort into his or her product. This person wants to know you find the product as interesting and exciting as he or she does. Excitement is communicated by showing enthusiasm for the marketing problem and its solution. Conversational understanding means not confusing vocabulary or facts about the client's marketing situation. Excitement is destroyed by memorized laundry lists of facts, and monotone speech.

2) Your arguments must be understandable and visible. Throughout your presentation, the reasons for your suggestions must be easy to follow. In visual materials, the suggestions and reasons are key elements. Not all arguments can be introduced during a presentation. When you have lots of support for your less important arguments, you can make summary statements which tease questions from the audience during later question and answer sessions.

3) What you say must communicate precision, depth and thoroughness. Your client is an expert. Your references to his or her product must use precise language and no mistakes in terminology or facts. Depth is communicated by telling the client a few facts about the product or market that he or she didn't know. It's also communicated through analytical statements. For example, instead of presenting a historical and chrono-logical history of the market, present an analysis of the forces which have changed the market. This tells the client you not only know the history, you understand what the important variables are. Thoroughness is commun-icated when all major details are covered. There must be no surprising omissions.

4) You must establish linkages between strategies. *Structured strategies* is a concept created to make the linkages between strategies more apparent. When you connect marketing strategy, sales promotion strategy, advertising strategy and public relations strategy, the connection commun-icates integration and thoroughness. There are other important linkages to establish, as well. At least briefly, a client wants to know how the new strategy presented is connected to his or her past strategy. This connection is important because it tells the client the new strategy is compatible with past marketing efforts.

5) Aim for presentation recall. Effective presentations are memor-able. There are several keys to recall. People remember three items better than four. When possible support for arguments should be written in groups of three. Major points should be in groups of three. Two groups of three are better than one group of six items. Buzzwords or keywords for your presentation should repeated, so the audience can recall them.

The presentation dialogue should demonstrate your competence. Your competence will be connected to your company. A sale cannot be made without these connections. Now, let's look specifically at advertising presentations.

Presenting Advertising

For years, students have been exposed to a traditional method of presenting advertising information. It's a sequential presentation of advertising facts and decisions. The normal sequence of steps is: situation analysis, prob-lems and opportunities, marketing strategy and target market, advertising objectives, creative strategy and tactics, media strategy and tactics, cam-paign evaluation and budgeting. There are several inherent dangers to this sequencing: 1) less interesting discussions at first, like the situation anal-ysis, can take important time away from exciting creative presentations; 2) extra long and boring media presentations can destroy the spontaneity of an earlier creative segment; 3) separation of the strategies can result in a lack of integration between marketing, advertising, sales promotion, and publicity proposals. Being aware of the dangers makes them somewhat avoidable. Certainly, this is not the only method of presenting a campaign.

One way to integrate the strategies more clearly would be to insert a strategic overview between the situation analysis and marketing strategy . By showing how the strategies relate to one another, it would provide a roadmap for later individual discussions.

Looking at your own presentation, you must determine what its strengths and weaknesses are. Strengths must be promoted; there must be workable solutions for its weaknesses. It's very important for a presentation to build to a crescendo before closing. Too much glitz at the front can make later presentations look flat. Too much extra detail can bore an audience to death. Here are a few quick observations about the individual parts of many advertising presentations.

Situation analysis. It's easy to get lost in history and market detail in the situation analysis. What you're trying to do is place your client's product in the context of the market and competition. You need to show that you know what forces have been, and will be, important in the marketplace. You need enough competitive surveillance information to show opportunities for your client. You must demonstrate that you know the client's product well, and that you understand the product's purchasers.

Problems and opportunities. Care must be taken if problems are discussed. The client can't be insulted, embarrassed or made uncomfortable by the discussions. Using the limiting factors approach discussed earlier offers an alternative which may be more palatable. Opportunities should be stated in terms of the product identity, competitive distance and target market changes. These are understandable and defensible.

Marketing strategy. In many instances, corporate marketing strategy, goals and sales objectives have been previously established. When these goals have been previously fixed, they should be re-stated accurately. For smaller clients, marketing decisions and goals for the product, competition and target market should be clearly stated with justification. Budget parameters should be acknowledged, only when they are constraints to strategy.

Advertising objectives. Based on strategic research, the goals for an advertising campaign should be realistic. The effects predicted should be within the realm of possibility. A strategic overview would integrate general advertising objectives with creative and media objectives.

Creative strategy and tactics. Assuming the creative product is workable and acceptable, the major deficiency in the presentation of creative strategy is that it is often not tied to marketing strategy. The strategy, and the advertisements and commercials presented, must be compatible and effective. If the creative strategy was established first, then the marketing strategy should be adjusted to match the creative strategy. It may be a surprise to many students, but not professionals, that many successful campaigns began with a creative idea, rather than a marketing analysis. The *campaign presentation* should be an experience in consistency.

Media strategy and tactics. Many presenters forget that media presentations are about potential purchasers, not numbers. Media presentations should present the major arguments for using a medium, and the justification for using specific vehicles. Efficiency formulas, estimated reach and frequency, and editorial environment are important, but may be provided in supplementary materials. Advertising performance data for media, if available, is the strongest support for any media argument.

Evaluation and budgeting. Many evaluation plans are often far too complex. A general rule-of-thumb is to evaluate using the simplest measure for the advertising objective being evaluated. Remember that the evaluation budget is determined by the overall campaign budget, so the evaluation should match the campaign objectives.

Budgets are budgets. They should be clear. Most people show budgets for media, and overall campaign budgets. Don't forget production costs and contingencies when they're needed.

Get ready for questions! Following most presentations, and during some, the audience will ask many questions. Novice presenters are terrified. Veteran presenters like the opportunity to show what they know, and how well they've thought out the client's advertising problem. If you go back to the concept of the strategic framework, with arguments for all decisions, *every major question you get will be related to the strategic arguments.* If the question isn't related to the strategic framework, it may be unimportant or unanswerable. In the next section, we'll examine what visual support is needed for your presentation.

Presentation Visuals

The technology for making presentation visuals has made tremendous leaps in recent years. Today, color overheads, color slides and computer screen overhead projectors are available. *What you put on the visual is far more important than the specific technology you use.* Flip charts can be used as effectively as slides; storyboards have advantages over videotape for commercial presentation. *The single most important production variable for visuals in a presentation is continuity.* Visuals should look like they belong to a set. Type sizes should be standardized and the style should be consistent. Here's how to prepare the visuals.

Once your strategic arguments are written, and the presentation order established, sit down with a newsprint pad or large piece of paper. Prioritize your arguments. Which ones do you think will need the most support; which ones will need the least support? Use presentation visuals, like flip charts, storyboards, etc., for these important arguments. When much supporting material is needed for your arguments, make presentation summary tables which can be handed out. On the newsprint or paper, make boxes for the illustrations you will need. Keep copy to a minimum, write key word arguments. Remember, audience members will recall sets of three. Here are a few limitations and strengths of each visual medium.

Overhead transparencies. Technology has improved overheads, so color overheads can be attractive. Hand written or poorly produced overheads look terrible and sloppy. People who use overheads tend to use the transparencies for their speech notes, rather than using the overhead to support their arguments. Overheads do lack the brilliance of projected images, but they do allow eye-contact with the audience, because moderate room lighting can be used.

Flip charts. Flip charts are underrated as an effective presentation medium. Carefully prepared newsprint charts, or boards, can be used to reinforce strategic arguments. They're great as a conversational medium because audience contact is continuous. Additional media must be provided for creative presentations when flip charts are used. Flip charts are extremely flexible, and easily adaptable to changing presentation situations. Unobtrusive notes can be pencilled on flip charts. Multiple sets of flip charts can't be prepared easily.

Slides. Slides are an overused medium. They can be dramatic; but while the lights are out, audience attention is diverted away from the presenter. If they're used, the number of slides must be reasonable. Slides should look like they belong to a set, rather than a group of unrelated strangers. The new computer slide technology is amazing. Outstanding slides can be produced rapidly. Judicious use of slides can be effective, overuse can be deadly.

Film, videotape, and multi-media presentations. The more complicated the technology, the more difficult it is to coordinate. If coordination is bad, it makes the presenter look bad. Poorly produced films or videotapes do more to damage the presenter's reputation, than artist-produced storyboards. For large clients, multi-media presentations are warranted. In these cases, the presentation should be carefully scripted, and visuals should be computer-controlled.

A Few Reminders and Hints

Never read a presentation. Presentations are supposed to look spontaneous and exciting, even though all are carefully prepared. Know what you're presenting and make it sound like you have conversational knowledge of the product and its environment. Before you present, have friends ask you questions about the strategic arguments behind all strategic decisions. You'll be ready for most questions. Do not use academic language or unusual jargon. Speak precisely in simple arguments. As a presenter, don't do what you don't do well. If you can't tell jokes, don't try to tell them in a presentation. If you can't sing, by all means don't try to sing in a presentation. Do what comes naturally. Relaxed and conversational doesn't mean loose and informal. Relaxed means you project a comfortable image to the audience. Conversational means you can quickly relate product facts and information about the product. There are no study questions, here. What you know about presenting is secondary to how well you perform. Practice makes the performance and the presenter.

Index

230